W9-CYU-759

HISTORY OF
BOXING

HISTORY OF BOXING

Peter Arnold

CHARTWELL
BOOKS, INC.

Photographic acknowledgments
All Sport Photographic, London, 101, 106 bottom, 107 left,
113 top, Alvin Chung 113 bottom, Tony Duffy 105 centre,
Duomo 104 centre, 188, John Gichigi 100 bottom right,
Trevor Jones 104 bottom, 112 bottom, Steve Powell 95, 100
bottom left; Associated Press, London, 73, 107 top right, 179,
183; BBC Hulton Picture Library, London, 43, 58, 60, 167
top; Boxing News, London, 38 top, 38 bottom, 41, 47, 52,
53, 55 top, 55 bottom, 56, 65, 67, 71 top, 72, 111 top, 121,
123, 124 left, 124 right, 126, 129, 130, 132, 135, 144 bottom,
164, 168, 169, 173; The Cleveland Museum of Art, Ohio, 45;
Camera Press, London, 98; Deans International Publishing,
London, 14, 15, 21, 22, 25 top, 25 bottom, 26, 158; Deans
International Publishing/John R. Freeman, London, 13 top;
C. M. Dixon, Canterbury, 9; Mary Evans Picture Library,
London, 17, 18, 19 top, 20 top, 23, 24, 33, 36 top, 36
bottom, 37, 116, 161, 165; Focus on Sports, New York,
86–87, 88, 88–89, 90, 91 top, 91 bottom, 100 top, 103
bottom, 104 top, 153, 154–155, 184, 187; The Illustrated
London News Picture Library, London, 64–65; Mansell
Collection, London, 8, 10, 11, 13 bottom, 16, 19 bottom, 20
bottom, 27, 29, 56–57, 76 bottom, 117; Don Morley, Reigate,
Surrey, 108, 112 top, 147, 149; Harry Mullan 103 top;
National Portrait Gallery, London, 35; Peter Newark's
Historical Pictures, Bath, 31, 39, 40, 48, 51, 66, 114, 115,
118, 122, 127, 159, 160, 163, 167 bottom, 171; The Photo
Source, London, 61, 63, 68, 70, 71 bottom, 74, 75 top, 75
bottom, 76 top, 77, 78, 93 bottom, 94 top, 97 top, 97 bottom,
105 bottom, 110 top, 110 bottom, 111 bottom left, 111
bottom right, 128, 131, 133, 136, 141, 142, 144 top, 145, 174,
175, 177, 180–181, 185; Popperfoto, London, 32, 50 top, 50
bottom, 79, 80–81, 82, 83, 84, 85, 92, 93 top, 96, 99, 105 top,
106 top, 107 bottom right, 109 top, 148, 152, 180; Press
Association, London, 102 bottom; Ronald Sheridan's Photo
Library, London, 7; Sport & General Press Agency, London,
94 bottom, 102 top, 109 bottom, 125, 137, 138, 143, 146,
150, 151, 156; Topical Press, London 139

Author's acknowledgments
Several books have been consulted during the research for
this book, and I am particularly indebted to the authors of
the following, whose books are thoroughly recommended:
Andre, Sam and Fleisher, Nat *A Pictorial History of Boxing.*
Hamlyn, London, revised edition 1981.
Butler, Frank *A History of Boxing in Britain.* Arthur Barker
Ltd., London, 1972.
Egan, Pierce *Boxiana.* Facsimile of 1812 edition, Vince
Harvey Publishing, Leicester, 1971.
Ford, John *Prizefighting: the Age of Regency Boxiana.* David
and Charles, Newton Abbot, 1971.
Golesworthy, Maurice *Encyclopedia of Boxing.* Robert Hale,
London, various editions.
Grombach, John V. *The Saga of the Fist.* A. S. Barnes and
Company, South Brunswick and New York, and Thomas
Yoseloff Ltd., London, 1977.
Menke, Frank G. *The Encyclopedia of Sports.* A. S. Barnes
and Company, South Brunswick and New York, and Thomas
Yoseloff Ltd., London, 5th revised edition 1975.
Odd, Gilbert *Boxing: The Great Champions.* Hamlyn,
London, 1974.
Odd, Gilbert *Encyclopedia of Boxing.* Hamlyn, London, 1983.
Sugar, Bert Randolph *The Great Fights.* Windward, London,
1981.

I would also like to thank my picture research colleague
Sheila Corr for finding such an excellent collection of boxing
pictures to illustrate the book.

Front cover:	Marvin Hagler v. Roberto Duran (Focus on Sports, New York)
Back cover:	Muhammad Ali v. Larry Holmes (Focus on Sports, New York)
Title page:	Jack Randall v. Martin the Baker (Mary Evans Picture Library, London)

For copyright reasons this edition is only
for sale within the U.S.A.

This edition published 1985 by
Chartwell Books, Inc.
A division of Book Sales, Inc.
110 Enterprise Avenue
Secaucus, New Jersey 07094

Prepared by
Deans International Publishing
52–54 Southwark Street, London SE1 1UA
a division of The Hamlyn Publishing Group Limited
London · New York · Sydney · Toronto

Copyright © 1985 The Hamlyn Publishing Group Limited
ISBN 0 89009 736 4

All rights reserved. No part of this publication
may be reproduced, stored in a retrieval system,
or transmitted in any form or by any means,
electronic, mechanical, photocopying, recording
or otherwise, without the permission of The Hamlyn
Publishing Group Limited.

Printed in Spain

CONTENTS

1 THE ORIGINS OF BOXING

Opposite: A mural at Thera in Greece shows children boxing, dating from some time in the 16th century BC.

Using the clenched fists in aggression or self-defence is one of those activities like running or hunting, so necessary to the existence of early men that its origin can only be said to be as old as mankind itself. With no inanimate weapon to hand, the fist is one of the best we have.

Sparring for recreation is likely to have developed quickly. It is natural that men would be proud of their proficiency with their fists and would spar with neighbours for fun and practice. No doubt spectators enjoyed the combats. It would soon be apparent that fist-fights were a means of settling grudges, and a grudge fight would attract even more onlookers, as it does now.

The earliest records of boxing date from before the great days of the Greek and Roman Empires. Egyptian hieroglyphics from about 4000BC suggest that a sort of combat between soldiers was practised. Thongs were wrapped round the hands and forearms in a primitive forerunner of the boxing glove. Slabs found in a temple near Baghdad also show fights with leather-wrapped fists from about the same time.

Records of early Greek and Roman times show that man-to-man combat was common in various games and festivals celebrated throughout their empires.

The word pugilism comes from the Greek *pugme* through the Latin *pugil*, a boxer, from *pugnus*, fist, and *pugnare*, to fight with the fist. The term boxing is believed to arise from the action of clenching of the fist, the folding of fingers and thumb into a box, and its roots also are in the Greek and Latin, *puxos* and *buxus*.

Homer in the *Iliad* and Virgil in *Aeneid* both refer to fist fighting. Odysseus, who knocked Irus cold with a right swing, was particularly adept.

About 900BC pugilism was sponsored in a brutal way by Theseus, son of Aegeus, a Greek monarch. To keep his warriors occupied and satisfy his lust for carnage, Theseus devised a method of fighting where the combatants sat facing each other on flat stones, their fists enclosed in leather thongs. Given a signal, they began punching each other. The battles ended only when one contestant beat the other to death. Naturally this took a long time, so Theseus introduced metal studs into the thongs, and then spikes, called *myrmekes*. A few blows would smash a man's face, and subsequently a few more could finish him off altogether.

Boxing was introduced into the ancient Olympic Games in 688BC, 92 years after the first records were kept of Olympics. Onamastus was the first champion. Bouts were not to the death and contestants wore leather wrappings which extended from around their knuckles almost to their elbows. Like today's boxers they also used headguards and punchbags in training.

Boxing was followed in the Olympic Games by the *pancratium*, a brutal mixture of boxing and wrestling which allowed almost anything short of biting and eye-gouging. Nevertheless the Greeks of the period prized skill above everything in their boxing. The champions were sponsored by their cities or states, celebrated by the poets and commemorated on vases and in statues.

Types of *cestus*, forerunners of the boxing glove. From the top: rawhide, cut into circles with holes for the fingers; leather, bound round the knuckles and up to the elbows, with protruding fingers; leather, completely binding the fists, and into which metal spikes and studs were at one time fixed; leather, protecting the knuckles and back of hand.

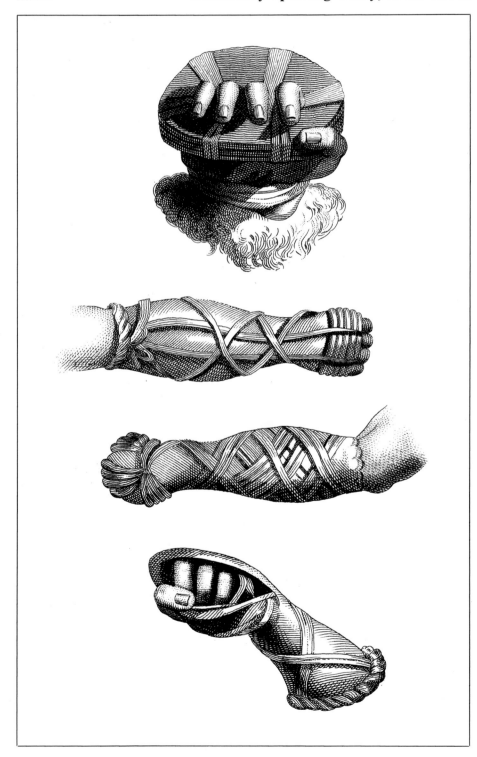

Theagenes of Thrace, in the fifth century BC, and Cleitomachus 250 years later each won both the boxing and *pancratium* at Olympia, and were early 'world champions' whose fame spread throughout Greece.

The influence of the Romans led to the decline of boxing. Their liking for gladiatorial combat led to the re-introduction of iron studs in the thongs. The lethal 'gauntlet' thus formed was known as a *cestus*.

While boxing continued in the Olympics, without the iron studs and in a manner which would be considered reasonably sporting today, from about 250BC Roman feasts and holidays would often include gladiatorial contests using an iron-studded *cestus*. The Emperor Caligula imported pugilists from Africa, matching them and awarding the winners maidens as prizes. These gladiators, while they lasted, formed a sort of professional circuit. But eventually common sense and the view that fighting to the death, or near-death, was not the best training for warriors, prevailed. The *cestus* was banned. Without the prospect of the pugilist being killed, public interest in the sport declined. In 393AD the Emperor Theodosius the Great terminated the Olympic Games and boxing as a spectacle disappeared for about 1300 years. It resurfaced in England, sometimes called the 'Cradle of Pugilism', in the 17th century, when it was closely linked with fencing. Masters who taught the necessary art of fencing, particularly those who specialized in teaching the backsword to the common populace, were often instructors in boxing – the science of self-defence – also. For publicity they would stage exhibition fights, with and without weapons, where the single-edged backsword was likely to provide plenty of blood without the contestants coming to permanent harm.

Samuel Pepys reported seeing one such exhibition in 1662: 'I came and saw my first prizefight . . . between one Mathews . . . and one Westwicke who was cut several times both in head and legs . . . all over blood . . . strange to see what a deal of money is flung to them both between every bout.'

Note the use of the term 'prizefight', preceeding its application to boxing, to which it soon came to be applied exclusively.

Gradually, fighting with the fists began to be a popular form of entertainment. Strong men with an aptitude for the sport began to roam the countryside, usually in small groups, with a length of rope. They would attract a crowd and one of them would issue a challenge, inviting any of the audience who fancied his chances to fight for a guinea. Spectators would form a circle with the rope (hence the 'ring'), into which, to accept the challenge, an onlooker would throw his hat (hence 'tossing one's hat into the ring,' meaning to accept a challenge).

Should there be no challengers, two of the party would box each other. In each

case, there would be a collection and the party would move on to the next village.

Travelling fairs might have a boxing booth, in which professionals would challenge the public or box each other, with spectators paying to watch.

A man who showed strength and aptitude would become a champion of his village or locality, and his neighbours would support him in challenges to other local champions. A 'purse' might be put up for the winner, and there would be plenty of betting.

Occasionally a local squire would back one of his household against the visiting pugilists or neighbouring champions,

and it was not uncommon for gentlemen of the aristocracy to stage matches among their servants and tradespeople to find the best.

Thus the first report of a boxing match in England, from the *Protestant Mercury* of January, 1681:

'Yesterday, a match of Boxing was performed before His Grace the Duke of Albemarle, between the Duke's footman and a butcher. The latter won the prize, as he had done many times before, being accounted, though but a little man, the best at that exercise in England.'

A bronze figure of Cleitomachus, who won the boxing and the *pancratium* at the 141st Olympic Games, 216 BC (National Museum, Rome).

A 'match of Boxing' did not resemble a boxing match of today. The fighters were stripped to the waist, but did not wear gloves. Kicking, biting and gouging the eyes were not allowed, nor hitting or grabbing below the waist. But most other things were. Wrestling was an essential part. The opponent could be knocked or thrown to the ground, either by picking him up round the waist or by a popular move known as a 'cross-buttock'. This involved getting beside him, putting an arm round his neck, grabbing his loose arm with the other hand and then, by shifting to his front and sticking a hip or buttock into his crutch, tossing him over a shoulder. Having thrown an opponent it was permissible to fall on him as heavily as possible.

It was not allowed to strike a man or otherwise inflict damage (apart from falling on him) once he was down. A round ended when a man was down, and there was a break of 30 seconds before the next. Rounds could therefore be of any length and, similarly, fights were carried on until one man was unable to continue. There were no referees, however, or need for them. The spectators were the guardians of fair play.

As more began to follow the sport, the ring formed by spectators holding a rope was found to be unsatisfactory, as its shape could not be maintained under the pressure of supporters surging back and forth in their excitement. So stakes were

used, around which the rope was wound. Later, an outer ring was also required for the big fights, to accomodate time-keepers, umpires (less to render decisions than to represent and see fair play for each boxer), whips and important gentry like those who had put up the money. The whips were equipped with short whips to keep the crowd from interfering with the battle. The time-keeper used a whistle or gong to indicate when the 30 seconds had elapsed between rounds – he was not required to time the rounds themselves, of course.

The two contestants occupied diagonal corners and each was allowed supporters, usually two. These men were usually fighters themselves, who might be engaged for a second supporting bout, or to provide a substitute bout should the main one finish quickly. Because of their secondary nature these men were known as 'seconds', as they still are. One second used his knees as a seat for the boxer between rounds; the job of the other was to revive his man if necessary and send him out fit for the next round: he was known as the 'bottle-man', and even now boxers still receive a mouth-wash from a second.

A line was scratched across the centre of the ring dividing it into two halves. At the start of the contest the boxers 'toed the line' an expression in general use to this day, and when the whistle blew, or the bell rang, or the gong was struck to

Many matches in the 17th and 18th centuries were organized by the gentry among their workpeople and tenants. This private 'turn-up' took place in the drawing room of a noble marquis.

begin a new round, each boxer had to toe the line again. The timekeepers would allow eight seconds for a boxer to come up to the mark – if he were unable to do so he lost the bout, i.e. he failed 'to come up to scratch', and was 'counted out of time', hence a count-out, now popularly known as a knock-out. The prize ring gave many other expressions to the language. Another comes from the habit of tying the boxers' purses to the stakes (so that they could see that nobody was making off with the cash while they fought). This became 'stake money', used now in horse-racing and gambling of all kinds.

The first champion of the bare-knuckle era is generally acknowledged to be James Figg (or Fig), from Thame, in Oxfordshire. He was skilled in the use of the backsword and quarterstaff, and also practised boxing. In 1719 he opened an academy in Tottenham Court Road, London, called 'Fig's Amphitheatre'. Here he taught the gentry the arts of self-defence. In a year or so he moved a short distance to Oxford Road (now Oxford Street) and the famous artist William Hogarth drew him a business card, copies of which were distributed at the fairs around the south of England. A Hogarth picture of Southwark Fair shows Figg challenging any of the crowd to enter the lists with him, 'for money, for love, or a bellyfull'.

Figg was more proficient as a fencer or cudgeller than as a boxer. It was largely through the writings of one of his clients, Captain Godfrey, that he became acknowledged as champion, but he confirmed his title by beating his only serious challenger, Ned Sutton, 'The Pipemaker', of Gravesend, three times.

Early in Figg's 'reign' there was a challenge from abroad when a gondolier from Venice, called Carini, offered to break the jaw-bone of any man who would fight him. Figg found Bob Whitaker to fight the awesome Venetian, who with his first blow knocked Whitaker clean off the stage of Figg's Amphitheatre. However, as Captain Godfrey described, an 'English peg' in the stomach knocked the wind from Carini, who was ultimately forced to retire.

George I and the Prince of Wales were among the spectators, and in 1723 George I sanctioned the construction of a 'Ring' in London's Hyde Park for the general use of any who wanted a fight. This gave some respectability to prize-

fighting for nearly a century until the Bow Street police dismantled it in 1820.

Figg died in 1734 (some authorities say 1740), when the title was claimed by George Taylor, one of his pupils who had himself built a great booth in Tottenham Court Road, and included among his patrons Frederick, Prince of Wales, the father of George III. There were other claimants, the most notable being Tom Pipes, but both Taylor and Pipes were beaten by another pupil of Figg, Jack Broughton, the second great name in prizefighting.

Broughton was born near Cirencester, Gloucestershire, in 1704 and went to London to become a Thames waterman. He defeated George Taylor around 1734 to claim the championship. Taylor fancied his chances and began confidently on the attack, but in 20 minutes Broughton had laid him flat. Taylor was jealous of Broughton's prowess and tried to find men to beat him, but to no avail.

The business card designed by the artist William Hogarth for James Figg, the first champion of England.

In 1741, Broughton beat George Stevenson, a Yorkshire coachman, at Taylor's booth. The Duke of Cumberland (the 'butcher of Culloden') had a good wager on Broughton (his brother, the Prince of Wales, backed Stevenson), and became his patron, lending him £300 to open an academy of his own, in Hanway Yard, Tottenham Court Road, behind that of the late Figg.

Stevenson was so battered in the 35-minute contest that a few days later he died. The tragedy upset Broughton and in an effort to ensure that it would not happen again, he called some of his patrons to his academy and drew up a set of rules. These were published on 16 August 1743 and read as follows:

1. That a square of a yard be chalked in the middle of the stage; and every fresh set-to after a fall, or being parted from the rails, each second is to bring his man to the side of the square, and place him opposite to the other, and till they are fairly set to at the lines, it shall not be lawful for one to strike the other.

2. That, in order to prevent any disputes, the time a man lies after a fall, if the second does not bring his man to the side of the square within the space of half a minute, he shall be deemed a beaten man.

3. That in every main battle, no person whatever shall be upon the stage except the principals and their seconds; the same rule to be observed in by-battles, except that in the latter, Mr. Broughton is allowed to be upon the stage to keep decorum, and to assist gentlemen in getting to their places, provided always he does not interfere in the battle; and whoever pretends to infringe these rules to be turned immediately out of the house. Everybody is to quit the stage as soon as the champions are stripped, before set-to.

4. That no champion be deemed beaten unless he fails coming up to the line in the limited time; or, that his own second declares him beaten. No second is to be allowed to ask his man's adversary any questions, or advise him to give out.

5. That in by-battles, the winning man to have two-thirds of the money given, which shall be publicly divided upon the stage notwithstanding any private agreements to the contrary.

6. That to prevent disputes in every main battle, the principals shall, on the coming on the stage, choose from among the gentlemen present, two umpires, who shall absolutely decide all disputes that may arise about the battle; and if the two umpires cannot agree, the said umpires to choose a third, who is to determine it.

7. That no person is to hit his adversary when he is down, or seize him by the hair, the breeches, or any part below the waist; a man on his knees to be reckoned down.

Broughton's Rules did much to improve the sport. They remained in force for nearly 100 years. Broughton also invented, or rediscovered, the boxing glove. It has been suggested that seeing a statue of a Greek boxer wearing the *cestus* gave him the idea for a padded glove. Broughton's gloves were lightweight 'mufflers' and used only in sparring – matches were still bare-knuckle. They were really to prevent damage to his aristocratic patrons. Broughton, an intelligent man, also introduced science into the ring, developing blocking and the art of the counter-punch.

Broughton beat numerous challengers over the next ten years, but in 1750 he had the misfortune to argue with a pugilist named Jack Slack at Hounslow Races. Broughton threatened to horsewhip Slack, Slack challenged him, and the result was a contest in Oxford Road on 11 April. Broughton was 46 years old, overweight, and not inclined to train properly for the bout. Slack, a butcher who had come from Norfolk to London to try his skill at pugilism, was 16 years younger. Broughton paid Slack ten guineas on the eve of the fight, fearing that without a bribe Slack would not appear. Slack bet the money on himself.

Broughton's superiority from the start was such that the odds were 10–1 in his favour – odds accepted by the knowing ones, including the Duke of Cumberland, who wagered several thousand pounds on him.

Suddenly, Slack made a jump at Broughton and caught him a desperate blow between the eyes, closing both of

them. For two or three minutes Broughton groped around feeling for his man like a drunk, at which the Duke of Cumberland cried: 'What are you about Broughton? You can't fight. You're beat.' Broughton replied 'I can't see my man, Your Highness. I am blind, but not beat – only let me be placed before my antagonist and he shall not gain the day yet.'

There was nothing the distressed Broughton could do, however, and in 14 minutes he was beaten. The Duke was disgusted, and announced Broughton had sold him out. He had Broughton's amphitheatre closed by order of the legislature. Broughton never fought again and brooded on the injustice of the allegations against him – but eventually he made peace with the Duke of Cumberland, was made a Yeoman of the Guard and died a very rich man.

Above: Jack Broughton (left) in his battle with George Stevenson, 'The Coachman', whose death led to Broughton's rules. The illustration is from a mezzotint by John Young after John Henry Mortimer (British Museum Print Room).

Left: An engraving from a bust by Sivier of Jack Slack, of Bristol, who conquered Broughton by blinding him with a blow between the eyes.

13

Tom Johnson (left) in his victorious defence against the giant Isaac Perrins, who was over 40 pounds (18kg) heavier.

Broughton's surprise defeat was considered to be entirely due to lack of training – perhaps a hard judgement on a man of 46. This is Pierce Egan, a popular recorder of the fight game in the early 19th century, in *Boxiana*: 'Hear it, ye Champions! Weep for the veteran's downfall! and profit by his loss – BE NOT TOO CONFIDENT – and *remember*, that it was occasioned by one fatal error – neglect of *training*!!!'

Slack was not a great champion, and during his reign prizefighting began to get an unsavoury reputation: many fights were suspected of being 'fixed'. He was certainly rough, perfecting a 'chopper' blow, something like a rabbit punch. He saw off a Frenchman named Pettit, but not before he had been half choked.

Eventually he lost his title in 1760 to Bill Stevens, 'The Nailer', at the Tennis Court, Haymarket, London. Ironically, the Duke of Cumberland, Broughton's backer, supported Slack to the tune of £100 against the Duke of York. When the outsider, Stevens, won, the Duke of Cumberland gave up his patronage of boxing and began campaigning against the sport.

Stevens held the title for less than a year, losing it to George Meggs, who was

managed by Slack. Stevens admitted that he sold the fight, thus bringing shame on 'nailers', or blacksmiths, throughout London.

For nearly 30 years the championship was as often bought as not. It was a period of double-cross. George Milsom, a baker, Tom Juchau, a paviour, Bill Darts, a dyer, Tom Lyons, a waterman, Peter Corcoran, an Irishman who was a coal-heaver and sailor, Harry Sellers, a protégé of Slack's from the west country, and Duggan Fearns, an Irish boatswain, all held the title in these years.

The best of them was Peter Corcoran, from Athoye, County Carlow, who came to England as a youth, found his way to London, defeated several pugilists, and took on Darts at Epsom on Derby Day, 18 May 1771. The fight was arranged by Colonel Dennis O'Kelly, a celebrated sportsman of the Turf. He was a great gambler, who owned the famous racehorse Eclipse (bred, incidentally, by the Duke of Cumberland) and made the historic winning bet: 'Eclipse first, the rest nowhere'.

Corcoran won the fight in one round and claimed the championship. But O'Kelly won several thousand pounds, and it was rumoured he had paid Darts

Richard Humphries (left) and Daniel Mendoza at the start of their fight at Odiham, Hampshire, in 1788, which Humphries won. Mendoza was the first in a tradition of great Jewish boxers.

£100 the day before the fight to lose it.

There were also suspicions about the way Corcoran lost the championship to Harry Sellers at the Crown Inn, Staines, Middlesex, on 16 October 1776. Corcoran, after putting Sellers down, appeared to allow his opponent to win. Sellers himself lost the title in less than five minutes to another Irishman, Duggan Fearns, in a match that cost gamblers dear and was reckoned to be a double-cross.

Respectability returned to the prize-ring with the arrival of Tom Johnson (real name, Jackling), from Derby, who built up a string of victories from 1783, and was generally acclaimed as champion by 1787. His best victory was against Isaac Perrins, a 17-stone (238lb – 108kg) strong man from Birmingham. Fortunes fluctuated violently before Johnson won after 75 minutes and 62 rounds.

Johnson lost his title to Big Ben Brain, from Bristol, another giant at 6ft 4in (1.93m) and 16st 6lb (230lb – 104kg). Brain, backed by the Duke of Hamilton, had earlier forfeited his deposit of £100 when falling ill after being matched with Johnson at £1,000-a-side. At Wrotham, Kent, he brought Johnson's reign to an end after 18 rounds of battling. But the effort took its toll of Brain. He did not defend his championship, and died in 1794, after arranging to meet Will Wood. His liver was found to be injured by the blows he took.

Meanwhile two smaller men had captured the imagination of the public. Richard Humphries, styled 'The Gentleman Boxer' because of his appearance and behaviour, was an attractive south-paw (one who boxes right foot forward) who was watched by the Prince of Wales, the Duke of York, and many of the French nobility, including the Duke of Orleans, when he beat Sam Martin, 'The Bath Butcher', at Newmarket in 1786.

Next year another up-and-coming pugilist, Daniel Mendoza, also beat Martin – but in 20 minutes, whereas it had taken Humphries 105 minutes. Humphries acted as second for Martin against Mendoza and gradually the two came to dislike each other. Humphries had Mendoza arrested over a debt (he was quickly released) and they nearly came to blows at an inn in Epping. A battle in the ring was a 'natural'. Excitement was high when the two champions were matched for 400 guineas in Odiham, Hampshire, in January,

1788. Mendoza, a Jew from Aldgate, London, was only 5ft 7in (1.70m) and weighed 168lb (12st – 75.6kg). Thousands watched and thousands of pounds were wagered as the bout commenced, with Humphries the favourite. Rain had made the ring slippery, and Humphries had difficulty keeping his feet. Jewish backers put their money confidently on Mendoza as Humphries was down six times in succession. But Humphries rallied, caught Mendoza in the groin and followed up with a blow to the neck, which caused Mendoza to fall awkwardly. He sprained an ankle, fainted with pain, and that was the end. The fight lasted 29 minutes.

Humphries sent his backer, a Mr. Bradyl, who had been unable to attend, a note: 'Sir, I have done the Jew and am in good health'. Mendoza's supporters released a black pigeon to take the news back to the East End of London.

The two met again, on 6 May 1789, at Stilton, famous for its cheeses, in Huntingdonshire. The betting was fairly even but this time Mendoza outboxed Humphries, who went down without a blow in the 22nd round, which should have meant defeat, but Humphries and his seconds argued so vehemently against this that other fights appeared likely to break out. Eventually Mendoza agreed to continue, and further punished Humphries, who eight minutes later again fell without a blow, this time not contesting the verdict that Mendoza had won.

A third match was arranged in Doncaster, at an inn yard surrounded by houses except on one side where the river Don flowed. Hundreds rowed over the Don and tore out palings to join the 500 who had paid half-a-guinea each to see the decider. Mendoza was only a narrow favourite in the betting, Humphries' reputation being still high, but he won easily, earning approval for the manner in which he did not punish a game rival unnecessarily.

By twice defeating Bill Warr, of Bristol, Mendoza claimed the championship of England in 1794. He was regarded as the most scientific boxer of all the champions till then, and his matches with Humphries were regarded as the best since the days of Broughton. Boxing became fashionable, academies sprang up (Mendoza's, in the City of London, was particularly well patronized), and the Prince of Wales, the Royal Dukes and many others of the aristocracy were among its supporters.

When Mendoza came to lose his championship, it was to another great figure of the prize ring, Gentleman John Jackson, so-called because of his careful dress and manners. Remarkably, he fought only three times. He beat William Fewterell, of Birmingham, a big man but no match for Jackson, in 1788, but next year was unluckily defeated by George Ingleston, a brewer, slipping on the wet ring and breaking a small bone in his left leg when well on top.

On 15 April 1795 Jackson fought Mendoza for 200 guineas a side in Hornchurch, Essex. Jackson appeared slightly the superior for four rounds, then in the fifth grabbed Mendoza by the

John Jackson, called 'Gentleman John', and a friend of the poet Byron, was a great champion and organizer of boxing through his Pugilistic Club.

hair, and repeatedly battered him till he fell to the ground. The umpires decided on appeal that this tactic was fair, and Mendoza never recovered, being beaten in 10½ minutes.

Despite this savagery, Jackson, who retired to open a boxing academy in Bond Street, London, enjoyed the popularity and patronage of the nobility, his academy becoming the centre of the sporting fraternity. He became a defender of the rules, and, like Broughton, helped in the development of gloves by insisting his patrons wore them. Among these were the Royal Dukes and Lord Byron, the poet, who included Jackson in his verse:

And men unpractised in exchanging
   knocks
Must go to Jackson ere they dare
   box

Jackson formed the Pugilistic Club in 1814, which brought together a number of regular patrons of prizefighting. Annual subscriptions enabled the Club to provide purses for boxers, thus taking over the role previously held solely by the private sponsor. One aim was to prevent fixed fights. The Pugilistic Club might have assumed similar authority in boxing to that which the MCC had in cricket and the Jockey Club in horse-racing, but its influence lasted only ten years.

When Queen Caroline was barred from Westminster Abbey on the coronation of her husband, George IV, in 1820, Jackson was asked to provide a bodyguard of 18 prizefighters to keep order in case of trouble. There was no trouble, and a gold medal awarded the boxers was raffled among them and won by Tom Belcher.

Belcher's older brother, Jem, from the stronghold of fistic prowess, Bristol, was the next to claim the title. He was a grandson of Jack Slack, also a butcher by trade, came to London when 18 years old, and after several wins, claimed the championship when beating Andrew Gamble near a famous gibbet on Wimbledon Common in 1800. Because Jackson was undefeated, and considered the best around, Belcher was not generally regarded as champion until 1803, when he disposed of Jack Fearby, 'The Young Ruffian'.

Belcher lost an eye at rackets, but continued fighting, even after losing his championship to Hen Pearce. Late in his career he twice fought Tom Cribb, one of the outstanding champions. He was an innovator, tying a yellow silk handker-

Boxing instruction at the rooms of Gentleman John Jackson. Patrons sparred with 'mufflers'. Notice also the fencers (R & G Cruikshank from Pierce Egan's 'Life in London').

17

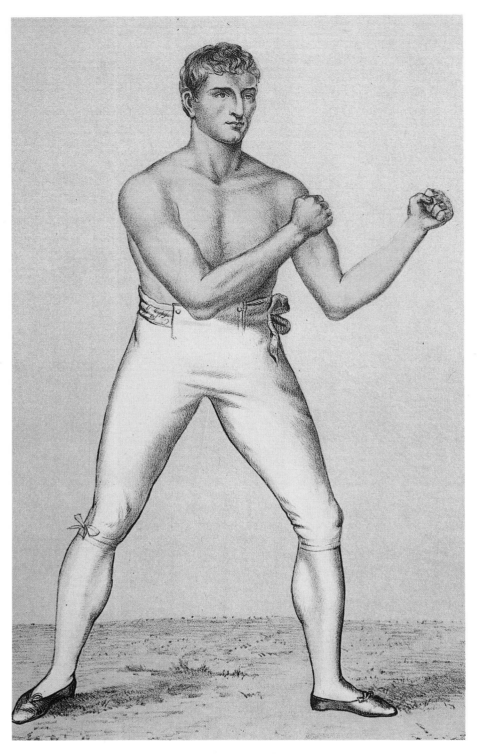

Jem Belcher, a heroic champion, who resembled Napoleon, fought with one eye and eventually died aged 31.

and he challenged Pearce (600 guineas to 400) for the championship. The Game Chicken won over 64 rounds in Hailsham, Sussex, on 8 October 1805.

He was then challenged by his idol, Belcher, jealous of his protégé's fame. Pearce had no difficulty winning, declining on occasion, to hit Belcher: 'Lest I hurt thine other eye'.

Alas, life in London was too much for Pearce, who liked the company of sporting men, and 'poured down copious libations at the shrine of Bacchus'; he also enjoyed 'the fond caresses of the softer sex', two attractions which have been the downfall of many boxers through the ages. Pearce's health became impaired, and sensibly he returned to Bristol, and gave up being a pugilist to become a victualler.

Gully, as The Game Chicken's closest rival, claimed the championship, and established his merit with two narrow victories over Bob Gregson, the 6ft 2in (1.88m) champion of Lancashire, who was the 'Poet Laureate' of prizefighting. Gully retired immediately, and his subsequent career was one of the most successful of all boxers. He made a fortune on the Turf as owner and bookmaker (his gambling duels with William Crockford, founder of the famous Club, were not always honest), became the owner of coalmines and was elected MP for Pontefract, in Yorkshire.

Tom Cribb was the next champion. From Hanham, near Bristol, he came to London when 13 to be a bell-hanger, but soon became a wharfsman. He beat former champion Jem Belcher, easily disposed of Bill Richmond, a black American slave brought by his master to challenge the British pugilists, and then, a little luckily, defeated Gregson over 23 rounds, after which both men were utterly exhausted. A second victory over a fast-fading Belcher (his last fight) and Cribb assumed the title of champion of England.

Cribb was now challenged by Tom Molineaux, another Virginian slave who had been sent to England to follow in the footsteps of Richmond, who seconded him. Molineaux had beaten some prominent men, but was not expected to trouble Cribb when they met at Copthall Common, near East Grinstead, Sussex, on 18 December 1810. It was the first big fight to capture international attention, and the first for the title between black and white opponents.

chief to the post in his corner – such colours were known for years as 'Belchers'.

The one-eyed Belcher began to suffer ill-health and depression and Henry Pearce, a friend and pupil, also from Bristol, became champion. Pearce's name was shortened to 'Hen' by his companions and this in turn led to the sobriquet 'The Game Chicken'.

Having beaten all the known contenders, Pearce sought out a fellow-townsman, John Gully, who was in the King's Bench Prison for a debt of his father's. They fought with mufflers and Gully did well, so his debts were paid

Above: Sparring in one of the academies in the 19th century. The pictures on the wall include some of the great prize-ring champions, including the Game Chicken.

Left: An unknown artist's impression of a fight between John Gully and Bob Gregson. Gully twice beat Gregson, but after the first fight was insensible for five hours and there were fears for his life.

Cribb won, but only after 39 rounds and 55 minutes, and not without some gamesmanship on the part of his seconds. The story of the fight is described in Chapter 8.

Three days later Molineaux issued a challenge for a return, but was kept waiting by Cribb who had announced his retirement. Molineaux accordingly beat Joe Rimmer and claimed the title. Cribb thereupon agreed to a return for £600 a side, at Thistleton Gap, Leicester, on 28 September 1811. This time Cribb trained hard for the fight at the Scottish estate of his backer, Captain Barclay, and was fit, whereas Molineaux was not in the same condition as the year before.

Public interest was enormous, with upwards of 20,000 making their way to the Midlands from all parts of the country. Cribb this time won easily, Molineaux being carried out senseless after only 11 rounds and 19 minutes. Cribb was fêted by the crowds all the way back to London. He had fought off the foreign challenge, as the Venetian gondolier had been resisted nearly 100 years before.

Tom Cribb (left) about to receive the silver cup presented to him in 1811, bought with 80 guineas given 'by the higher flights of the Fancy, as a remembrancer of their approbation of the manly combats and pugilistic qualities of the champion of England' (R & G Cruikshank from Pierce Egan's 'Life in London').

Part of an engraving showing the adventures of the Fancy on the road to a fight at Moulsey Hurst, a popular venue for fights around the end of the 18th century.

Cribb established a sporting parlour, where he was introduced to Tom Winter, a 17-year-old boxer from Hereford. Winter changed his surname to the more promising season of Spring, and under Cribb's coaching beat a succession of leading pugilists. When he beat Tom Oliver in 1821, Cribb retired again and handed the championship to Spring.

However the championship was also claimed by Bill Neat, who beat Tom Hickman, 'The Gas Man', on 11 December 1821 in a fight immortalized by William Hazlitt in an essay, 'The Fight'. The literary world was taking an increasing interest in prizefighting. John Keats, Thomas Moore and later John Clare, in addition to Byron, were poets who followed the fights. Neat challenged Spring, and they met on 20 May 1823 near Andover, Hants, Spring winning over eight rounds and 37 minutes.

Spring was beaten only once, in a return with Ned Painter, battling for 42 rounds with a bad eye injury sustained in the first. He was one of the best and most scientific of the prizefighters. His last two fights, against Jack Langan, the Irish Champion, in 1824, lasted 77 and 76 rounds respectively. Battering Langan so injured Spring's hands that he did not fight again.

Interest in prizefighting then declined for a while, partly because magistrates began to take a firmer line. Two boxers

were prosecuted after a match at Moulsey Hurst, by the Thames just outside London, which had become a regular venue for contests organized by John Jackson's Pugilistic Club and Jackson then closed his premises at 13 Old Bond Street.

Prizefighting had been illegal since 1750. Therefore matches could not be advertised. Those sportsmen, patrons and gentlemen from London who followed the fight game (called the 'Fancy' or 'Corinthians') knew where matches were to be, of course, but local spectators often discovered them only by following the procession of those in the know.

Naturally, prize money could not be paid from a 'gate' which might not materialize. Most prize money, therefore, came from stakes put up by the boxers themselves or their backers. These were large in the case of the champions – 500 guineas a side for Pearce v Belcher and Cribb v Gregson and £600 for the second Cribb v Molineaux match – but not necessarily equal. Pearce beat Gully putting up 600 guineas to Gully's 400; Cribb, who was called 'The Champion' for a dozen years till 1823 without defending, asked £1,000 to fight Neat to deter the younger and, no doubt, stronger man.

Fortunes were made betting, and boxers often received rewards from their backers. Where it was possible to raise

The first fight between Tom Spring and Jack Langan at Worcester racecourse. For the first time in boxing a grandstand was erected. There were 30,000 spectators, and one was killed and several injured as twice during the fight parts of the stand collapsed.

The Fives Court, in London, the scene of many great bouts in the 18th and 19th centuries. Randall and Martin are seen sparring with 'mufflers', around 1805. Many of the champions are represented in the foreground, including Gentleman John Jackson, Molineaux and Cribb.

gate money from spectators it was shared equally among the boxers. The loser would also receive the proceeds of a collection made by the tough men (usually boxers themselves) employed to keep the space clear between the inner and outer ring, to prevent the boxers being interfered with. They used their short whips to encourage the watchers to put money into their caps – hence the expression, still used for any sort of collection, a 'whip round'.

While it was the duty of the local magistrates to prevent prizefights and arrest the principals, the fact that they were frequently sponsored by the local aristocracy, and that Royalty might be interested, made the actions of the guardians of the law in any particular instance unpredictable. Sometimes they turned a blind eye, on other occasions not. Where necessary, decoy fights were set up to lead the authorities astray, or fights were arranged near County borders so that escape over the boundaries was easy.

A fight between Mendoza and Bill Warr, scheduled for Stoken Church, Oxfordshire, on 22 June 1791, was postponed on notice of an intended visit

from the magistrates. The championship match between Belcher and 'The Young Ruffian' was arranged to take place at Newmarket, but, the magistrates interfering, the party travelled out of the county to Linton, about 15 miles (24km) away, where the fight took place. Belcher more than once attracted the attention of the police. He spent 28 days in prison, and was also fined for disturbing the peace after his last fight (with Cribb). Two days before Gully's second title fight with Gregson, the Marquis of Huntingdon announced in the *County Chronicle* that he had notice of the intended 'riotous assembly' near Dunstable, and that as *Custos rotulorum* (Keeper of the Rolls) he had taken steps to detect and punish all persons aiding and assisting in the breach of the peace. It was decided that the fight should move to Sir John Sebright's park in Hertfordshire, several miles away, and the carriages, carts and horsemen formed a great procession as they moved off.

The increased interest the law took in prizefighting around this time arose from the general air of unrest among the working population following the Luddite risings and the movement towards trades unionism. Large gatherings of work-people were discouraged, even if given some respectability by the presence of the Fancy. Prizefight crowds included, of course, elements out to appropriate the easy money always present where gambling is rife – pickpockets, ladies of easy virtue and tricksters.

Boxing could not be suppressed altogether, however. Tom Cannon, 'The Great Gun of Windsor', beat Josh Hudson for £500-a-side at Warwick in 1824, but lost in 1825 to Jem Ward who claimed the title. Ward was from London's East End, and at 16 was working in a coal yard, which earned him the title of 'The Black Diamond'. Before winning the title he had thrown a fight by accepting £100 to 'lie down' against Bill Abbott, an admitted sin for which he was forgiven. He lost the title to Peter

DESCRIPTION OF A BOXING MATCH. June 9th 1812

From a Coloured Etching by ROWLANDSON

Captain Desmond Coke

A Thomas Rowlandson illustration of a prize fight between Jack Ward (or Warr) and a fighter called Quirk, at Padnal Corner, Epping Forest, in 1806. Quirk won when Ward could not come up to scratch for the 13th round.

Opposite top: James Burke, 'The Deaf 'Un,' who fought Simon Byrne for 3 hours and 16 minutes (99 rounds), after which Byrne died. Burke went to fight in America and was nearly killed by gangsters.

Opposite bottom: William Thompson, 'Bold Bendigo', who twice won the title and had some bitter fights with Ben Caunt.

Below: Joshua Hudson, the 'John Bull fighter' who twice fought Tom Cannon the 'Great Gun of Windsor' in 1824. He was unable to beat him and Cannon claimed the championship.

Crawley, 'Young Rump Steak', on 2 January 1827. Crawley retired immediately and Ward resumed his reign, but there was little interest in the ring at the time. After beating Simon Byrne in 1831 Ward was given a championship belt – the first boxer so honoured.

Ward retired and James Burke, known as 'The Deaf 'Un', took over the championship. Burke, another Cockney, specialized in long fights, beating Bill Fitzmaurice over 166 rounds (3 hours) in 1829 and losing to Bill Cousins in 111 rounds (2 hours 50 minutes) ten weeks later, when still only 19 years old. After beating eight more men, Burke took on the Irishman Simon Byrne in 1833. This fight, just outside London, lasted 99 rounds (3 hours 16 minutes) and was of unremitting savagery, with both men nearly out several times. The seconds were criticized for forcing them to continue, and more than once the public tried to intervene. Burke won to become champion, but Byrne did not recover from a coma and died three days later. Byrne himself had earlier caused the death of Sandy McKay, badly beaten in 47 rounds in 1830. McKay died from his injuries, and Byrne was tried for manslaughter, but acquitted.

Sam O'Rourke, who claimed the Irish championship, now sought revenge for the death of his countryman Byrne, but Burke was reluctant to fight. O'Rourke went to America as 'world champion', claiming that Burke was dodging him, but Burke followed and caught up with him in New Orleans, where O'Rourke had opened a boxing school. A match was made in New Orleans, but O'Rourke, a gangster, stood little chance with Burke, and after only three rounds his mob broke up the fight and attempted to kill Burke, who luckily escaped although it was first reported in London that he had been assassinated. He reached New York and beat Paddy O'Connell there. O'Rourke turned to smuggling and was eventually murdered in a lumber camp in Canada.

In March 1838 Bill Phelps, a lightweight known as Brighton Bill, died after being beaten by Owen Swift, and the Broughton Rules of 1743 were revised in an attempt to prevent such tragedies in future. The principal change required that at the beginning of a round a boxer must toe the line unaided, and could not be carried to the centre of the ring by his seconds. This rule might have saved Byrne as both he and Burke were brought up to the centre of the ring when they might not have made it unaided – in fact it was said that Burke was revived to go out for one round by a second biting through his ear. Another new rule meant fighters going down without being hit were disqualified. The new rules, which became international, were known as the London Prize Ring Rules.

When Burke returned from America he found other fighters had risen to prominence, notably William Thompson and Ben Caunt. Burke pointed out he was still champion and issued a challenge to all-comers. The first to take him on was Thompson, who was one of triplets (from a Nottingham family of 21) nicknamed Shadrack, Meshach and Abednego. William's nickname became Bendigo when he fought, and he was sometimes called 'Bold Bendigo'.

JOSH. HUDSON,
(THE JOHN BULL FIGHTER)

He took the championship over ten rounds at Heather, Leicestershire, on 12 February 1839, when Burke was disqualified for butting. Bendigo, who was taught by his mother, had previously fought Caunt twice, winning the first fight when Caunt was disqualified for dashing across the ring to hit Bendigo in his corner. Bendigo, at 5ft 9¼in (1.77m) and 165lb (74.3kg) was something of an acrobat, and a difficult man to pin down and he had taunted Caunt, 6ft 2½in (1.89m) and 210lb (94.5kg) on his impotence. In the return, Bendigo was disqualified for going down in the 75th round (1 hour and 20 minutes) without a punch (although it was probably a slip, and Bendigo's supporters attacked Caunt for claiming the fight).

Bendigo hurt his knee and retired for a time after beating Burke. Nick Ward, brother of Jem, beat Burke in 1840 and claimed the title. In 1841 he first defeated Caunt (disqualified through a low blow) then lost to him over 35 rounds (47 minutes) at Long Marsden, Yorks. Caunt was awarded a championship belt and went to America to seek challengers. Although he claimed to find none, he did decline a challenge from Charles Freeman, who at 6ft 10in (2.08m) and 270lb (121.5kg) dwarfed even Caunt. Instead Caunt brought Freeman to England where he fought William Perry, 'The Tipton Slasher,' on 10 December 1842, but after 70 rounds they were forced to stop because of darkness. It was ten days before the battle was resumed, and the Slasher was disqualified for going down without a blow. Freeman, on this performance, might have become champion, but he contracted tuberculosis and died in 1845.

Caunt was anxious to beat Bendigo again when the latter recovered from his knee injury, and the two fought for the championship on 9 September 1845. Bendigo was now nearly 34, but Caunt could not beat him, despite his size advantage and being four years younger. The fight was rough, with Caunt attempting to lift Bendigo by the neck and fall on him over the rope, but eventually Caunt was forced to go down without being hit and the match and championship belt were awarded to Bendigo. Bendigo defended successfully five years later, when Tom Paddock was disqualified after 49 rounds for hitting Bendigo on the ground, but he was clearly past his best and immediately

retired. Bendigo, a wild man when drunk, was imprisoned 28 times during his life for various offences concerning breaches of the peace, but later became a Methodist preacher, causing Lord Longford to ask him to treat the Devil better than he had poor Ben Caunt. Bendigo told his Lordship to back him against the Devil, as he had against Caunt.

Paddock, who had had the better of the fight with Bendigo before the disqualification, claimed the title but lost it after only six months, being disqualified again for a foul blow in the 27th round against the Tipton Slasher at Woking, Surrey, on 17 December 1850.

The Slasher himself lost the title through a foul blow to Harry Broome, from Birmingham, at Mildenhall, Staffs, on 29 September 1851. Broome lost to Paddock five years later, on 19 May 1856. Paddock could now call himself a champion who had won in the ring and he was presented with a new belt. Since his fight with the Tipton Slasher he had spent a period in jail when he and his opponent Harry Poulson were arrested for disturbing the peace by fighting.

Meanwhile a new fighter was capturing all the attention – Tom Sayers, from Brighton, who although barely 10 stone (140lb – 63kg) was beating all the big men. His battle for £200-a-side with the Tipton Slasher on 16 June 1857 at the Isle of Grain, Kent, was claimed to be for the Championship of England. Sayers won in ten rounds (1 hour and 42 minutes), despite giving away about four inches (10cm) and 40lb (18kg).

Exactly a year later, Sayers confirmed his title by beating Paddock over 21 rounds in 1 hour and 20 minutes. He then beat Bill Benjamin and prepared for the fight which really set alight world interest in boxing – his great match with John C. Heenan, of the United States, for the 'world championship'. This fight took place at Farnborough Common, Hampshire, on 17 April 1860 (see Chapter 8). After 2 hours and 6 minutes it was called a draw when the police interrupted, with each side claiming the superiority.

Heenan was champion of America, where prize-fighting had begun later than in England, gaining momentum with the emigration of many Englishmen in the early 19th century when fights were often staged around the taverns at the ports of arrival.

It is accepted that the match between Jacob Hyer and Tom Beasley, in New York in 1816, was the first real prizefight in the United States. It is believed that Hyer broke an arm and Beasley claimed the verdict. Hyer did not fight again.

On 9 September 1841 Jacob Hyer's son, Tom, fought George McChester, known as Country McCluskey, at

The arrangement of the prize ring in 1841, soon after the London Prize Ring Rules came into force. The ring is 24ft (7.31m), and there is an outer ring patrolled by beaters. The fight is Broome (later to be champion of England) versus Hannan.

Caldwell's Landing, New York, winning in 101 rounds (2 hours and 55 minutes), but boxing in America received a setback in 1842 when Chris Lilly, an Englishman, knocked out Tom McCoy, an Irish-American, in 120 rounds (2 hours and 40 minutes), and McCoy subsequently died. A boxer called Yankee Sullivan, who had advised Lilly, was arrested and went to prison. From then onwards prizefighting was strictly illegal in the USA, and continued only with the connivance of sympathetic politicians.

Many of the better American fighters were Irish immigrants, or of Irish descent like Yankee Sullivan. Born in Ireland as John Ambrose, and an ex-convict, he sought to gain influence and notoriety by subjecting Tom Hyer to continuous abuse and the ill-feeling roused between the two resulted in a challenge match for $5,000-a-side at Rock Point, Maryland, on 7 February 1849. Hyer won in 16 rounds in a fight

usually taken to be the first American championship bout. Hyer failed to entice William Perry, the Tipton Slasher, to the States, declined a return with Sullivan for less than $10,000-a-side and in effect retired.

The Irish then began to dominate American boxing, particularly with John Morrissey, born in Templemore, County Tipperary, who had come to America, aged three, in 1834. He matched a friend, John Willis, with a friend of Hyer's, George Thompson, and gambled heavily on his man. Thompson, well ahead, deliberately fouled his opponent to avoid trouble from Morrissey and his men. Morrissey himself then fought Sullivan for Hyer's vacant crown at Boston Corners, New York, on 12 October 1853, forcing Sullivan to retire in the 37th round.

Morrissey's next opponent was John C. Heenan, who was born in West Troy, New York, where Morrissey's parents

The presentation of belts to Tom Sayers and John Camel Heenan at the Alhambra Palace in London. Heenan is wearing his belt, and Sayers receiving his (seen above).

The Great Prize Fight Fizzle. Jem Mace of England and Joe Coburn of the USA 'fought' in Canada in 1871, but there was little action and the restive crowd forced the referee to call it a draw. Six months later they repeated the performance at Bay St Louis, Mississippi.

had settled. He was known as 'The Benicia Boy' because he had moved to the Pacific Coast and found employment in the workshops of the Pacific Mail Steamship Company in Benicia, San Francisco. Here he built a reputation as a pugilist before returning to New York. Ill feeling developed between the two men and he and Morrissey fought on 20 October 1858 at Long Point, Canada. Heenan broke his right hand on a post early in the fight and he lost in 11 rounds.

Morrissey retired, operated gambling dens in New York and Saratoga and served in the US Congress. He was elected to the Senate but was taken ill and died, aged 47, before he could serve. He thus followed the route of gambling, laying the odds and public service taken by the English champion, John Gully, elected to Parliament the year after Morrissey was born.

Heenan was recognized as champion after the retirement of Morrissey, partly because Morrissey had refused him a return after his bad luck in their first fight, and partly because there were no other challengers. It was this lack of challengers which forced Heenan to challenge Tom Sayers in England and led to the encounter on Farnborough Common in 1860.

There was a lull in interest in Britain after the Sayers–Heenan fight. Sayers would not easily be followed, and there was a reaction against the brutality of the fight. Questions were raised in Parliament and the railway criticized for taking the Fancy to their illegal destination. The police, the clergy and the magistrates became more determined to hinder the sport. Even its defenders were dismayed when Sayers became ill and died aged 39.

Tom Paddock, now 36, once again claimed the title but was beaten by Sam Hurst, 'The Stalybridge Infant', who was 6ft 3in (1.91m) and over 15 stone (210lb – 94.5kg). Hurst won in 5 rounds (9½ minutes) in Berkshire on 5 November 1860.

The best boxers around, however, were Jem Mace, who became one of the outstanding champions, and Tom King. Mace, born in Beeston, Norfolk, was a scientific boxer who stood only 5ft 9½in (1.77m) and whose weight was usually between 150 and 160lb (67–72kg). Though only a middleweight he was well built, having developed his physique on the anvil, his father being a blacksmith.

He toured the country with the fairs, playing a violin and boxing in the booths. He fought the Stalybridge Infant on 13 June 1861 for £200-a-side, and won in eight rounds (40 minutes).

Mace next fought Tom King, a Cockney from Stepney, who served in the Royal Navy and then became a dockyard worker. King became a friend of Jem Ward and advanced rapidly in the pugilistic profession, meeting Mace for the championship on 28 January 1862. They fought at Godstone, Surrey, for 43 rounds and 68 minutes, by which time King had had enough. However, in a return on 26 November of the same year, at Medway, Kent, Mace, who was comfortably in control, took a terrific blow on the temple, which two rounds later caused him to retire after 21 rounds and 38 minutes.

King announced his retirement after this match, and Mace was regarded as champion. On 1 September 1893 he successfully defended against Joe Goss in London. Goss, from Northampton, was of a similar size and weight to Mace, both men being used to opponents much bigger than themselves. Mace won over 19 rounds in 1 hour and 55 minutes.

John C. Heenan returned to England and challenged King for the world championship. King was persuaded by public opinion to accept the match, which was for £1,000-a-side, and this took place at Wadhurst, Kent, on 10 December 1863. Heenan was much heavier and stronger, but was not quite the force he had been against Sayers, and King was much the better boxer. After 24 rounds (35 minutes) The Benicia Boy was forced to give best. He thereupon retired, and King did the same, for the second time. King could claim to have retired while still champion of England and maybe the world. He turned to horse racing, became one of the Turf's best-known figures and had built a fortune of £50,000 by his death in 1888.

Meanwhile, Joe Coburn, who was born in Middleton, County Armagh, Ireland, but early went to the States to fight, returned to England with the American title and challenged Mace for the world crown, a bout being arranged for 4 October 1864 near Dublin, Ireland, at £500-a-side. However Coburn refused to accept any referee but his friend, James Bowler. In the end no referee was appointed, and they fought a 'drawn' exhibition bout for 75 minutes.

COBURN shies his castor in the Ring,

Then shies himself.—At the same moment JEM MACE appears.

Round the First.—Slashing work—Foot to foot; hilt to hilt—Furious onslaught.

Round the First continued—Superhuman endurance—Fierce counters taken and exchanged—the old glory of the P. R. revived.

JEM made a fearful lunge at COBURN, who made a lightning double counter, which would have spoiled JEM's beauty—if, however—

COBURN came up briskly to the scratch; JEM was promptly on hand;

But COBURN, whose memory was a little out, mistook the game for a foot-race, and made for his corner,

Amid cries of "May the best man win!"

The Men again at it—JOE takes his gruel like a glutton—JEM will not be denied—The death-struggle—*Time*, 75 minutes; *distance*, 300 yards.

COBURN game to the last—Wonderful stamina—"Sponge on, I will endure. Where is he? Don't hold me!"

Unnecessary interference of the Canadian Authorities.

Reading the Riot Act, when no Riot was intended.

"My watch is gone," he cried. *A Voice:* "Jest so. Watches was made to go."

Utter rout of the Authorities.—"Her Majesty's Own," bowled over.—Freedom triumphant. Downfall of tyranny.

THE GREAT PRIZE-FIGHT FIZZLE.

29

Mace drew with Joe Goss on 24 May 1866 near Meopham, Kent, over one round which lasted 65 minutes. Mace was accused of not trying and fought Goss again on 6 August, giving him a severe beating in 21 rounds packed into 31 minutes.

The anti-boxing lobby was now getting stronger and stronger in England. Mace and Ned O'Baldwin, called 'The Irish Giant', from Lismore, were prevented from boxing, and many of the leading pugilists went to the States, among them Tom Allen, Joe Goss, Joe Wormald, Ned O'Baldwin and Mace himself.

Tom Allen, from Birmingham, won the championship of America on 12 January 1869 at Chester Island, beating Bill Davis over 43 rounds for $2,000-a-side. Exactly five months later, Mike McCoole, who had claimed the championship with a win over Davis in 1866, beat Allen on a foul over nine rounds at Foster's Island, Mississippi. He refused to meet Allen again. Mace therefore fought Allen at Kennerville, Louisiana, on 10 May 1870, and won over ten rounds.

On 30 November 1871 Mace fought his old adversary Joe Coburn, six years after their abortive meeting in Ireland. The fight took place at Bay St Louis, Mississippi. Coburn was no match for Mace, who was now 40 years old, but the fight lasted for 3 hours and 48 minutes, with little action in the 12 rounds. The referee then decided to call it a draw. Mace went off to Australia and New Zealand in disgust.

It was not the end of Mace. In 1890 he fought Charlie Mitchell, who had won the heavyweight championship of England (with gloves) in 1882. The referee stopped the fight in Mitchell's favour in the third round in Edinburgh. Mace at the time was 59 years old. He was a champion of the prize ring who had fought into the era of gloves. In America there was a counterpart.

After Heenan had relinquished his American crown, Joe Coburn and Mike McCoole, two Irishmen, met on 5 May 1863 at Charlesworth, Maryland, Coburn winning in 70 minutes to claim the title. Three years later, on 19 September 1866, McCoole beat Bill Davis over 34 rounds (35 minutes) near St Louis, claimed the title for himself and arranged a return with Coburn in Indiana for 27 May 1868. But Coburn had been arrested, and McCoole, who entered the ring alone, was confirmed as champion by default until his defeat the following year by Tom Allen.

Meanwhile Jimmy Elliott had also claimed the title when Coburn refused to fight him, and confirmed his standing with a win over Bill Davis on 10 May 1867 at Point Pelee Island, Lake Erie, Canada. He also beat Charley Gallagher, who was born in Canada, over 23 rounds (77 minutes) at Peach Island, near Detroit. Elliott was finally stopped on 8 May 1879 by Johnny Dwyer, of Brooklyn, at Long Point, Canada, retiring after an injury to his ribs. Dwyer claimed the title.

Charley Gallagher had beaten Tom Allen on 23 February 1869 in St Louis in two rounds (3 minutes), establishing a title-claim for himself. He fought Allen again later the same year (after Allen had lost to McCoole) and lost, although the referee declared it a draw. It made little difference as Gallagher died of tuberculosis two years later.

A surer line lies with Allen, who after taking back the title from McCoole, lost it to Joe Goss, who had also arrived in the States from England, and who indeed fought Allen on both sides of the Atlantic. Goss won on a foul over 27 rounds fought in two rings in Kentucky on 7 September 1876. The whole picture was complicated.

The championship of America was at last undisputed when a new giant appeared on the scene, Paddy Ryan, an Irishman from Thurles, Tipperary, who like other famous fighters before him had crossed the Atlantic to live in Troy, New York. At 5ft 11in (1.80m) and 200lb (90kg) he was known as 'The Trojan Giant'.

Ryan beat Goss at Collier Station, West Virginia, on 30 May 1880, in 87 rounds (84 minutes). He lost the championship in his next fight to an even greater man, John L. Sullivan, from Roxbury, Massachusetts, a suburb of Boston. A man of enormous strength, Sullivan was known as the 'Boston Strong Boy'. On 7 February 1882 he fought Ryan for the title and $2,500-a-side at Mississippi City, and he took both by beating him into submission in nine rounds lasting just over ten minutes.

Charlie Mitchell, the Birmingham-born scrapper who was to beat the ageing Jem Mace in 1890, won middleweight and heavyweight competitions in Lon-

don in 1882 and immediately went to America with the intention of knocking out the new wonder boy, Sullivan. They met, wearing gloves, on 14 May 1883 at Madison Square Garden, New York. Mitchell was only a middleweight and stood no chance against the Boston Strong Boy, who was 5ft 10½in (1.79m) and weighed 190lb (85.5kg). However, Mitchell knocked him down (the only man to do so) in the first round but was himself knocked from the ring in the second, and when he was down in the third, the police intervened and stopped the fight.

Sullivan beat a Maori challenger, Herbert A. Slade, but a second fight with Mitchell was cancelled when Sullivan, who loved the rip-roaring life and was a broth of a boyo, arrived drunk at the hour of battle – he apologized from the ring in evening dress.

In 1887 Sullivan visited England and was met at Liverpool with tremendous enthusiasm, particularly by the Irish. He boxed exhibitions, including one for the Prince of Wales, and made a handsome

profit. It was arranged that he should meet Mitchell again, under London Prize Ring Rules, but bare-knuckle fighting being now almost impossible in England, the venue was fixed across the Channel, in France.

The battle took place before a limited number of spectators (who included Sullivan's girl-friend, dressed as a boy) behind the racing stables of Baron Rothschild's estate at Chantilly, on 10 March 1888. Rain for 36 hours beforehand, which continued spasmodically during the fight, made the conditions muddy and difficult. Mitchell, who was giving away over two stone (28lb – 12.6kg), fought a brilliant defensive battle. After 39 rounds lasting three hours and 11 minutes, gendarmes broke up the fight and arrested the boxers. The seconds agreed it was a draw, though both factions thought their man was winning.

The boxers were in an equally sorry state in the cells. Mitchell would not pay bail and was kept overnight. Sullivan paid and fled to England, avoiding his

John. L. Sullivan, the American champion, gets a blow to the chin of Charlie Mitchell in their fight in France in 1888. It was called a draw when the fight was stopped after 39 rounds.

sentence of three days imprisonment and a 200-franc fine.

Sullivan returned to America, where he became ill with typhoid fever, and did not help his physical condition with his liking for the whisky. Sullivan had turned down a challenge from Jake Kilrain, imported from Ireland to take his crown, leading to Richard Kyle Fox, who owned the *Police Gazette*, an influential sporting newspaper which devoted much space to boxing, claiming the title on Kilrain's behalf. Sullivan engaged William Muldoon, a famous wrestler and weight-lifter, to get him in condition. Muldoon decided that in view of Sullivan's declining condition, he had better fight Kilrain sooner rather than later and put his man on a water diet. Kilrain had recently fought Jem Smith, who was claiming the British championship after beating Jack Davis on 17 December 1885, one of the last important bare-knuckle fights in England. Smith's fight with Kilrain, held on the *Isle des Souverains* on the River Seine, in France, had been drawn after 106 rounds lasting two hours and 30 minutes, when darkness fell.

The Sullivan-Kilrain fight, originally scheduled for New Orleans on 4 July 1889 but put back four days because the New Orleans authorities banned it (although the referee, John Fitzpatrick, was the Mayor) was for a side bet of $10,000 and aroused tremendous public interest. It was eventually held at Richburg, Mississippi, under what was described as blistering hot sun which scorched the backs of the fighters, although a rare photograph shows spectators wearing jackets. After 75 rounds, lasting two hours and 16 minutes, Kilrain could not continue, and Sullivan was declared the winner. On the strength of Kilrain's draw with Jem Smith, Sullivan claimed the world title.

Sullivan was himself all but exhausted after the contest, and declared that he would not fight again with bare knuckles. He went on the stage, got out of condition, but put his title on the line against James J. Corbett in 1892. The fight was under Queensberry Rules, and the boxers wore gloves. It is generally recognized as the first fight for the heavyweight championship of the world (see Chapter 8).

Thus John L. Sullivan in America joined Jem Mace in England as a great champion who spanned the bare-knuckle days of the London Prize Ring Rules and the days of boxing gloves and the Queensberry Rules. Charlie Mitchell, who fought both, as well as Jim Corbett for the heavyweight title, also boxed right through the transition.

The last prize ring fight of any note was on 23 December 1889, when Jem Smith, who claimed to be champion of England, fought Frank Slavin, an Australian who claimed the British Empire championship, in Bruges, Belgium. The fight was a throwback to the worst days of the prize ring. A large bet was made on Smith by Squire Abingdon Baird, who gambled heavily on boxers and was not particular how he won. He hired a squad of ruffians

John L. Sullivan and Jake Kilrain clinch in the seventh round of their championship fight at Richburg in 1899. Note the hats and jackets on a 'blistering hot day'. This was perhaps the last great prize fight.

to go to Bruges, where during the fight they hit Slavin with sticks whenever he came within range of the ropes. The brave Slavin nevertheless was on top and about to knock out Smith in the 14th round when the mob invaded the ring and the timid referee, probably for his own safety, declared the result a draw. British sportsmen of the Pelican Club, which arranged the match, insisted that Slavin have the stake money (£500-a-side). Slavin went to America and beat Jake Kilrain, wearing gloves.

The prize ring era had lasted about 170 years. Most of the significant activity was in Great Britain and Ireland, there being no prizefighting in Europe, except when fights were taken there from England to avoid the law. In America it developed from the English settlers, but it was not until bare-knuckle boxing was coming to its end that a champion emerged there to rank with the best British fighters.

The prize ring could be cruel. The fights were brutal, with boxers smashed into insensibility in a way that would not be tolerated today. Several fights are known which lasted for over four hours. The longest fight is believed to be of six hours 15 minutes between James Kelly and Jack Smith, near Melbourne, Australia on 19 October 1856. Mike Madden and Bill Hays fought for 185 rounds (six hours three minutes) at Edenbridge, Kent, on 17 July 1849. The prizes for the lucky ones could be great, both in terms of future financial prosperity and in public esteem.

Too many heroes died young. Of those whose feats are prominent in this chapter, most did not reach 50 years of age. James Figg died at 39, Jem Belcher at 30, Tom Johnson 46, Big Ben Brain 48, Henry Pearce, the Game Chicken, 32, Tom Molineaux 34, James Burke, the Deaf 'Un 35, Nick Ward 38, Ben Caunt 46, Tom Paddock 39, Tom Sayers 39, John C. Heenan, the Benicia Boy, 38, Joe Goss 44, Charley Gallagher 22, Paddy Ryan 48. Some fell victim to illnesses of the time, principally tuberculosis, but the deaths of all were hurried by the fearful punishment they took.

The esteem in which the champions were held is marked by some of the memorials erected to them, particularly those of the 18th and 19th centuries who lived to a more respectable age.

John Broughton, who brought rules to the prize ring, lived to 86 and left £7,000, has a stone in the floor of Westminster

Abbey to commemorate his name. Gentleman John Jackson, who lived to 76, has a memorial sculpted by Thomas Butler, which shows Jackson's physique and a crouching lion above his tomb, in Brompton Cemetery, London. Tom Cribb, who reached 66, has a huge monument of Portland stone, put up by public subscription in Woolwich churchyard, London, showing a lion grieving for the dead warrior, while Tom Spring, who died at 56, has an imposing memorial in Norwood Cemetery, London and William Thompson, Bold Bendigo, who became a preacher and lived to be 79, has a large memorial in Nottingham.

Tom Sayers, one of the gamest of all the champions, who was only 39 when he died five years after his last fight, so captured the public imagination that a magnificent memorial was built for him in Highgate Cemetery, London.

The monuments reflect the esteem in which all the prize-ring heroes were held by both the aristocratic Fancy and the men from whose ranks they rose – butchers, blacksmiths, dock workers, bricklayers. They were truly the gladiators of modern times.

An illustration from a French magazine showing Peter Jackson, the West Indian who fought in Australia and America, in his fight with Frank Slavin, the champion of Australia, at the National Sporting Club in 1892. Jackson won in the tenth round.

2 THE COMING OF GLOVES

The biggest step towards boxing as we know it today came with the publication of the Queensberry Rules in 1867. At the time important matches were fought under the London Prize Ring Rules, which were adapted in 1838 from Broughton's Rules of 1743 (see Chapter 1) and which were revised in 1853 and 1866.

The 29 London Prize Ring Rules generally set out Broughton's Rules at greater length and in greater detail, specifying fouls more explicitly. The main changes were:

1. The 'square of a yard' in Broughton's Rule 1 was replaced by the old 'scratch' line.

2. After the 30 seconds between rounds, and the umpire's call of 'Time', each man was required to walk to the scratch unaided, and was allowed eight seconds to do so. This prevented seconds from carrying boxers to the scratch who were, in reality, unfit to continue.

3. There was more attention paid to the boxers' dress, in particular limiting spikes on boots.

4. A man wilfully going down without a blow was deemed to have lost the battle.

5. Fouls, such as butting, gouging, biting, scratching, kicking, the use of stones, etc. in the hand, squeezing on the ropes, were set out fully.

6. Provisions were made regarding wagers in the event of postponements, cancellations, interference by the law or darkness, boxers quitting the ring and other unforseen circumstances.

The Queensberry Rules were not, in fact, devised by Lord Queensberry at all, although he may have helped. They were drawn up by a fellow-student at Cambridge University called John Graham Chambers (some authorities claim he was Arthur Chambers, who later went to the States and won the world lightweight title in 1872, but this is not universally accepted). As the Queensberry name was valuable in publicizing the rules, Chambers sought out the patronage of the eighth Marquess of Queensberry, under whose name the Rules were published. They took most of the brutality from the ring, introducing gloves and the concept of a three-minute round.

The Queensberry Rules were as follows:

1. To be a fair stand-up boxing match in a twenty-four foot ring, or as near that size as practicable.

2. No wrestling or hugging allowed.

3. The rounds to be of three minutes' duration, and one minute's time between rounds.

4. If either man fall through weakness or otherwise, he must get up unassisted, ten seconds to be allowed him to do so, the other man meanwhile to return to his corner, and when the fallen man is on his legs the round is to be resumed, and continued till the three minutes have expired. If one man fails to come to the scratch in the ten

seconds allowed, it shall be in the power of the referee to give his award in favour of the other man.

5. A man hanging on the ropes in a helpless state, with his toes off the ground, shall be considered down.

6. No seconds or any other person to be allowed in the ring during the rounds.

7. Should the contest be stopped by any unavoidable interference, the referee to name the time and place as soon as possible for finishing the contest; so that the match must be won and lost, unless the backers of both men agree to draw the stakes.

8. The gloves to be fair-sized boxing gloves of the best quality and new.

9. Should a glove burst, or come off, it must be replaced to the referee's satisfaction.

10. A man on one knee is considered down, and if struck is entitled to the stakes.

11. No shoes or boots with springs allowed.

12. The contest in all other respects to be governed by revised rules of the London Prize Ring.

Notice that, although there were to be three-minute rounds, there was no mention of any limit to a bout, and the prize-ring concept of fights being to a finish continued. It was the organizers of fights who began to specify time limits.

Originally a 'fight-to-the-finish' came to be regarded by some promoters as 45 rounds (this being 2 hours 15 minutes of actual boxing, enough time usually for a decision). Later the limit became 20 rounds, and then 15 (in Europe 12) which is a world title distance today.

The concept of a 'points' win began in Britain in the early days of glove-fighting, when the referee was required to award five points to the winner of a round, and less to the loser – $4\frac{3}{4}$ for a close round, $4\frac{1}{2}$ if the loser had been well beaten, i.e. put down for a count or otherwise punished. Nowadays there is a variety of ways of scoring around the world, with the maximum points per round being usually ten rather than five, but the cumbersome method of using only part of the range of marks per round is still the rule, even, sometimes, with the unnecessary convention of half-marks.

For a while, fights with gloves under the Queensberry Rules were held while

prize-ring contests were still being fought, some boxers flitting from one style to the other.

Boxing in Britain took another step in the direction of law and order with the formation in London of the National Sporting Club in 1891 following the demise of the Pelican Club. Although boxing was still illegal, it had 'retired' indoors, where matches held in large rooms in public houses or in sporting clubs under Queensberry Rules were largely tolerated by the authorities.

The Pelican Club, however, as described in Chapter 1, had promoted a notorious bare-knuckle fight in Belgium between Jem Smith and Frank Slavin, in 1889. This led to its closure, as many members resigned in disgust, including

The man who gave his name to the famous rules of boxing, the eighth Marquess of Queensberry, in profile as seen by Phil May.

J. Kilrain.
Champion of America

C. Mitchell
Boxing Champion

S.T. DADD.

J. Swain Eng.

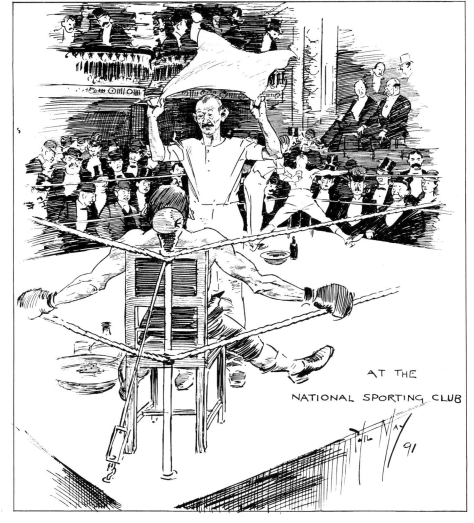

AT THE

NATIONAL SPORTING CLUB

John Fleming, who, with Arthur 'Peggy' Bettinson, began the National Sporting Club.

The membership of the National Sporting Club was wide, embracing not only the aristocracy but the wealthier businessman, and the atmosphere was the opposite of that of the old prize ring. Spectators wore evening dress, and silence was observed during rounds. Applause was limited to inter-round periods. The Club was a popular venue for boxers, and rapidly became the nearest thing to a governing body in England, promoting and hosting British title fights. A famous contest in its early days was for the 'British Empire Heavyweight Championship' in 1892, in which Peter Jackson beat Frank Slavin of Australia.

At this time there were no clearly defined weight classes, although interest was by no means confined to the heavyweights. Matches were made at weights suitable to the fighters, who came to be known as lightweights, roughly below $9\frac{1}{2}$ stone (133lb – 60kg) or middleweights, up to about 11 stone (154lb – 70kg). Subsequently bantam, feather and welterweight classes were added, then light-heavy, which was

PHIL MAY 97

Opposite top: Jake Kilrain, called by the *Illustrated Sporting and Dramatic News* the 'champion of America' (Sullivan was) and Charlie Mitchell, just 'boxing champion' in their fight at the Westminster Aquarium in 1887.

Opposite bottom: A representation by Phil May of boxing at the National Sporting Club in 1891. The NSC was a club for well-to-do boxing followers who dressed for the fights.

Left: Another Phil May view of the National Sporting Club in 1897. After the turn of the century the NSC formulated the weight divisions and assumed control of British boxing.

known in England as cruiser, and, for the very small men, flyweight. But there was little agreement at the end of the 19th century as to the divisions.

One of the best of the lighter men in the early days of gloves was Jack Dempsey, who was born John Kelly in County Kildare, Ireland, in 1862. He won the world middleweight championship on 30 August 1884 when he beat George Fulljames in 22 rounds in Toronto. Dempsey was called 'The Nonpareil' because nobody could be found at his weight to beat him. He remained champion until 1891 when he lost to Bob Fitzsimmons, although he was knocked out by George La Blanche in the 32nd round in San Francisco in 1889. La Blanche used a 'pivot punch', a backhander delivered with a swivel of the heel, which was declared illegal.

Dempsey's defeat by Fitzsimmons, himself one of the immortals of the ring, cost his backers a fortune. A purse of $1,000 was put up by the Olympic Club of New Orleans, Louisiana, which the following year, 1892, became famous for staging the first world heavyweight championship bout under Queensberry Rules. The contestants were John L. Sullivan, generally acknowledged as the bare-knuckle champion, and James J. Corbett, a former bank clerk, and an educated man who studied Sullivan and worked out how to beat him. 'Gentleman Jim', as he was known, was a clever, scientific boxer.

Corbett won by a knockout in the 21st round (see Chapter 8), to become the first heavyweight champion of the world. This distinction is often claimed in the United States for Sullivan on the basis of

Below: Jack Dempsey, 'The Nonpareil', and his fight with the Australian champion Billy McCarthy at New Orleans in 1894. The result was a draw over 20 rounds. Dempsey had won by a 28th round knock-out four years earlier.

two previous victories. The first is Sullivan's defeat of Paddy Ryan in 1882, after Ryan had beaten Joe Goss, then claiming the British championship, in 1880. It is difficult to see how this makes Sullivan world champion but not Ryan. The second strand to the claim rests on a fight between Sullivan and Dominick McCaffrey in Cincinatti, Ohio, on 29 August 1885. This was billed as 'six rounds to decide the Marquis of Queensberry glove contest for the championship of the world' – natural promoter's hyperbole. The fight ended in some confusion. After six rounds the referee left for Toledo. He was not required to make a decision. It is reported there was

a seventh round, Sullivan hoping to knock out his opponent. He failed, and himself left. Two days later the referee was asked who won, and said Sullivan, a verdict upheld by the newspapers. This, it is said, makes Sullivan the first of the Queensberry champions. However, it was not said before 1936, and the fact that Sullivan actually 'won' a fight wearing gloves does not substantiate such a strong claim.

Sullivan was, in fact, world bare-knuckle champion by universal consent in 1892, as Jem Mace, Britain's last undisputed prize-ring champion, was 61 by then, and there had been no serious challenger to Sullivan for a while. The defeat by Corbett left Sullivan the last bare-knuckle champion, and made Corbett the first Queensberry Rules champion.

Corbett had come into prominence by beating Joe Choynski and Jake Kilrain, and boxing a draw over 61 rounds with Peter Jackson. Jackson was a black West Indian, born in 1861, who went to Australia to become a boxing champion and then on to the States, where he challenged Sullivan, who refused to fight him because of his colour. Some think he was the best heavyweight of his time, and his draw with Corbett, when he was already 30 years old, suggests this might be true. Jackson impressed the following year, when at the National Sporting Club in London he knocked out Aus-

JACK DEMPSEY

Jim Corbett knocks out Peter Courtney especially for the Edison Kinetoscope. The theatre, known as the 'Black Maria' was built on tracks so that it could follow the sun round.

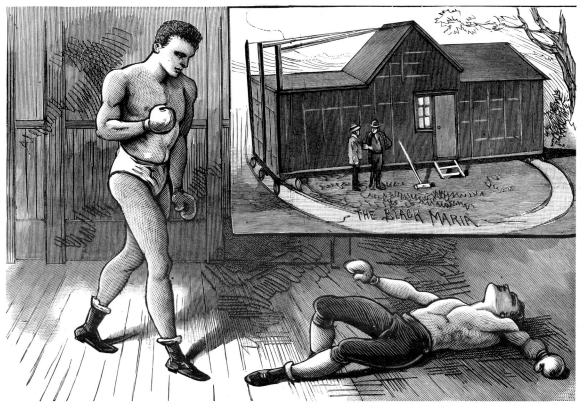

THE BLACK MARIA

38

tralian Frank Slavin in the tenth round. Like Sullivan and Corbett, he went on the stage, starring for six years in 'Uncle Tom's Cabin'. When he was 37 he fought James J. Jeffries, who, like Corbett, won the world title a year after meeting Jackson. Jackson died when he was 40 years old of tuberculosis.

The affairs of Corbett after he became champion were taken over by William A. Brady, a theatrical impresario. He kept Corbett on the stage in a play 'Gentleman Jack' for five years, during which Corbett defended his title against England's Charlie Mitchell, knocking him out in three rounds in Jacksonville, Florida, on 25 January 1894. Corbett then announced his retirement, choosing Peter Maher, an Irish heavyweight from Galway, as his successor.

This did not impress Bob Fitzsimmons, who was Corbett's main challenger for the title. Fitzsimmons was a Cornishman who had left England as a child for New Zealand, where he became a blacksmith's apprentice and built up a very muscular upper frame. He won a boxing competition organised by Jem Mace and took up the sport as a profession, going to America, where he could earn most money. He beat the great Jack Dempsey, 'The Nonpareil', to win the world middleweight championship in 1891 and subsequently challenged for the heavyweight title.

Fitzsimmons' reaction to Corbett's retirement was to knock out Peter Maher in the first round in Langtry, Texas, on 21 February 1896. The public were reluctant to recognize him as champion, however, until he had beaten Corbett.

The Fitzsimmons-Maher battle was the second attempt to make a moving picture of a fight. On 8 September 1894 Corbett fought Peter Courtney at the Edison Laboratory in Orange, New Jersey, in front of a 'Kinetoscope'. This involved the use of a huge Kinetographic theatre which had to be moved around so that the sun shone directly onto the 'ring'. Rounds lasted as long as the film – about 90 seconds. Intervals were longer. It was claimed to be a legitimate fight – Corbett won by a knockout in the sixth round to collect $5,000 to Courtney's $1,000 – but it was no doubt an arranged exhibition. The films were never shown.

The attempts to film the Fitzsimmons-Maher fight were amusing. Edison made the arrangements without informing the boxers. Fitzsim-

mons got to hear, however, and demanded extra payment, which was refused. Fitzsimmons had his revenge by knocking out Maher in 95 seconds – before the cameraman could get the machine working! Three weeks later, in New York, Fitzsimmons and Maher recreated their battle for the Kinetoscope Company, who circulated the film as the actual fight. Needless to say, Fitzsimmons collected a fee this time.

Corbett made no secret of his contempt for Fitzsimmons, publicly tweaking his nose in a hotel in 1895. He was reluctant to meet a man who was really a middleweight. The match was made, however, but took a long time to come to fruition, many states refusing to allow it because of possible trouble from the huge crowd expected. The boxers were actually arrested in Arkansas for conspiring to commit a breach of the peace.

Peter Jackson, the best black heavyweight of his day, boxing a 61-round draw with James J. Corbett, soon to be the world champion, at Las Vegas in 1891.

39

The fight took place, eventually, at Carson City, Nevada, on 17 March 1897, in a specially built open-air arena. Nevada legalized boxing in order that the fight might be staged. The purse was $15,000, and there was a $5,000 side bet. Fitzsimmons was 13lb (5.9kg) lighter at 157lb (70.7kg) to 170lb (76.5kg). He was down in the sixth round, but fought back to win with his 'solar plexus' punch in the 14th. The fight is described in full in Chapter 8. It was the first real contest to be filmed.

Fitzsimmons cashed in by means of a theatrical tour similar to those which had proved so lucrative for previous heavyweight champions. He and his wife, Rose, who had previous stage experience, knocked out the drama from a play called 'The Honest Blacksmith'.

The first challenger to Fitzsimmons was James J. Jeffries, a big man, but considered too slow to trouble Fitz. Once again the fans were in for a surprise. The fight took place at the New York holiday centre, Coney Island, on 9 June 1899. The physical advantages were overwhelmingly with Jeffries. At 6ft 2½in (1.89m) he was 2½in (7cm) taller; at 220lb (99kg) about 56lb (25kg) heavier; at 76in (1.94m), his reach was nearly five inches (14cm) longer; and, at 24 to Fitzsimmons' 36, he was 12 years the younger. His extra weight was all muscle.

Jeffries fought from a crouching position, and 'Fitz' found it difficult to reach the target. The bigger man also used his weight cleverly, going into many clinches and laying on his opponent. Fitzsimmons tried hard and got in some telling blows but was eventually worn down by Jeffries' huge swings. In the 11th round Jeffries brushed aside Fitzsimmons' leads, hit him with two swinging rights and a left, and, as Fitzsimmons stood helpless, put him down for the count with another left.

The most prominent heavyweight of the 1890s among those who did not win the title was Tom Sharkey, who fought three world champions and 'beat' two of them, although in strange circumstances. In 1896, Sharkey, an ex-sailor who had a sailing ship under a five-pointed star tattooed on his chest, fought Fitzsimmons in San Francisco after Fitz had despatched Maher in one round. Wyatt Earp, the famous Wild West Marshal, was the referee, and also the $10,000 stakeholder. Fitzsimmons knocked out Sharkey in the eighth round, but was amazed to hear Earp disqualify him for a low blow and hand the winning cheque to Sharkey. Earp then buckled on his gun and challenged anybody to dispute the decision.

Fitzsimmons secured an injunction to prevent the cheque being cashed and later claimed in court a conspiracy involving the referee. One of Sharkey's sparring partners, Billy Smith, testified that Sharkey's manager and two local sportsmen had fixed the fight with Earp. The $10,000 purse had been staked on Sharkey in advance at 3–1, the four conspirators to collect $10,000 each. However the judge stopped the case, pointing out that boxing was illegal anyway in California, and Earp and his fellow-swindlers kept the proceeds of their crime, and Sharkey the decision.

In 1898 Sharkey fought Corbett, by then ex-champion. During the ninth round, Corbett's second, Connie McVey, crawled through the ropes into the ring. The referee, 'Honest John' Kelly, immediately awarded the fight to Sharkey on a foul, but called all bets off. There was more talk of another swindle, but an investigation did not probe very deeply.

There was no suggestion that Sharkey himself was a party to any double-cross. In 1899 he fought James J. Jeffries for the world title and put up a tremendous show, fighting bravely to the end of 25 brutal rounds despite two broken ribs and severe facial cuts. He lost on points and was taken to hospital.

In the last 20 years of the 19th century boxing was tolerated, although illegal, in many centres in America. In some, like

James J. Jeffries (left) shakes hands with Bob Fitzsimmons before taking the title from him in 1899. Ed Graney is the referee.

California, even bare-knuckle fights could be held, while other states would turn a blind eye on gloved contests only. Thus the first bout for the heavyweight championship of the world, between Sullivan and Corbett in New Orleans, was held without hindrance, although against the law.

The first state to permit boxing was New York in 1896 (closely followed by Nevada) using the Horton Law, which allowed matches for purses and side-stakes. But generally there was no control over the promotion of bouts, individual promoters in various towns throughout the States arranging whatever matches they thought would attract the public.

In 1882 the original Madison Square Garden arena at Madison Avenue, New York, staged its first boxing match. The first bout held there concerned John L. Sullivan, who had issued a challenge to anybody to stay four rounds with him. He offered $100, later $500, to a successful opponent, a sum which remained unclaimed after a triumphant tour of the states. On the opening of Madison Square Garden to boxing, an English middleweight, Joe Collins (known as Tug Wilson) by clinching and going down often managed to last the four rounds and became the only man to collect the cash. Next year Sullivan beat Charlie Mitchell at the venue, which was rebuilt in 1890 and hosted many fights until 1925, when a new Madison Square Garden was built on Eighth Avenue. It was replaced in 1968 by today's 13-storey building over Pennsylvania Station.

Tom Sharkey, who gained dubious victories over Corbett and Fitzsimmons but lost a tremendous battle with Jeffries for the heavyweight championship in 1899. Note the cauliflower ear.

Kid McCoy, once middleweight champion, at the end of his career. He fought in two styles: one, brilliant, was the 'real McCoy', the other was somewhat controversial.

In the early days of gloved fights under Queensberry Rules, when they were still fought to a finish, although over three-minute rounds, there were of course, some marathon contests. Most of these occurred in the late 1880s and 1890s. The longest recorded was between Andy Bowen and Jack Burke, who boxed for 110 rounds in New Orleans on 6 April 1893. After seven hours and 19 minutes the boxers refused to continue, and the referee announced a draw. Bowen had been in another long fight in 1891, when he was knocked out in the 48th round by Austin Gibbons. Danny Needham and Patsy Kerrigan drew after 100 rounds (six hours and 39 minutes) in San Francisco in 1890. The longest fight under Queensberry Rules in which there was a decision was between Harry Sharpe and Frank Crosby in Nameski, Illinois, on 2 February 1892. Sharpe knocked out Crosby in the 77th round (five hours and six minutes).

Among the boxers who made reputations and drew the admiration of fight fans in the last years of the 19th century were many who fought at the lighter weights which, without being standardized, were gaining recognition. An American named Billy (real name Amos) Smith seemed to win so often that a newspaper column asked who was this 'mysterious' Billy Smith, and the prefix stuck. Mysterious Billy Smith was recognized as world welterweight champion after beating Danny Needham in 1892, and although he lost the title to Tommy Ryan in 1894, he reclaimed it in 1898 when Ryan moved up a division, and held it until beaten by Jim 'Rube' Ferns in 1900.

Tommy Ryan put his welter title on the line, and at the same time challenged for the middleweight title relinquished by Bob Fitzsimmons, when he fought Charles 'Kid' McCoy in 1896. McCoy won, but Ryan regained the welterweight title, and after McCoy had moved up to the heavyweights, Ryan himself moved up and won the vacant middleweight title which he held until his retirement in 1904.

Kid McCoy would have been one of the greatest ever boxers at light-heavyweight, but this division was not recognized until 1903, when McCoy was a veteran of 31. He then fought for the title but lost to Jack Root. He was not heavy enough to get a title fight at heavyweight, losing the chance with a defeat by Jack Sharkey, but fought former champion Jim Corbett in 1900, when it was thought he threw the fight. McCoy tricked Tommy Ryan in their double title bout. He told Ryan he was dying of consumption and needed the prize-money for doctor's bills. Ryan did not bother to train too hard, and was knocked out by a fully fit McCoy in the 15th round. McCoy, on this occasion, was undoubtedly the 'real' McCoy, and gave his name to an expression which became universal in the English language. He later made films in Hollywood, before committing suicide in 1940.

There were some good men in the lightweight class. Jack McAuliffe, born in Cork, Ireland, in 1866, was fighting in America by the time he was 18. He was American champion and is generally recognized as world champion from 1886 to 1893, although this is hard on the ten-years-older English champion Jem Carney, who went to Revere, Massachusetts, to fight McAuliffe in 1887. The match, held in a huge barn to avoid the police, was billed for the world championship. The crowd held it up in the 70th round, when McAuliffe was about to be counted out, and stopped it altogether in the 74th, when it appeared Carney had again delivered a knock-out blow. To save the local bets, the referee called the fight a draw. Otherwise, McAuliffe was never beaten.

George Lavigne, the 'Saginaw Kid', claimed the lightweight title in 1896, when he beat the English champion, Dick Burge, in London. He had previously beaten Andy Bowen, the marathon fight specialist mentioned earlier, knocking him out with such force in the 18th round that Bowen struck the boards with his head and died. Lavigne lost his title to Frank Erne in 1899.

In the featherweight category, a boxer from Auckland, New Zealand, Billy 'Torpedo' Murphy, won a match with Irishman Ike Weir, billed for the world championship in San Francisco in 1890. He then lost to Young Griffo (Albert Griffiths) in his home town of Sydney, Australia, eight months later. Young Griffo was never fully recognized as world champion, even though he was possibly the best defensive boxer of all time. He fought for many years in America, sometimes when the worse for drink, and he died of over-indulgence in an asylum when 58 years old.

Several other boxers briefly claimed the featherweight crown in the 1890s, notably George Dixon, of Canada, known as 'Little Chocolate' because he was brown and only 5ft 3½in (1.61m), Solly Smith, of Los Angeles, Dave Sullivan, of Cork, Ireland, Ben Jordan, of Bermondsey, London, and Eddie Santry, of Aurora, Illinois.

The first champion among the smallest men, fighting in what was then the bantamweight class, is usually recognised as Tommy Kelly, the 'Harlem Spirit', in 1890, but English boxers dominated the class and Billy Plimmer, of Birmingham, went to America and outpointed Kelly in 1892. He fought in America for three years but on returning to England lost the title to Tom 'Pedlar' Palmer of Canning Town, London, whose father was a prizefighter, the fight being stopped after Plimmer's brother intervened and climbed into the ring in the 14th round.

Palmer was not recognized as champion in America, however, where Jimmy Barry was favoured after he beat Caspar Leon in 1894. Barry went to London and fought Walter Croot for the world title in 1897, winning by a knockout. Croot died of a brain injury, and Barry was charged with manslaughter, but cleared. Barry was upset by the accident, however, and after holding his crown by means of two draws with Leon, he retired undefeated. Terry McGovern claimed the 'vacant' title, and in 1899 Palmer went to New York to settle the difference of opinion as to the rightful champion with him.

The McGovern-Palmer fight at Tuckahoe, New York, on 22 September 1899, was a strange one. Soon after the start, the timekeeper struck the bell accidentally, and the referee sent the boxers to their corners to begin again. Second time round, Palmer proffered a glove to McGovern, who replied by swinging a right to the chin which knocked him out. The official time was 75 seconds. Palmer's career virtually ended when he was jailed for five years in 1907 after being convicted of manslaughter following a fight on a train.

At the end of the century, therefore, boxing was in the curious position of being immensely popular and of boasting champions who were rich and famous, and yet was still illegal in most parts of the world, although becoming increasingly tolerated. More fame and riches were yet to come.

3 THE BEGINNING OF THE BOOM

The Horton Law which allowed boxing in New York State was repealed as the 20th century began. The main reason was a fight between James J. Corbett and Kid McCoy in August, 1900, at Madison Square Garden, New York. Corbett won by a knockout in the fifth round, but his opponent was not the 'real' McCoy and the general opinion was that McCoy had thrown the fight. Public boxing was banned by the repeal of the Horton Law, but it was replaced by the Lewis Law, which allowed the staging of boxing tournaments only for members of properly constituted clubs.

At the National Sporting Club (NSC) in London a death in the ring led to a test case which went in boxing's favour. On 4 April 1901 Jack Roberts, a featherweight, knocked out a boxer called Billy Smith, who struck his head on falling and died. Roberts and nine leading members of the NSC were charged at the Old Bailey with 'feloniously killing and slaying' Murray Livingstone, the real name of Smith. The prosecution admitted that the object was to stop boxing rather than to inflict punishment on the defendants. The judge, Mr Justice Grantham, upheld the desirability of differences in ordinary life being settled with fists in preference to weapons, and the desirability of organized boxing being run under proper rules.

The jury found that the death occurred in a properly regulated boxing contest, was accidental, and that the defendents were therefore 'not guilty'. The result was that the police authorities concerned themselves only with keeping order at boxing matches and did not question the legality of properly run fights again.

The National Sporting Club, having overcome this crisis, went from strength to strength for a while, and did much for boxing in tte early days of the century, perhaps the most important being the establishment of weight classes. Before these were standardized, the poundage fluctuated in each class, boxers and promoters claiming that fights at any odd weight they cared to announce were for a 'championship'. Even in classes which were generally acknowledged, champions fixed weight limits to suit themselves. When Bob Fitzsimmons took Jack Dempsey's middleweight title in 1891, for instance, the limit was 154lb (69.3kg), but Fitzsimmons, being heavy for a middleweight, raised the limit by 4lb (1.8kg) for his defence against Dan Creedon, of Australia, in 1894.

In 1909 The National Sporting Club announced fixed poundages for eight classes as follows:

Flyweight	8st (112lb – 50.4kg)
Bantamweight	8st 6lb (118lb – 53.1kg)
Featherweight	9st (126lb – 56.7kg)
Lightweight	9st 9lb (135lb – 60.75kg)
Welterweight	10st 7lb (147lb – 66.15kg)
Middleweight	11st 6lb (160lb – 72kg)
Cruiserweight	12st 7lb (175lb – 78.75kg)
Heavyweight	over 12st 7lb.

This welcome enterprise was applauded and accepted throughout the boxing world, except for the term 'cruiserweight' in America, where there was already a 175lb class called 'light-heavyweight'. This had been suggested by Lou Houseman, a Chicago news-paperman, in the interests of Jack Root, who was between the recognised middle and heavyweight limits, and was agreed to by the boxing press, so that the fight between Root and Kid McCoy in 1903 was advertised as being for the light-heavyweight championship of the world.

The British eventually changed their name for the class from 'cruiser' to 'light-heavyweight' in 1937, and in 1979 a new 'cruiserweight' title was introduced by the World Boxing Council, with a limit of 13st 13lb (195lb – 87.75kg). Other new intermediate classes had been introduced since the 1920s, and there are now 15 weight divisions.

To go with their new weight classes, the NSC persuaded their President, Lord Lonsdale, to give his name to the famous series of belts, to be won by boxers in each class. This was to give authority to the Club's rule that British

championship matches could only be held on their premises. It helped to deter other promoters and to establish a monopoly for the NSC over the titles in the new classes, the holder of a Lonsdale Belt being the champion. In effect it made the NSC a sort of ruling body of the sport in Britain for many years.

The Fifth Earl of Lonsdale provided the first belt himself. It was won by Freddie Welsh, when he beat Johnny Summers for the lightweight title on 8 November 1909. The other first winners were:

> Flyweight: Sid Smith,
>   4 December 1911
> Bantamweight: George 'Digger'
>   Stanley, 17 October 1910
> Featherweight: Jim Driscoll,
>   14 February 1910
> Welterweight: Aschel 'Young'
>   Joseph, 21 March 1910
> Middleweight: Tom Thomas,
>   20 December 1909
> Cruiserweight: Dick Smith,
>   9 March 1914
> Heavyweight: Billy Wells,
>   24 April 1911

A painting by George Bellows, called 'Stag at Sharkey's', dated 1907. At this time boxing matches in New York were allowed only in private clubs. No points decisions were rendered.

A boxer winning three title bouts in the same division keeps his belt and a new one is issued. All the above won original Lonsdale belts outright except Smith, Joseph and Thomas. The original belts in these classes were won by Jimmy Wilde (flyweight) Johnny Basham (welter) and Pat O'Keefe (middle). Only one boxer has won three Lonsdale belts outright – heavyweight Henry Cooper. Provision was made for an outright winner of a Lonsdale belt to receive a pension of £1 a week when he reached the age of 50. After the demise of the original NSC in 1929, the British Boxing Board of Control maintained the Lonsdale Belt tradition.

Another famous venue of the time, in which the spectators were far less sedate than the well-heeled NSC patrons, was Wonderland, at Whitechapel Road in London's poor East End district. Originally the Effingham Music Hall, it began to put on an occasional boxing tournament in 1899, and then came under the control of Harry Jacobs, who staged twice-weekly shows there until the building burned down in 1911. The year before, Dick Burge, a former lightweight champion, and Tom Pritchard converted a disused chapel in Blackfriars Road, South London, and began promoting weekly shows. This became known as The Ring (the building itself was octagonal) and was a popular venue for many years. After the First World War, during which Dick Burge died, his wife continued operations, being the only woman boxing promoter. The building was destroyed in the Second World War.

The sport began to establish itself in the early 20th century in many parts of the world which previously had no boxing traditions. It was introduced into the 1904 Olympic Games in St Louis, USA, but nearly all the competitors were American (as they were in the Games as a whole) and they won all the medals in the seven boxing classes. Incidentally, women's boxing was a display event at St Louis.

Australia already had a flourishing fight business, largely due to the influence of Jem Mace. Frank Slavin, Young Griffo, the West Indian Peter Jackson and the English world champion Bob Fitzsimmons have already been mentioned as leading fighters in Australia. Canada also had produced excellent boxers, such as George Dixon.

Boxing took much longer to get going in Europe, although from the Middle Ages the French had long practised a form of combat of their own, *savate*, combining the use of fists and feet with canes and sticks. This rough form of battle developed around 1820 into the more sophisticated *chausson*. One Parisian teacher, Charles Lecour, in the house of Lord Seymour, fought with an English bare-knuckle boxer, Owen Swift, and was defeated. He decided to combine *savate* with English boxing and invented *la boxe Francaise*. For a time the sport was taken up by society and literary men – Alexander Dumas and Theophile Gautier took lessons – and around the turn of the century there were 100,000 enthusiastic participants. In 1908 the world amateur champion was Georges Carpentier. Although *la boxe Francaise* has not died out (there was even a revival in the 1970s), it was rapidly overtaken in popularity by *la boxe Anglaise* from the early years of this century. Carpentier became world light-heavyweight champion of 'English' boxing also and he and Charles Ledoux were European champions before the First World War.

There was a short period of boxing popularity in Germany in the 19th century, including a public tournament in Hamburg in 1899, but the police were more successful in suppressing boxing in Germany than elsewhere, and it did not resurface there until after the First World War.

Denmark had boxing before 1900, and in 1908 had the world lightweight champion in Battling Nelson. Italy, in 1909, began producing good boxers and many went to America to find boxing fame, the first to win a world championship being Johnny Dundee in 1923. Later Primo Carnera became Italy's best-known boxing export, winning the world heavyweight championship in 1933, while one Italian-American, Rocky Marciano, became one of the all-time greats.

Boxing reached Belgium and Holland before the First World War, but neither country has made any impact on the international scene. Most other European countries did not introduce boxing until as late as the 1920s and 1930s and only one has caused a ripple on boxing's pond, although that ripple was more like a wave when Sweden's Ingemar Johansson won the world heavyweight title in 1959.

Way back before the First World War the big name in boxing was a heavy-weight whose successes led to race riots. But the man still in control of the title at the turn of the century was James J. Jeffries, the 'Boilermaker'.

On 11 May 1900 he defended his title against the former champion, James J. Corbett, at Coney Island. Jeffries was managed by William A. Brady, who had previously steered Corbett to the title and was the only man to manage two world heavyweight champions. The clever Corbett put up one of his best performances in outpointing the giant Jeffries for 22 rounds. He had no difficulties in avoiding the lefts the cumbersome Jeffries poked out, and was winning the fight easily when he care-lessly got caught on the ropes in the 23rd round. Jeffries' punishing left finally connected and Corbett was knocked out. Corbett would have won on points had the bout gone the scheduled 25 rounds, but with this defeat he became more popular than he had been when toppling the idol, John L. Sullivan, eight years earlier.

Jeffries fought another ex-champion in 1902: Bob Fitzsimmons, from whom he had won the title three years earlier. By now, Fitzsimmons was 39 years old, but public opinion wanted the return. Fitzsimmons was fit and still had his punch, and for four rounds outboxed and hurt Jeffries, who bled badly from nose and mouth. But the years and weight were even more difficult for Fitzsimmons to give away than in their first fight. A couple of huge body blows in the fifth slowed Fitzsimmons. He still gave more than he received, but another left to the body in the eighth had Fitzsimmons retreating and finally a left hook to the stomach and a crushing thump on the chin forced him to the floor, from where he was unable to rise.

Next year, Jeffries again fought Gentleman Jim Corbett, who had been inactive for three years. He was now 37 years old, nine years older than Jeffries. This time he was knocked out in the tenth round.

By now, William Brady was having difficulty in finding credible opponents for Jeffries. An inexperienced miner, Jack Munro, had the temerity to put the champion down in a minor exhibition bout during a Jeffries tour. He was given a title bout in 1904, but was knocked out in two rounds. Jeffries then retired,

powerful, unbeaten, a worthy champion, but one who had never attracted the same enthusiasm as John L. Sullivan.

On 3 July 1905 Jeffries refereed a contest between Marvin Hart and Jack Root, the former light-heavyweight champion, in Reno, Nevada, and when Hart won by a knockout in the 12th round named him as the new heavy-weight champion of the world.

Although Hart is included in the records, most of the public at the time did not take all this very seriously. Neither Hart nor Root was any more than a light-heavy, and it is ludicrous to think either would have stood much chance with Jeffries. Hart, from Jefferson County, Kentucky, held the title for less than a year. On 23 February 1906 he took on Tommy Burns in Los Angeles and was outpointed over 20 rounds.

Burns was born Noah Brusso in Chesley, Ontario, Canada, on 17 June

Tommy Burns, the only Canadian to hold the world's heavyweight title. At only 5ft 7in (1.70m) he was easily the shortest champion, but his record was impressive until he met Johnson.

1881, and was himself not a real heavyweight. He was only 5ft 7in (1.70m) tall and also was not taken seriously – at least at first. How could he have stood up to Jeffries who was, after all, a hugely-built giant?

However, Burns did all he could to justify his title claim. More or less managing himself, he defended his title twice in 1906, three times in 1907 and no less than seven in 1908. He disposed of Jim Flynn, drew with the light-heavy champion Philadelphia Jack O'Brien, and then beat both him and Australian Bill Squires. Then he went on a world tour and beat Gunner James Moir, the British champion, and Jack Palmer, both in London; Irishman Jem Roche in Dublin in 88 seconds, a record for the division; Jewey Smith and Bill Squires again in Paris; and Bill Squires for a third time and Bill Lang, both in Australia. All these bouts, apart from those with Philadelphia Jack O'Brien, were won by knock-outs.

Then he came up against Jack Johnson, the first black boxer to fight for the heavyweight championship. When Johnson began his boxing career it was practically impossible for a man of his race to win the title. For a start, black boxers in America were considered inferior in every respect, and found it difficult to get fights against leading white opposition, except when there was no chance of winning. Secondly, any white fighter could 'draw the colour line' to avoid a meeting with a black man who might be dangerous. John L. Sullivan 'drew the colour line' after he became champion, refusing in particular to meet Peter Jackson, who was the obvious contender. Jackson got a chance against Jeffries, but by then was 37 years old and had been out of the ring for six years. Otherwise Jeffries, too, was reluctant to fight a black boxer.

The best of the black boxers in America were forced to fight each other time and again. Indeed the best way for many of them to earn much money was the 'battle royal', in which a dozen or so were put into a ring together and left to eliminate each other until a single winner remained.

Three black boxers of the early days of the century are regarded now as men who could possibly have won the heavyweight title, apart from Johnson: Sam Langford, Joe Jeannette and Sam McVey.

Langford was regarded by some as the equal of Johnson although they met only once, in 1906, when Johnson won on points over 15 rounds. After Johnson had won the title, Langford challenged him persistently, but having been dodged for so long himself Johnson was not interested in risking the championship against Langford.

Langford was born in Weymouth, Nova Scotia, Canada, and boxed out of Boston, becoming known as the 'Boston Tar Baby'. He stood 5ft 7½in (1.72m) and was only a middleweight, but had hugely developed shoulders, and fought mostly heavyweights. In 1909 he knocked out the British heavyweight champion William 'Iron' Hague in four rounds in London. Langford fought Harry Wills, a fellow black heavyweight, 25 times, mostly in no-decision bouts, but winning twice and losing to the 6ft 4in (1.93m) giant six times. Langford also fought

Jack Johnson, facing camera in the fight with Tommy Burns, from whom he won the world heavyweight title at Sydney, Australia, in 1908.

McVey 15 times and Jeannette 14. He was forced to give up boxing through failing eyesight when 44 years old and, sadly, spent the last 30 years or so of his life blind.

Joe Jeannette fought Johnson nine times before the latter became champion. Twice Johnson won on points, once Jeannette won on a disqualification, two bouts were drawn and four were no-decision affairs. He also fought McVey four times, one a tremendous battle in Paris in 1909, when Jeannette was down 21 times in the first 37 rounds. McVey went down 19 times thereafter and Jeannette another six, and it was McVey who gave best, collapsing and being counted out as he tried to come up for the 49th round. McVey fought and lost to Johnson three times, but for a period, 1910–15, was a genuine title-contender.

Johnson was born in Galveston, Texas, in 1878, and took up professional boxing in 1897. He was knocked out twice early in his career, but otherwise was victorious until he fought Marvin Hart in San Francisco in March, 1905. Hart was given the decision on points over 20 rounds, and a little over three months later was given the heavyweight championship of the world after knocking out Jack Root. Some thought both decisions were flattering to Hart.

Johnson resumed his winning ways and in 1907 went to Australia to record a couple of knockouts. Then he followed the new champion, Burns, to London, where The National Sporting Club proposed a title fight between the two. That idea was dropped when Burns demanded £6,000, then an unheard-of sum, whatever the result, and Burns took off for Australia.

Soon Johnson was also invited to return to Australia by Hugh D. McIntosh, a Sydney caterer who dabbled in sporting events and was to become a big boxing promoter both in Australia and London, where he became known as 'Huge Deal' McIntosh. McIntosh had promoted fights featuring both Johnson and Burns during their visits to Australia and knew that a heavyweight championship match between the two would be a money-spinner. He offered Burns the £6,000 he demanded, and the champion could run away no further.

McIntosh built a large outdoor arena at Rushcutter's Bay, just outside Sydney, for the fight. It took place on 26 December 1908 before 16,000 spectators, who paid £26,000. It was the first white-v-black match for the title, and a triumph for McIntosh, who both refereed the match and made himself a fortune.

Another triumph was that enjoyed by Johnson, and 'enjoyed' is the word, as the much bigger and heavier man toyed with his opponent. Johnson stood just over 6ft (1.83m) and weighed nearly 14st (195lb – 87.6kg). He had Burns down in the first round, and from the seventh onwards punished his opponent unmercifully. The fight was scheduled for 20 rounds, but the police stopped it in the 14th and Johnson was the new champion. Throughout the fight, Johnson flashed his golden smile at the spectators and Jack London, the novelist, reporting the fight in the London *Daily Mail*, said: 'Jeffries must emerge from his farm and remove that smile from Johnson's face' – a view echoed throughout America.

Jeffries was reluctant to come out of retirement, and a desperate search was begun for a 'white hope' to beat Johnson, who was the most hated man in America – among the whites, of course.

Unfortunately for his enemies, he was unbeatable. In 1909, the middleweight champion of the world, Stanley Ketchel, was put up as a challenger, and on 16 October the two met at Colma, California. Ketchel was fast and a hard puncher, and the fans went mad in the 12th when he caught Johnson and knocked him down. Johnson got up, however, and as Ketchel rushed in, timed a right uppercut to his chin so perfectly that Ketchel was immediately knocked out by a blow that left two of his teeth embedded in Johnson's glove.

Now the clamour increased for Jeffries, in the eyes of white America the 'rightful' champion, to come back and teach Johnson a lesson and Tex Rickard, a boxing promoter with a huge success behind him in the staging of a lightweight championship in 1906 (described later in this chapter) saw the opportunity of another big coup. As soon as Jeffries had agreed to fight Johnson, Rickard outbid everybody with an offer of $101,000 for the match, 75 per cent to go to the winner and 25 per cent to the loser.

Independence Day was chosen for the contest – 4 July 1910 in Reno, Nevada, the only state which would allow the fight. Rickard built a special arena, into which he packed 15,760 spectators, with

Above: One of boxing's most surprising knockdowns. Heavyweight Jack Johnson being put on the deck by middleweight champion Stanley Ketchel in 1909.

Right: The unbeaten Jeffries (left) made a comeback to try to stop Johnson at Reno in 1910, but Johnson was too good for the former champion.

more trying to get in. Johnson won by a knockout in the 15th round, as described in Chapter 8, but the 38-year-old Jeffries, although beaten for the first time, at least collected well over $100,000 for his pains, with his share of the gate and film rights.

In the event the film was banned, as it was regarded as likely to inflame the race riots which broke out in various parts of America at this defeat of the white man by the black man.

Blacks, celebrating with a few drinks, could not help showing their satisfaction at the result, and no doubt there were plenty ready to do a little boasting, and worse. Some whites, on the other hand, were only too anxious to look for provocation to exact revenge for their hero's defeat. Several people were killed, hundreds seriously injured and thousands arrested in incidents in many parts of the country. Some of the more serious riots were in the capital, Washington, Kansas City, Jacksonville, Norfolk, Virginia, and Los Angeles. In some places lynching parties were out. And all this because Jack Johnson had won the world heavyweight championship.

The only boxer around likely to give Johnson a close match was Sam Langford, but such a contest was unattractive to promoters. Plans to match Johnson with the British champion, Bombardier Billy Wells, in London in 1911 were thwarted by the Home Office, fearing adverse effects on the Empire should a black man beat the British best. Johnson did not fight for exactly two years; then, on 4 July 1912 in Las Vegas, the referee stopped his fight with Jim Flynn in the ninth round.

Johnson's liaisons with white women then led him into trouble with the law. He was sentenced to a year and a day in prison, but fled to Europe, where he set up in style and lived expensively from money made by appearances on the stage, mainly in London and Paris.

In Paris, Johnson drew with Battling Jim Johnson, another black boxer, and beat Frank Moran, a white American brought over to challenge. Late in 1914 he went to Buenos Aires, Argentina, and knocked out Jack Murray in the third round.

Back in America, the 'white hope' search was frantic. In 1913 the best prospect appeared to be Luther McCarty, but he died after collapsing from a first-round punch from Arthur Pelkey – it appeared a previous injury from a fall from a horse was responsible. When Pelkey was knocked out by Gunboat Smith in 1914 the latter claimed 'the white heavyweight championship of the world'.

The man who came to the fore as the likeliest contender for the real title, however, was a giant cowboy from Pottawatomie, Kansas. Jess Willard was no great shakes as a boxer, but he stood 6ft 6¼in (1.99m) and weighed around 17st 12lb (250lb – 112.5kg). Carefully managed by Billy McCarney, with maximum ballyhoo, Willard was selected by promoter Jack Curley to be the next to try to topple Johnson.

Johnson could not box anywhere in the States, of course, and the fight was originally intended for Mexico, but eventually took place on the racecourse in Havana, Cuba, on 5 April 1915 (see Chapter 8). It was suggested to Johnson by Curley that if he lost he would be allowed back into the States without serving his sentence, and when, after outboxing Willard comfortably for 25 rounds, he was knocked out in the 26th (when he lay 'shading his eyes from the sun'), Johnson maintained that he lost deliberately. It did not save him from going to prison when he returned home, and the truth of the matter has never been satisfactorily resolved.

Tex Rickard, the most famous of all promoters, who staged fights involving Gans, Jeffries, Willard, Johnson, Dempsey, Carpentier and Tunney among others, and promoted the first million-dollar fight.

The 'Giant Cowboy' fought Frank Moran in a 'no decision' bout at the Madison Square Garden in 1916, and retained his title to the end of the First World War.

The no-decision contests were the result of the Frawley Law, which came into effect in 1911, limiting bouts in New York State to ten rounds and forbidding decisions. While the referee could not name a winner, unofficial victors were nominated by the press. Under this law, a champion could only lose his title if knocked out and many boxers who fought in this period have 'no-decision' verdicts among their records.

Outside the heavyweight division, many boxers wrote their names in the record books of the greats in the years between the turn of the century and the First World War, and one was former world middle and heavyweight champion, Bob Fitzsimmons. He also won the light-heavyweight title in 1903, beating George Gardner on points over 20 rounds in San Francisco to become the first of the few men to win world titles at three weights.

Fitzsimmons held the title for a year, and was then knocked out by Philadelphia Jack O'Brien (Joseph F. Hagan), who had earlier fought undefeated in Britain. He was one of the cleverest of defensive boxers, who chose to fight among the heavyweights rather than defend his title; and drew with Tommy Burns in a challenge for the top prize. After nearly losing his light-heavy crown when Stanley Ketchel knocked him down in a no-decision bout (the final bell saved O'Brien when the referee's count

reached 'eight'), he retired in 1912 and was succeeded by Jack Dillon, who had been claiming the title since 1909. He was called 'Jack the Giant Killer' as he consistently took on and beat men bigger than himself. He lost the championship in 1916 to 'Battling' Levinsky, whom he'd previously beaten. Levinsky fought both Jack Dempsey and Gene Tunney, future heavyweight champions, during his career.

The middleweight division continued producing those fights which make this the most keenly contested class of all. Tommy Ryan, one of the best champions, ruled for nine years before being succeeded, in 1907, by Stanley Ketchel, who proved even greater.

Ketchel lost the championship briefly in 1908 to Billy Papke, who threw a right instead of touching gloves, but won it back a few weeks later. In 1909 Ketchel knocked out the light-heavyweight champion, and then, as related, had the nerve to challenge Jack Johnson, the heavyweight champion, a venture which ended painfully. Ketchel was murdered by a jealous rival in love in 1910, and the title was reclaimed by Papke, who then lost it on points to 'Cyclone' Johnny Thompson in Australia. Thompson gave up the title in 1911 because of weight problems, whereupon Papke claimed it yet again. But he was beaten by Frank Klaus, Klaus by George Chip and Chip by Al McCoy, and these were the champions recognized in America until 1917.

However, Australia, having won the title, was not disposed to give it up when Thompson did, and recognized Eddie

Stanley Ketchel (left) and Billy Papke before their first fight in 1908. They had three bitter encounters.

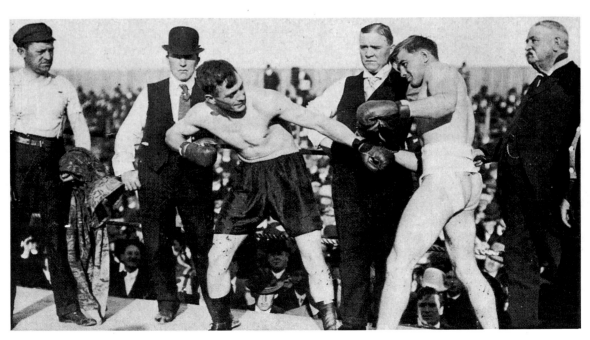

McGoorty as champion. Jeff Smith and Mick King then held it until Les Darcy took it from Smith in 1915. The brilliant Darcy knocked out George Chip, one of the American claimants, in nine rounds, and seemed to have the stronger claim to the world title. He went to America by invitation of Tex Rickard to settle the disputed crown in 1917 but was criticized for avoiding the war, couldn't get a bout and died of fever and, the romantics say, disappointment. He could have been one of the all-time great middleweights but was denied the chance to prove it. Mike O'Dowd knocked out Al McCoy in Brooklyn six months after Darcy's death, and was recognized universally as champion.

Among the welters, a tiny boxer, Joe Walcott, known as 'The Barbados Demon' made a huge reputation by beating men bigger than himself. Although only 5ft 1in (1.55m) and little more than 10st (140lb – 63kg), he knocked out Joe Choynski, one of the leading heavyweights, and also beat middleweights Dan Creedon and Joe Grim. He won the welter title from Jim 'Rube' Ferns in 1901 and in a spell when the title frequently changed hands, lost it finally in 1906 to Billy 'Honey' Mellody. Mike 'Twin' Sullivan won it from Mellody, and then moved up a division. There were then several claimants: Jimmy Gardner, Jimmy Clabby, Harry Lewis, Ray Bronson, Waldemar Holberg, a Dane who beat Bronson in Australia, two English boxers, Tom McCormick and Matt Wells, and Mike Glover.

Then Jack Britton, from New York, outpointed Mike Glover in Boston in 1915, but two months later was himself beaten by Ted 'Kid' Lewis, from Aldgate, London. Thereafter these two held the title between them for seven years, beating each other and all-comers. In all, they met 20 times in various towns of the United States, many of them no-decision bouts.

Joe Gans was the king of the lightweights in the early days of the century, even boxing a draw with the welterweight champion, Joe Walcott. Gans featured in the fight that made Tex Rickard into the leading promoter of the day after a rough, tough Dane, Oscar 'Battling' Nelson, had beaten Jimmy Britt to claim the 'white' championship of the world.

Rickard owned the leading gambling saloon in the small town of Goldfield,

Oscar 'Battling' Nelson, the Dane who became world lightweight champion, a rough-tough scrapper.

Nevada, and when citizens of the town were discussing how to put Goldfield 'on the map', Rickard suggested a world title fight between Gans and Nelson. He planned to stage it himself, making his debut as a promoter.

Rickard put up the astonishing sum, for lightweights, of $30,000, and when the press came to Goldfield to see what it was all about, put the money in his window in gold dollar pieces. He publicized the battle as a grudge fight, and as a race fight. He built an open-air arena for 8,000 spectators. His hype succeeded and the match was a sell-out.

On 3 September 1906, the fight commenced in the hot afternoon sun, scheduled for 45 rounds. Nelson had insisted on two-thirds of the purse, and a weight limit of 9st 7lb (133lb – 59.9kg), 2lb (0.9kg) less than usual. The elder Gans was weakened by the reduction, but outboxed and outfought Nelson, who needed all his strength and stamina to stay in the fight. Every time Gans began to tire, and Nelson looked to have a chance, Gans would stop his opponent's wild efforts with superb boxing, until finally Nelson's face was cut to ribbons. In the 42nd round the well-beaten Nelson deliberately fouled Gans by punching him in the groin and was disqualified.

Goldfield was in the news, and Rickard made a handsome profit, going on to make even more lucrative matches.

Nelson won the title two years later, knocking out Gans in 17 rounds in San Francisco. He in turn lost to Ad Wolgast by a knockout in the 40th round of a bloody battle in which there was a no-foul rule, in 1910. Wolgast preferred to fight with his own referee, Jack Welch. In 1911 he met Owen Moran, from Birmingham, England, who had knocked out Nelson. Moran was counted out in the 13th round, having taken a fierce blow to the stomach.

There followed a remarkable fight with a Mexican challenger, Joe Rivers, which almost ended in a double knock-out. The two battered each other for ten rounds, with Rivers, the favourite with the Los Angeles crowd, having the better of it. In the 11th a clinch led to both men crashing to the canvas and almost out of the ring. In the 13th Wolgast began hitting low, but Rivers would not be denied and threw a tremendous right, flush on Wolgast's chin. At the same time Wolgast was swinging a left which struck Rivers on the groin. Both went down, Wolgast completely out and Rivers writhing with pain on his haunches.

The referee began counting over Wolgast, and then, seeing him stir, lifted him up and supported him while completing the count over an astonished Rivers. He then dumped Wolgast on his stool, announced him the winner, and hurried away. The referee justified his decision later on the grounds that in his view Wolgast had landed first and therefore he decided to count out Rivers. Although Wolgast's blow was definitely low, many spectators claimed Rivers had risen at 'eight' anyway. Despite a riot among the fans, the result stood. Wolgast lost his title in 1912, disqualified against Willie Ritchie in Daly City, California, when the referee was not Jack Welch.

A clever lightweight from Wales, Freddie Welsh, next won the title. Despite going to the United States, he had been dodged by Gans, Nelson and Wolgast. Eventually Charles B. Coch-ran, the theatrical impresario, persuaded Ritchie to meet Welsh at Olympia, London. Welsh was so anxious to get the title that he agreed to fight Ritchie for nothing and won narrowly over 20 rounds. He returned to America to cash in, and among those he beat was Wolgast, again disqualified for a low blow. Welsh held the title for three years, but when 31 lost it to a man ten years younger, Benny Leonard, who knocked him out in the ninth round of a no-decision bout at the Manhattan Casino, New York, in 1917. Leonard, one of the game's all-rounders who could both box and punch, held the title until after the First World War.

The feather and bantam classes in those pre-war days boasted Terry McGovern, from Johnstown, Pennsylvania, who moved up from winning the bantamweight title in 1899 to the featherweight title in 1900. 'Terrible Terry' was invincible for a spell, but surprisingly lost his championship to Young Corbett (William H. Rothwell, from Denver, Colorado). The fight is described in Chapter 8.

Corbett moved up to the lightweights, and Abe Attell claimed the crown. He was to reign for seven years, although not without controversy. In 1904 he was knocked out by 'Brooklyn' Tommy Sullivan, but held on to the title as Sullivan was over the weight limit. In 1908 he fought Owen Moran, from England, over 25 rounds in his home town of San Francisco, and Moran was very dissatisfied with the decision of a draw. They were rematched, and with Attell demanding a shorter bout of 20 rounds, and Moran disagreeing, the fight was fixed for the compromise of 23 rounds, the only title fight ever over such a distance. It did Moran little good. The second fight was also declared a draw.

In 1909 'Peerless' Jim Driscoll, the British, European and Empire champion, went to America to challenge Attell, who would only agree to a no-decision bout. Driscoll won every round by such a wide margin that in Europe, at least, he was regarded as the uncrowned champion.

Attell was finally deposed on 22 February 1912, when Johnny Kilbane outpointed him over 20 rounds in Vernon, California. Kilbane kept the title until after the war. Driscoll, on the other side of the Atlantic, boxed a draw over 20 rounds with Owen Moran.

Left: Freddie Welsh (right) on his way to the world lightweight championship, which he took from Willie Ritchie at Olympia, London, in 1914.

Below: Terry McGovern, 'Terrible Terry', whose all-action, hard-hitting style made him invincible for a couple of years and earned him the world bantam and featherweight titles.

The bantam division was ever-changing, the small men usually moving up in class after winning the title. Harry Harris, Harry Forbes, Frankie Neil, Joe Bowker and Jimmy Walsh reigned while there was disagreement between Europe and America over the title not resolved until Kit Williams (born Johnny Gutenko in Copenhagen, Denmark, but raised in Baltimore, Maryland) beat both Eddie Campi and Johnny Coulon in 1914. In 1917 he lost the title to Pete Herman, from New Orleans.

Meanwhile a British flyweight title had come into being in the weight limit set by the NSC in 1909. Previously many small men had called themselves flyweights and even paperweights, but the class was hazy. The first British titleholder was Sid Smith, of Bermondsey, who beat Eugene Criqui, of France, in 1913 to be acknowledged as the first world champion. He relinquished the title, as did Percy Jones, the next claimant, both moving up to bantam.

The great Jimmy Wilde, from Wales, claimed the championship with a knockout of Joe Symonds in 1916, and was challenged by Young Zulu Kid, the American contender. Wilde won by a knockout (see Chapter 8) and remained champion for seven years.

With the Frawley Law proving a hindrance to boxing in the United

Opposite: Georges Carpentier first brought women to boxing in large numbers. The fashionable crowd at Olympia in 1914 watch the critical moment of the 'white heavyweight championship' fight. Carpentier slipped to the canvas and 'Gunboat' Smith was disqualified for a blow while he was down.

Below: Jimmy Wilde (left), the world flyweight champion, attacking Pal Moore, the American bantamweight, whom he beat in 1919.

States, the situation in Britain was flourishing as the First World War approached. There were several tournaments a week in London at 'The Ring' and, until it burnt down in 1911, Wonderland. Wonderland was replaced almost immediately by Premierland, which promoter Harry Jacobs built from an old warehouse. Hugh McIntosh, from Australia, promoted at Olympia, as did C. B. Cochran. Most cities had a boxing arena, the original Liverpool Stadium, then known as the Albert Hall, opening for boxing in 1911. Arnold Wilson promoted there, later becoming one of the leading promoters in London.

In this period the National Sporting Club began to lose its influence on British boxing. As a club with limited seating it could not compete with the purse offers of commercial promoters. It retained until after the war its monopoly of the championships through the Lonsdale belts, but increasingly the champions, having won the title at the NSC, were drifting away to make money elsewhere.

Britain had some of the world's best boxers in the lighter weights, but in the heavier classes were rarely challenging for world championships. The man who held the British heavyweight title from 1911 till the end of the war was Bombardier Billy Wells. He stood 6ft 3in (1.91m), but at 13 stone (182lb – 82kg) he did not carry the corresponding weight to challenge the world's best.

He went to America to stake his claim to being the 'white hope' of boxing but was knocked out by Al Palzer and

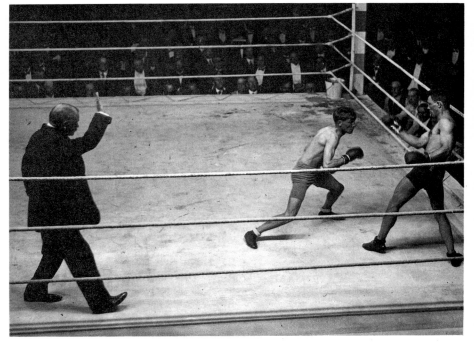

56

Carpentier being chaired after his first-round knock-out of British champion Billy Wells to win the European heavyweight title at National sporting club in 1913.

'Gunboat' Smith. The fight with Palzer was advertized for the 'white championship' and Wells began by outboxing Palzer and dropping him for a count. But Palzer was 3st (42lb – 19kg) heavier, and his rugged swings soon got to Wells and put him away. However Wells knocked out Tom Kennedy and Boer Rodel. His fights rarely went the distance.

Wells was also British Empire champion when, at the Ghent Exhibition in Belgium, in 1913, he fought Georges Carpentier for the European championship. Carpentier was the first boxing hero of France and was European welter, middle and light-heavyweight champion. This time Wells had all the physical advantages of 4in (10cm) and 17lb (7.7kg). In the first round the 19-year-old Carpentier was down and almost out, but Wells stood off and failed to finish his groggy opponent. In the fourth Carpentier caught Wells to the body and, as he dropped his hands, finished him with a right to the chin. It was a totally unexpected victory, cheered by a 10,000 crowd, many of them miners who had come across from Carpentier's home town of Lens. Six months later Carpentier met Wells in a return at the NSC and knocked him out in 73 seconds.

Just before the war, Carpentier met the American Ed 'Gunboat' Smith for the 'white heavyweight championship' at Olympia, London. In the sixth, Carpentier was dropped for a count, but Smith followed up with a blow to the head. It seemed Smith tried to hold it back, and that it was only a light blow, but Carpentier's manager, Francois Descamps, jumped into the ring claiming a foul, and his boxer was awarded the verdict.

Carpentier was still only 20 years old, and a very handsome man. He was idolized in France and the fights between 'Gorgeous Georges' and the upstanding 'Beautiful Billy' Wells first attracted women in any great numbers to the game.

Boxing was still not quite at ease with the law. At big contests the boxers would still be visited by the police in their dressing rooms, and warned that they were liable to prosecution should anything happen to their opponents. Carpentier received such a warning before his second fight with Wells. Not speaking English, he didn't understand it, and demolished Wells in little more than a minute.

Carpentier, with most of the boxers of Europe, was on active service from 1914 onwards. Carpentier was decorated for bravery and had his reward after the war, when he took part in what Tex Rickard described, probably with no feelings of shame, as 'The Battle of the Century'.

4 THE MILLION-DOLLAR DAYS

Boxing in New York was liberated after the First World War by an Englishman. The Frawley Law was repealed in 1917, and boxing once more outlawed in the State. The Englishman who made it legal again was William A. Gavin, who arrived in New York in 1918 and formed an organization based on the National Sporting Club, with his own version of the Queensberry Rules.

Before the operation could begin, legislation was required to permit boxing again. Gavin handed his rules to the New York State senator, James J. Walker, and the Walker Law was passed in 1920, legalizing boxing. The main beneficiary of the new Law was not Gavin himself but the promoter Tex Rickard, who had agreed to be match-maker at Gavin's club. Rickard saw greater possibilities, and before the Walker bill was passed obtained a lease on Madison Square Garden.

Walker, later Mayor of New York, also instituted the licensing of boxers and all others connected with the game – referees, managers, trainers, seconds etc – under the control of the New York State Athletic Commission, which was specially formed with three commissioners selected by the Governor of New York State.

Other States legalised boxing along the same lines as the Walker Law and there were attempts to form a federation of all of them so that the sport could be controlled throughout the land by one body. William Gavin was instrumental in forming the National Boxing Association in 1920 as part of his plans for his International Sporting Club.

The Association, however, was not successful, because only 13 states became members. The strongest states, in boxing terms, New York, Pennsylvania, California and Massachusetts, decided that their experience and organizational skill were not to be sacrificed to a new and unproven body, or rather those in control declined to forgo their power. However, the National Boxing Association remained in being, and in 1962 became the World Boxing Association.

In Great Britain, a Boxing Board of Control was formed in 1918 with members from various interested organizations, but the largest number of members came from the National Sporting Club, so control of boxing hardly changed.

An International Boxing Union was formed in Paris in 1920, consisting of Great Britain, the USA, France, Australia, Canada, Denmark, Holland, Italy, Norway, Sweden, Switzerland, Brazil and Argentina. The object was the formulation of international rules, with in particular the administration of world championships. In practice, the USA did not participate, so in 1922 Great Britain withdrew, and the absence of one body regulating world championships remains one of boxing's biggest bugbears to this day.

When the First World War ended and boxing fans could redirect their attention to the less damaging hostilities of the ring, the heavyweight in charge of the championship was the giant cowboy, Jess Willard. But during the war a rough and tough heavyweight from the West had been building a reputation with a

Jess Willard being counted out in the first round of his fight with Jack Dempsey in 1919. The bell had saved Willard, however, and Dempsey's reign as champion was delayed for two more rounds.

series of wins. Jack Dempsey had revenged a knock-out defeat by Jim Flynn, and in 1918 recorded 18 knock-out victories himself. He was managed by Jack Kearns, known as 'Doc' because he took a black bag to his corner. Kearns guided Dempsey until he was the logical challenger to Willard.

Rickard realized the drawing potential of a Willard-Dempsey title fight and persuaded the champion to meet Dempsey on 4 July 1919 in Toledo, Ohio. Willard had been travelling with a circus for the three years since his previous fight, and had oil wells which were prospering, so he did not need the contest.

As usual, the critics favoured the champion. Dempsey, despite his record, was not thought big enough at 6ft 1in (1.86m) and 13st 5lb (187lb – 84.2kg) to beat Willard, who was 3st 11lb (53lb – 24kg) heavier. Dempsey and Kearns were confident, however, and bet their share of the purse, $10,000, that Dempsey would knock out the champion in the first round. The odds were 10–1 against them.

That first round was remarkable. Dempsey, sun-burnt, fit and eager, hit the pale, lethargic Willard with two-handed barrages from the first minute, and seven times in the first round Willard was down, the last time clearly unable to beat the count as he sat on the canvas. Dempsey left the ring thinking he had won his $100,000 bet, but the time-keeper pointed out to the referee that the bell had saved Willard, but had not been heard. Dempsey was recalled, the fight continued, and the inevitable end was delayed until the third round. Dempsey therefore fought without monetary reward.

There have been various explanations, of course, for the unheard bell. One is that in changing a bloody canvas before the big fight the lacings had been drawn over the bell, thus muting it, although it is not explained why this was not noticed at the bell to begin the fight. Another is that Dempsey did win in the time, but that the gambling fraternity had to find a quick way of reversing the outcome.

It was also suggested by one of his handlers that Dempsey had plaster of Paris in his bandages to help him collect his bet. There was no evidence of this, and all these stories, like many others in boxing, remain matters of conjecture.

Dempsey, known as 'The Manassa Mauler', knocked out a couple more challengers and appeared to have no real opposition. In these circumstances Rickard brought off perhaps his greatest coup in manufacturing 'The Fight of the Century'.

Dempsey was not popular in America, because he had obeyed Kearns' instruction to work in the shipyards instead of going into the army during the war, and he was called a 'draft dodger'. The man Rickard hit upon to challenge him was none other than handsome Georges Carpentier, the European heavyweight champion. Carpentier was a war hero, a man decorated for valour. It was an angle that the publicity highlighted – the elegant hero against the swarthy, bullying, slacker. It was an angle that paid off.

For a start, Rickard matched Carpentier with Battling Levinsky, the world light-heavyweight champion. On 12 October 1920 Carpentier knocked out Levinsky in the fourth round in Jersey City to take the title.

The heavyweight champion, Dempsey, met the light-heavyweight champion, Carpentier, on 2 July 1921 also in Jersey City. For his 'Battle of the Century' Rickard built a huge outdoor wooden arena at Boyle's Thirty Acres at which over 80,000 fans watched the fight, which grossed at the gate nearly four times the previous record: $1,789,238. It was the first million-dollar gate and also the first fight to have a running commentary broadcast by radio, the equipment being loaned by the US Navy Department through a technical officer, F. D. Roosevelt, who later became President of the United States.

The contest itself could not live up to the star billing. Carpentier could not give the weight away. Used to attacking, he found he was forced instead to fight off the charges of the heavier, stronger man. He caught Dempsey with a terrific right in the first round, but without checking him. In the second another great right did make Dempsey stagger and clinch, but the more permanent damage was to Carpentier, whose thumb was broken.

The stylish Frenchman, who had the fans on his side, now looked like a pale lamb for slaughter as the unshaven, rugged Dempsey forced the attack. In the fourth round Carpentier was quickly put down for a count, and as he rose a

Signing for the first million-dollar boxing match. Jack Dempsey is seated left, with his manager, Jack 'Doc' Kearns, standing behind him. Carpentier is seated second from right with his manager, Francois Descamps, on his left. Between the boxers are promoters William A. Brady, C. B. Cochran of London and Tex Rickard.

powerful right to the jaw knocked him unconscious for much longer than the required ten seconds.

The boxing boom had arrived, although not for the citizens of Shelby, Montana, where Dempsey was next to defend. A group of local businessmen, recalling Rickard's first great success in 1906, when he put Goldfield, Nevada, on the map and made a fortune for himself, decided to turn themselves into promoters. They staged the heavyweight championship on 4 July 1923, with Dempsey defending against Tommy Gibbons, another light-heavyweight, who, moreover, was 34 years old.

The Shelby promoters guaranteed Dempsey and Kearns $200,000 advance, plus $100,000 to be paid while the fight was in progress. Alas for Shelby, nobody was interested in this one-sided match, although in the event Gibbons boxed cleverly to last the distance and lose only on points. A mere 7,202 spectators paid, the receipts were well short of Dempsey's purse, and the result was that four Shelby banks went broke and the townsfolk faced heavy losses.

If that was dull, Dempsey's next match packed more action into its short duration than half-a-dozen normal fights. The opponent was Luis Angel Firpo, of Argentina, and the fight is described in Chapter 8. Dempsey retained his crown with a knock-out.

The logical challenger to Dempsey was Harry Wills. Wills was 6ft 4in (1.93m), about 30lb (13.5kg) heavier than Dempsey and a skilful boxer. Twice the match almost came off, once for Benton Harbour, Michigan, and once for Jersey City, 6 September 1924, where Rickard even had tickets printed. The trouble was Wills was black, and the fight was barred.

The New York State Athletic Commission (NYAC) wanted the match in 1925 but this time Dempsey declined to meet Wills. Rickard claimed that the Governor of New York had hinted that the contest was not desired there. Wills received $50,000 as compensation for his broken contract. Clearly the memory of Jack Johnson led white America to fear another black champion.

The NYAC barred Dempsey from fighting in New York after his refusal to meet Wills, and when Rickard fixed Dempsey's next defence for the Yankee Stadium, the Commission refused to sanction it. The fight was taken to the Sesquicentennial Stadium, in Philadelphia, where Dempsey's opponent was an ex-marine, Gene Tunney, former holder of the American light-heavyweight title. He was fit, strong and two years the younger. As a heavyweight he was as tall as Dempsey and weighed about the same. He was also a clever boxer, who had fought on the Dempsey-Carpentier bill, and studied the champion's technique.

This was another battle the public wanted to see. The live gate was the highest in history, 120,757. The receipts were a new record, $1,895,733.

Dempsey had not fought for three years, but was a warm favourite to win. The contest took place in pouring rain. The canvas was wet and slippery. Tunney handled the conditions well, was confident and fast, and constantly beat Dempsey to the punch. Dempsey, by his own standards, was lethargic. A punch to Tunney's throat in the fourth round had the challenger in trouble, but he survived, and in the end was a comfortable points winner over ten rounds.

A return was a 'natural', but first Rickard had to re-establish Dempsey. A eliminator arose when Jack Sharkey beat Harry Wills. Rickard promoted a Sharkey-Dempsey bout at Yankee Stadium, New York, on 21 July 1927. This was another million-dollar gate, with Tunney contracted to meet the winner.

Sharkey's speed was too much for Dempsey at first, but he made the mistake of mixing it. In the seventh round Dempsey hit Sharkey with what appeared to be a low punch. Sharkey turned to the referee, and Dempsey knocked him out with a hook. Sharkey claimed a foul, but to no avail. Rickard announced his Dempsey-Tunney return match.

This was, of course, another crowd-puller. For a second time over 100,000 watched a fight between these two boxers. The receipts were $2,658,660 and marked the high spot of the boxing boom. The fight, at Soldier's Field, Chicago, on 22 September 1927, became probably the most famous boxing match of all for its controversy. It was known as 'The Battle of the Long Count', and is described in Chapter 8.

Tunney won and defended only once after this, an easy win over New Zealander Tom Heeney. He married an heiress and was not persuaded to try a comeback.

Meanwhile, there was plenty of action at the lighter weights. Light-heavy-weight Georges Carpentier has already been mentioned. He took the world championship from Battling Levinsky in 1920, although most Europeans accepted him as the world's best long before this. Carpentier did not rule for long, however. On 24 September 1922 he was surprisingly beaten by a Senegalese boxer, Battling Siki. Siki was brought to Paris when he was ten years old by a dancer who took a liking to him, but he was later abandoned. He had his first fight at 16, enlisted during the war, and was awarded the *Croix de Guerre* for bravery. As a boxer, however, he was not thought to be in the same class as Carpentier.

It has been suggested that there was a scenario for this fight, which was to inaugurate the new Buffalo Stadium in Paris. Siki at first refused to fight the man who was his idol, but was persuaded to do so. It is said that Siki was to be allowed to go six rounds without undue punishment, but Carpentier was then to knock him out spectacularly to make a good newsreel film. But Siki either wasn't given the plan or he decided to ignore it. After Carpentier had put him down in the third round, the enraged Siki set about the surprised champion and eventually knocked him out in the sixth. He was then temporarily disqualified for tripping his opponent, but a threatened riot from the spectators

The fight which ruined a town. Shelby, Montana, could not pay the bills when Dempsey (right) held on to his title with a points win over the clever Tommy Gibbons (left).

63

The end of the fight in which Georges Carpentier was relieved of his light-heavyweight titles in sensational manner by the primitive Battling Siki at the Buffalo Velodrome, Paris, in 1922.

ensured him Carpentier's world, European and French titles.

Success went to Siki's head, and he took to extravagant behaviour, like walking about in Paris with a lion. He took to drink and made the mistake of defending his world title against the Irish American Mike McTigue in Dublin on St Patrick's Day, 17 March 1923. It was a time of Irish 'troubles', and in an atmosphere of nationalist fervour and with the sound of rebel gunfire being heard in the stadium, McTigue had the better of a 20-round bruising fight. Siki went to America, but continued his destructive behaviour, and ended his life in a Harlem gutter, murdered in a brawl when only 28 years old.

One man who beat him in ten rounds in America was Paul Berlenbach, who in May 1925 took the title from McTigue with a 15-round points win in New York. He was a southpaw and a former wrestler, who had taken part in the 1920 Olympic Games, but he lost in turn to Jack Delaney, after beating him in 1925. The return fight on 16 July 1926 was

watched by 49,186, who paid $461,789. The big money was not only for heavyweights. Delaney, however, soon moved up to the heavyweight class, which produced some confusion. Mike McTigue claimed back the crown, but Tommy Loughran beat him on points in New York on 7 October 1927, and was acknowledged champion.

Loughran, from Philadelphia, was one of the most skilful of boxers. In his second defence, he was down twice for long counts in the first round against the hard-hitting Leo Lomski but for the next 14 rounds he steadily outpointed his man. After six defences, he, too, moved up to the heavyweight class, leaving the title vacant again in 1929.

Among the middleweights, Mike O'Dowd, the champion at the end of the war, fought six times in 1919, but on his third defence in 1920 lost on points to Johnny Wilson.

On 31 August 1923, Harry Greb, 'The Human Windmill', beat Wilson on points at the Polo Grounds, New York. Greb was a great all-action fighter

and had shared it with Ted 'Kid' Lewis for over seven years before Walker took it.

Mickey Walker held the title for about half as long himself before, on 20 May 1926, he was outpointed in Scranton, Pennsylvania, by Pete Latzo. Walker immediately turned his attentions to the middleweights and won the world title at this weight seven months later, on 3 December. He held this world championship longer than his first, and did not lose it in the ring, relinquishing it in 1931 to move up yet again and take his chances with the heavy brigade.

Meanwhile, Latzo held the welterweight title for only 13 months and was then beaten on points by Joe Dundee. For six years after this the title was swopped around by a group who kept beating each other: Young Jack Thompson, Jackie Fields, Tommy Freeman, Lou Brouillard, a Canadian, and Young Corbett III, an Italian. Eventually Jimmy 'Baby Face' McLarnin knocked out Young Corbett III in the first round in Los Angeles on 29 May 1933 and brought some much needed stability to the division.

A light-welterweight division was created in 1922 at 10st (140lb – 63kg). It was the idea of an American boxing magazine called *The Boxing Blade*, and

Harry Greb, the 'Human Windmill', (right) and Johnny Wilson pose before the world middleweight title fight in New York in 1923, in which Greb became the new champion.

coming towards the end of a brilliant career, in which for the last few years he had fought with the sight of one eye only. The best of his six successful defences was against Mickey Walker in New York, a bruising points win over 15 rounds. Greb lost the title to the first black middleweight champion, southpaw Tiger Flowers, who beat him on points twice over 15 rounds in 1926. Flowers was champion for little more than nine months, being outpointed over ten rounds in Chicago by Mickey Walker.

Born in Elizabeth, New Jersey, Walker, like Greb, was one of the ring's indestructibles, boxing for 17 years. He was known as 'The Toy Bulldog'. He had moved up to middleweight from the welterweight class, where on 1 November 1922 he lad beaten Jack Britton on points in New York for the title.

Britton, from Clinton, New York, was a brilliant 'classic' boxer, and an excellent counter-puncher, who had a career extending over 22 years and 299 fights. He first won the welter crown in 1915,

Benny Leonard (right) shakes hands with Lew Tendler in New York in 1923. Leonard retained his title on points over 15 rounds.

the readers chose the first champion, Pinkey Mitchell, who defended against Nat Goldman in 1923. He lost to Mushy Callahan in 1926, and Callahan held the title until 1930.

The great lightweight of the 1920s was Benny Leonard, who was champion from 1917 to 1925. He had many exciting defences, with Lew Tendler, Johnny Dundee, Charley White and Richie Mitchell in particular giving him trouble, before he retired undefeated in 1925. Jimmy Goodrich became champion when knocking out Stanislaus Loayza of Chile, in the final of an eliminating competition. He quickly lost the title to Rocky Kansas, who just as quickly lost it to Sammy Mandell.

Two of Mandell's best defences were against Jimmy McLarnin in 1928 and Tony Canzoneri in 1929, Mandell beating both these great boxers on points. Canzoneri did gain the title however on 14 November 1930 when he knocked out Al Singer in one minute six seconds of the first round, Singer having caused a sensation earlier in the year by dealing with Mandell in a similarly rapid manner, knocking him out in one minute 46 seconds.

The 1920s saw the introduction of another new weight division, junior lightweight at 9st 4lb (130lb – 58.5kg). Johnny Dundee was the first champion, winning on a disqualification against George Chaney in New York on 18 November 1921. There were six cham-

pions from 1921 to 1933 but action was desultory and so was public interest. The class died out in 1933 but was revived in 1959.

Johnny Dundee also fought as a featherweight, winning the world title on 26 July 1923 with a points victory over Eugene Criqui, of France. Criqui, previously a successful flyweight, was a war hero who had had his jaw smashed by a German bullet. It was mended with a silver plate and plastic surgery, which perhaps helped him take a punch. As European featherweight champion he had gone to New York and taken the world title from veteran Johnny Kilbane with a sixth-round knock-out on 2 June 1923, ending Kilbane's 11-year reign, but was champion for only 54 days before Dundee relieved him of the crown.

Dundee had a 21-year career in which he had 322 fights, about half of them 'no decision' affairs. He had nearly won the featherweight title ten years earlier, when he boxed a 20-round draw with Kilbane. From Shaikai, in Italy, his real name was Joseph Corrara. When he took the ring name of Dundee, he was called 'The Scotch Wop'.

Dundee did not defend his featherweight title, moving up to lightweight. Louis 'Kid' Kaplan won an eliminating tournament for the title, beating Danny Kramer in the final. He, too, moved up a division, and Benny Bass won another eliminator. He lost on points to Tony Canzoneri, who was knocked out by a Frenchman, Andre Routis, who lost on points to the first man since Kilbane to hold the title for more than a year or so, Battling Battalino. Battalino won the title in his home town, Hartford, Connecticut, on 23 September 1929, and he defended five times, holding the crown into the 1930s.

In the bantamweight class, Pete Herman, who held the title when the First World War ended, swopped it around with Joe Lynch and Johnny Buff in the early 1920s before Abe Goldstein and Eddie Martin claimed it for a few months each. Then Charley (Phil) Rosenberg beat Martin on points in 1925 only to be deprived of the crown in 1927 when failing to make the weight for a defence against Bushy Graham.

There followed the usual confusion when an undefeated champion is stripped of his title, this time coloured by politics. Bud Taylor beat Tony Canzoneri to get NBA recognition; Panama Al Brown beat Videl Gregorio to get NYAC recognition. Taylor then retired from the division, and Brown decided to fight abroad, causing the NYAC to withdraw its support, so instead of two recognized champions there were none. Brown, however, was so good that he was acknowledged champion until well into the 1930s.

Jimmy Wilde, the flyweight champion who had retired after being beaten by bantamweight Pete Herman in 1921, was persuaded to go to New York two years later to defend the flyweight title he had never lost in the ring, against Pancho Villa on 18 June 1923.

Villa, a tough, strong 22-year-old Filipino was much too good for the 31-year-old Wilde, but the Welshman won even more friends in defeat for his tremendous bravery. He was dragged to his corner at the end of the second round after being knocked out by a blow delivered just after the bell, and from then on he fought groggily and partially blinded. But he kept coming forward in an attempt to knock out his tormentor until he was himself knocked out in the seventh round. It was a week before he recovered sufficiently to go home.

Pancho Villa came to a sad end himself. Two years later, on 4 July 1925, he fought Jimmy McLarnin in a non-title bout in Oakland, California. The day before he had had an infected tooth removed, but the blows he took on his jaw spread the infection. He went to hospital to have more teeth removed, but died ten days later when the poison spread through his body.

With Villa's death, the flyweight situation remained cloudy throughout the rest of the 1920s with the NBA and NYAC again in conflict. Two Olympic champions, Frankie Genaro and Fidel la Barba, were accorded recognition, as were at various times Newsboy Brown, Johnny Hill, from Scotland, Izzy Schwartz, Midget Wolgast, Albert Berlanger, a French Canadian, and Emile Pladner, a Frenchman from Clermont-Ferrand. When Pladner knocked out Genaro in Paris in 1929 for the NBA and IBU version of the title, the fight lasted only 56 seconds.

Eventually Young Perez, of Tunis, beat Frankie Genaro with a second round knock-out on 27 October 1931, and was then beaten by Jackie Brown in Manchester on 31 October 1932 in a fight

recognized by both the NBA and IBU as for the title.

The flyweight title thus returned to Britain where it remained for some years. Brown was champion until he was stopped by Benny Lynch in the second round in Manchester on 9 September 1935. A week later Small Montana beat Midget Wolgast on points for the American title. When Montana came to London on 19 January 1937 to lose on points to Lynch, the Scot became the first undisputed champion for many years.

One of the most significant developments in boxing in the 1920s was the launching of *The Ring* magazine by Nat Fleischer in February 1922. Fleischer presented a belt to each of the world champions at the time, and continued to award a belt to each new champion until he died in 1972.

The Ring was not the first magazine devoted to boxing but it became the most influential. Earlier in America, Richard Kyle Fox's *Police Gazette*, an illustrated sporting journal, dealt extensively with boxing from 1873 (it ceased publication in 1932). *The Ring* began its monthly ratings lists in 1925, and subsequently these and its annual record book gained international respect.

In 1925 the old Madison Square Garden was pulled down and a new one erected on Eighth Avenue and 49th Street. Built by Tex Rickard – it was called 'The House That Tex Built' – it cost $5.5

Jimmy Wilde (right) in his fight with Pete Herman at the Royal Albert Hall in 1921. Herman tricked Wilde over a weight agreement. Wilde was only persuaded to fight because the Prince of Wales was present, and he lost in the 17th round.

million, and for boxing could seat around 20,000. The first fight there was on 11 December 1925, a successful defence of the light-heavyweight title by Paul Berlanbach against Jack Delaney.

In Britain, London's Royal Albert Hall was first used for professional boxing in 1919, when Ted 'Kid' Lewis fought Matt Wells, and the new Wembley Stadium saw its first boxing when J. Arnold Wilson brought over the American heavyweight Tom Gibbons to knock out Jack Bloomfield in 1924.

In 1929 the Board of Control was reconstituted as the British Boxing Board of Control (BBBC), still with strong National Sporting Club influence, but run on more democratic lines. In 1937 the NSC ceased to operate as a club and lost its permanent seat on the Board.

The BBBC took over the administration of the Lonsdale Belts from the NSC, and indeed the control and regulation of boxing in Britain. The BBBC's jurisdiction was upheld in the courts in 1933 when the Irish heavyweight Jack Doyle sued them after having his purse withheld following a second round disqualification against Jack Petersen at the White City on 12 July 1933. The BBBC won the case on appeal.

The best British heavyweight in the 1920s was Joe Beckett, who took the title from Bombardier Billy Wells in 1919. Beckett, however, met his match in Georges Carpentier when he challenged at the Holborn Stadium in 1919 for the European championship. Promoter C. B. Cochran asked £25 for ringside seats, but spectators saw only 74 seconds, a fast Carpentier right stretching Beckett 'out for the count'.

Johnny Basham, a Welshman from Newport, had a fighter's name but it did not describe his method, for he was, in fact, a highly skilful boxer rather than a slugger. He held the British and Commonwealth welterweight titles, and laid claim to the British and European middleweight titles, although the NSC did not recognize this claim. Unfortunately for him he could never beat the crashing, dashing Ted 'Kid' Lewis, who relieved him of all his titles.

Tommy Milligan from Wilshaw, in Scotland, won the British and European welterweight titles from Ted 'Kid' Lewis, and added the two middleweight titles to his collection. An attempt at the world middleweight title resulted in him being knocked out by Mickey Walker in the tenth round in 1927.

Among the lighter men, Alf 'Kid' Pattenden and Terry Baldock, both bantamweight champions, will always be remembered for one of the greatest and bravest of fights at Olympia on 16 May 1929, while Johnny Hill, from Strathmigloe, Scotland, kept up the British tradition for flyweights by adding a version of the world title to his British and European titles when he outpointed Newsboy Brown in a brilliant bout. Hill lost only once, to Emile Pladner of France, a man he had already beaten, but by then, 7 February 1929, Hill was already ill. He won two more fights that year, and in October was due to fight Frankie Genaro for the NBA version of the world title. Unfortunately Hill collapsed in training and a few days later died.

The victorious Benny Lynch poses for a battery of cameramen after the defence of his world flyweight title against Small Montana at Wembley in 1937.

5 THE BROWN BOMBER ERA

In the United States, gangsters achieved enormous wealth and power during the Prohibition years of the 1920s and many of them had a strong interest in boxing. Deprived backgrounds and early violence were the common experience of both criminals and boxers. In the 1920s the mobs began to make inroads into boxing, taking over the roles of promoter and manager – or at least as the powers behind them. The object was to fix fights, both for gambling purposes and to promote protégés into championship class.

Evidence of the interest taken by the underworld could be seen in the ringside seats for the fight, in February, 1929, between Jack Sharkey and Young Stribling, one of an eliminating series designed to find a successor to Gene Tunney as heavyweight champion. Al Capone, Bugs Moran and Dutch Schultz, Three of the most notorious mobsters of the day, were there with their henchmen.

This fight should have been promoted by Tex Rickard, but he had died following an appendix operation shortly before and it was taken over by Jack Dempsey, in association with the Madison Square Garden Corporation. Sharkey got the decision on points after ten rounds and went on to knock out Britain's 'Phainting' Phil Scott after the latter had protested repeatedly for alleged fouls. After Germany's Max Schmeling had beaten Johnny Risko and Paolino Uzcudun, of Spain, Schmeling and Sharkey met for the heavyweight championship at the Yankee Stadium on 12 June 1930. Sharkey was outpointing Schmeling, but in the fourth round

doubled him up with a low blow. Schmeling was carried to his corner, his manager, Joe Jacobs, leapt into the ring to protest, the referee and one judge were not in a position to see the low blow, and confusion reigned for some time before referee Jim Crowley disqualified Sharkey on the evidence of the second judge. It was said that a journalist on a Hearst newspaper helped by threatening to get boxing banned again in New York if Schmeling did not get the verdict. Schmeling was the first champion to win the title on a disqualification. Even then he had officialdom to contend with. The NYAC confirmed Schmeling as champion a week later, but only on a 2–1 majority, one member claiming he had not proved himself the best. Then the NYAC declared the title vacant and banned Schmeling from fighting in the State when Jacobs turned down an immediate return with Sharkey.

Schmeling instead went to Cleveland, Ohio, where he defeated Young Stribling on a knockout in the 15th round with less than a minute remaining. For Young Stribling, 'The Georgia Peach', who had 280 fights from bantam to heavyweight, it was really a last opportunity. A colourful character, brought up in a circus and managed by his father, an ex-acrobat, he had a passion for speed and flew airplanes. Two years after his fight with Schmeling, he was killed on his motorcycle speeding to the hospital where his wife was having a baby.

On 21 June 1932 Schmeling gave Sharkey his return at Long Island, New York. Both boxers were tentative, but Schmeling appeared to do enough to win, and complained bitterly when Sharkey was given the decision on points. Manager Joe Jacobs, a voluble American Jew, made one of the more forceful and justified 'We wuz robbed' speeches afterwards. 'We should have stood in bed', he said.

Born in Binghampton, New York State, of Lithuanian parents, Sharkey's real name was Joseph Paul Zukauskas, but he was known as 'The Boston Gob', being an ex-Navy man. A favourite punch of his was the blow to the midriff, so his disqualification against Schmeling and the low blow which had earlier helped Dempsey to beat him were perhaps no more than his share of adverse decisions. An excitable man, he was prone to tears at reverses like this, and was sometimes called 'The Sobbing Sailor'.

Having beaten a German, Sharkey put up his new championship against Primo Carnera, an Italian, on 29 June 1933.

Carnera was a physical freak. He stood 6ft 5¾in (1.98m) and weighed 19 stone (266lb – 120kg), and was known as 'The Ambling Alp'. He was born in Sequals, Italy, on 26 October 1906 and was a strongman in a circus when a French manager, Leon See, had him taught the rudiments of boxing. After drawing the crowds and being successful in Paris and London, he went to America but was outpointed by Sharkey. But he then ran up a string of victories before challenging Sharkey again, this time for the title.

The career of Primo Carnera is the worst indictment of the influence of crooks in boxing in America at that time. He fell into the hands of the mob, who quickly dispensed with See and replaced him with Walter Friedman, who was connected with gangster club-owner Bill Duffy, killer Owney Madden and racketeer Dutch Schultz. It is accepted now that many of Carnera's fights in the States were fixed, especially in the early

Max Schmeling, the former champion, in training in Potsdam in 1935 for a fight with Max Baer for the heavyweight title – but Baer lost the title and Schmeling was sidestepped by Braddock.

Left: Jack Sharkey has his arm raised after the 'Boston Gob' had taken the heavyweight championship from Max Schmeling, being consoled, right, in 1932.

Below: Primo Carnera, the heavyweight champion in 1933–34. He was the heaviest of all the champions, and one problem his opponents had was to avoid being trodden on by those huge feet.

days when he was vulnerable to a skilled boxer.

On 10 February 1933 Carnera fought Ernie Schaaf prior to a shot at Sharkey's title. Schaaf collapsed in the 13th round of a dull fight and was found to be dead. This tragedy affected Carnera, although it was discovered that Schaaf died from brain damage probably caused by a beating he had taken from Max Baer.

Carnera beat Sharkey by a knockout in the sixth round in another controversial contest. Sharkey went down from a punch which some said missed by inches and later explained his performance by claiming that he saw a vision of his pal Ernie Schaaf, and stood around long enough to get knocked out.

Carnera lost the title in his third defence, when he fought Max Baer, 'The Livermore Larruper'. Baer had the physical equipment and talent to make a great champion. At 6ft 2½in (1.89m) and 15st 4lb (214lb – 96.3kg), he could take a punch and had a tremendous right of his own. He was a great draw, but unfortunately was something of a joker and playboy who clowned too much for his own good. Even in the world title fight he was able to joke when both men ended on the canvas together after one exchange. 'Last one up is a cissy', said Baer, but he had Carnera down 11 times in all in their encounter at Long Island, New York, on 14 June 1934, and eventually the referee stopped the fight in the 11th round.

James J. Braddock, the 'Cinderella Man', in 1929, before an unsuccessful attempt on Tommy Loughran's light-heavyweight title. Six years later Braddock was heavyweight champion.

Carnera fought on, winning some, losing others, including a bad beating from Joe Louis, but had not been allowed to keep any of his earnings when he finally returned to Italy on a cattle boat. Luckily, after the war, he was able to go back to the United States and make some money in the wrestling boom. He opened a liquor store, and was comfortably off when he finally returned home to Sequals. He died on 29 June 1967.

Meanwhile, Baer, who had his own radio show and was the hero of the lady fans, was champion for one day short of a year before losing his title to a man as different from him as possible.

James J. Braddock was a boxer whom fame had apparently passed by. By 1934 he was working as a dock hand to support his family, having more or less given up the ring with a record showing he had won little more than half his contests. But put on the Baer-Carnera bill as a stepping-stone for Corn Griffin, a promising youngster, he won, and two victories later he found himself matched with Baer for the title on 13 June 1935 at Long Island.

Braddock's rise from rags to the title-shot earned him the name 'The Cinderella Man'. Perhaps he was destined to win the title, with his forenames 'James J.'. Remarkably, of the first 14 heavyweight champions, he was the fourth 'James J.' following Corbett, Jeffries and Gene Tunney, whose actual names were James Joseph.

He certainly took his chance with determination. While Baer regarded the challenge lightly, and clowned throughout the contest, Braddock methodically outboxed him and won on points. He had been 10–1 against in the betting. The publicity ballyhoo for the fight spoke of an ambulance waiting to take Braddock to hospital.

While the heavyweight championship was changing hands so rapidly, a young professional from Lafayette, Alabama, was building up a record that everybody believed would take him to the title. Joe Louis was black, and no black heavyweight had been given the chance of the title since Jack Johnson. But Louis was clearly something special, and his handlers were making sure that none of the prejudice still alive from the Johnson era would halt him. Johnson was given the cold shoulder when he visited the Louis training quarters, and Louis was coached not to show his delight at victory over white fighters.

After a string of victories against well-chosen opponents, Louis battered former champions Primo Carnera and Max Baer into defeat; Carnera was stopped in six rounds and Baer suffered the first knock-out of his career in the fourth round, though many thought he could have stood up. But, as Baer said, 'Why take more?'. When Louis also knocked out the tough Paolino Uzcudun, he collected the name 'The Brown Bomber'.

It was another ex-champion, Max Schmeling, who halted the progress, albeit temporarily, of Louis' 27 consecutive victories. The fight was taking its expected course until Schmeling caught Louis with his famous right hand in the fourth. Although Louis rose, he took a beating from then on, and was finally knocked out in the 12th round. Joe quickly rehabilitated himself with a third round knock-out of another ex-champion, Jack Sharkey, two months later, but it was Schmeling who had the better credentials for a shot at Braddock's title.

However Louis' interests were being looked after by Mike Jacobs, a clever operator. Jacobs had begun as a ticket concessionnaire working closely with Tex Rickard, and had built up such power as a block buyer of tickets that when Rickard died he was himself able to start promoting. Early on in Louis' rise Jacobs obtained a promotional monopoly on him which enabled him eventually to control boxing in America.

The Madison Square Garden Corporation signed up Schmeling to fight Braddock for the championship, but Jacobs, through his Twentieth Century Sporting Club, fixed up a deal with Braddock that caused him to ignore the Garden deal and fight Louis instead. Schmeling protested and turned up for a 'weigh-in' on the date his contract stipulated but there was nothing he could do.

Braddock and his manager, Joe Gould, were reluctant to meet Schmeling because of the likelihood of the fight being boycotted by the Jewish fans – Schmeling was being wrongly reported at that time as a Nazi sympathizer. But more important was a deal which promised Braddock ten per cent of Jacobs' heavyweight championship promotions for the next ten years.

Whether the deal also included agreement as to how Braddock fought is not known, but when the fight went on in Chicago, on 22 June 1937, Braddock surprised everybody by throwing a right without preliminary at Louis' head and knocking him to the canvas. Thereafter, rather than boxing his usual cagey fight, which seemed to be his only chance, Braddock kept coming forward, bravely carrying the fight but gradually being reduced to bloodied impotence, with Louis ending the fight with one of his fiercest rights in the eighth round. Braddock, with both eyes almost closed, his face cut and his mouth spurting blood, was completely out.

The win established the reputation of Louis, restored some interest to the heavyweight class and set up some good pay days for Louis, Jacobs and, presumably, The Cinderella Man. Jacobs, with the heavyweight champion under his control, was now made matchmaker at Madison Square Garden, and gained a near-monopoly of world title fights.

Louis defended first against Tommy Farr, from Wales, in a fight that most British supporters thought Farr had won, but the judges estimated Louis's punches as being more effective than Farr's, and gave him the points verdict. On 22 June 1938 he gained his revenge over Schmeling, knocking him out in the first round (see Chapter 8).

Louis then went on a 'bum-of-the-month' campaign, beating 17 opponents between 1939 and 1942, all but one, Arturo Godoy, of Chile, by the short route. The best fight was against Billy Conn, who had relinquished the light-heavyweight title, on 18 June 1941. Conn, fast and confident, outpointed Louis for 12 rounds, only for Louis to connect and achieve a knock-out in the

Joe Louis (left) and Tommy Farr in their heavyweight title contest in 1937. Louis won a close points decision.

73

13th round (see Chapter 8). In 1942 Louis became an Army sergeant-instructor and the title was put on ice until after the Second World War.

The light-heavyweight division was confused after Tommy Loughran relinquished the title in 1929. Maxie Rosenbloom, the NYAC champion, finally gained universal recognition when he beat Lou Scozza, the NBA champion, on points in Buffalo, New York, on 14 July 1932.

Bob Olin beat Rosenbloom in 1934 but passed on the title to John Henry Lewis in St. Louis on 31 October 1935. After Lewis relinquished the title in 1938 to fight Joe Louis for the heavyweight crown, there was another disagreement on succession, between America and Britain. Melio Bettina won the vacant American version, soon losing to Billy

John Henry Lewis, the world light-heavyweight champion from 1935 to 1939, when he challenged Joe Louis for the heavyweight title. He failed a medical in London when due to fight Harvey and immediately retired with failing eyesight.

Conn, who also relinquished the title to fight Louis, whereupon Anton Christoforidis beat Bettina, but four months later he lost to Gus Lesnevich, who held the title throughout the war.

Meanwhile, in Britain, Len Harvey took a version of the title with a points win over Jock McAvoy on 10 July 1939. Harvey was near the end of a magnificent career, and he was 37 years old when knocked out by Freddie Mills to lose the title on 20 June 1942. Mills and Lesnevich met to sort out who would be undisputed champion in 1946, Lesnevich winning the first and Mills the second of two fights.

After Mickey Walker had relinquished his middleweight title in 1931, this division for a change lacked a really outstanding performer. The NBA, NYAC and IBU could not agree on a champion throughout the 1930s. The best claim was probably held by the Frenchman Marcel Thil, a man covered with hair except on his head, who was an aggressive body-puncher. He was regarded as champion by the IBU when he beat William 'Gorilla' Jones in 1932 and he saw off all challengers until 1937, when he lost in the tenth round to Fred Apostoli. Eventually, Billy Soose and Tony Zale emerged as NYAC and NBA champions respectively. When Soose relinquished his claim and Zale beat George Abrams on points in 1941, Zale was geNerally recognized, and he remained champion throughout the Second World War.

Jimmy McLarnin, who captured the world welterweight championship in 1933, had three tremendous battles with Barney Ross, losing the rubber and the title on 28 May 1935. These fights are described in Chapter 8.

Ross was one of the fighters who won titles across the feather, light and welterweight divisions in the 1930s, begun by Tony Canzoneri, who, after losing his featherweight championship in 1928, won the lightweight title in 1930. He lost this to Ross in 1933, but held it again after Ross relinquished it, losing it finally to Lou Ambers in 1936. Canzoneri also held the light-welterweight title twice between 1931 and 1933, when he lost it, again to Ross.

So Barney Ross had already taken Canzoneri's light and light-welterweight titles in 1933, and still held the latter when he first won the welterweight title from McLarnin.

Coming up behind Ross was Henry Armstrong, known as 'Homicide Hank'. Armstrong won the undisputed featherweight championship on 29 October 1937, knocking out Petey Sarron in the sixth round in New York. Previously Armstrong held the NYAC version. Before he relinquished this title, he won the welterweight championship from Barney Ross on 31 May 1938, and then took the lightweight title from Lou Ambers on 17 August 1938. He thus became the only boxer ever to hold world titles at three weights simultaneously.

Fritzie Zivic took his welterweight title in 1940, losing it to Freddie (Red) Cochrane in 1941. The lightweight title was regained by Ambers in a return on 22 August 1939 and then taken by Lew Jenkins and Sammy Angott. Angott caused confusion by announcing his retirement in 1941, only to change his mind four months later, when there were already new NYAC and NBA champions. The situation was not resolved until 1947 when Ike Williams, the NBA champion, beat Bob Montgomery, the NYAC champion, by a knock-out in Philadelphia.

The featherweight title, after Armstrong had relinquished it, was won by Joey Archibald, Harry Jeffra and Chalky Wright, before Willie Pep took it from Wright in 1942. There were many claimants during the war when Pep served in the army, but Pep soon established his superiority on his return to boxing.

The 'in-between' titles, light-welterweight and junior lightweight, both lapsed in the mid-1930s and were not revived until 1946 and 1959 respectively.

Bantamweight king Panama Al Brown, who reigned from 1929, finally lost his title in the ring when beaten on points by Baltazar Sangchilli, who was fighting in his home town of Valencia, Spain, on 1 June 1935. Before then, however, both the NBA and NYAC had decided to deprive Brown of the crown for the crime of defending it outside America. They named various champions before Sixto Escobar, of Puerto Rico, drew the strands together with a victory over Tony Marino on 31 August 1936. Escobar swopped wins with Harry Jeffra until both became overweight. Lou Salica took the vacant title in 1940, but lost in 1942 to Manuel Ortiz, who kept it for the rest of the war.

Left: Henry Armstrong, 'Homicide Hank', knocks Pedro Montanez to the canvas at Madison Square Garden in 1940 when retaining his world welterweight title.

Below: Panama Al Brown (left) a very tall bantamweight, was world champion from 1929 to 1935, when he lost the crown to Spain's Baltazar Sangchilli (right).

The flyweight title, meanwhile, was firmly in British hands in the 1930s. Benny Lynch became overweight in 1938, but Peter Kane, from Golborne, Lancs, who had already given Lynch two hard fights, the second a draw, beat the American Jackie Jurich for the vacant title to keep it in Britain.

Kane joined the RAF, but put his title at stake against Jackie Paterson, from Springfield, Ayrshire, in Glasgow on 19 June 1943. It was nearly five years since Kane had won the title, and he was knocked out in the first round, in 61 seconds to be precise. Paterson remained champion until boxing resumed fully in Britain after the war.

British boxing was booming in the 1930s. London's White City Stadium staged its first boxing tournament in 1933 when Jack Petersen, the British and

Empire heavyweight champion, defended against Jack Doyle, a singing Irish boyo who packed a terrific wallop in his right fist, but on this occasion persisted in punching low. Doyle was disqualified in the second round and his purse was confiscated – he sued the BBBC for it, and lost. Petersen could have been world champion had he been a little bigger and not suffered with eye problems. His three great fights with the German Walter Neusel were lost due to eye problems.

The Wembley Pool and Sports Arena opened for boxing in 1934 – Neusel was on the bill against Len Harvey, and they fought a draw. Harringay Arena first staged boxing in 1936. The popular Neusel was again on the bill, fighting Ben Foord of South Africa, who had taken the British Empire heavyweight title from Petersen. Neusel won on points.

It was at Harringay that the first contest to be televised took place, on 7 April 1938, when Len Harvey outpointed Jock McAvoy for the British light-heavyweight title, although this was not publicly screened. The first televised contest to go out on closed circuit to theatre screens was also held at Harringay – the classic between Eric Boon and Arthur Danahar for the British lightweight championship, which is described in Chapter 8.

Two boxers from Liverpool who just failed at world title attempts kept their fans happy over long careers throughout the 1930s. Ernie Roderick fought for 19 years from 1931 and held the British welter and middleweight titles. In 1939 he interrupted a string of knock-out victories by Henry Armstrong, but lost the points decision in his challenge for the world welter crown.

Nel Tarleton began boxing in 1926, and after pleurisy and pneumonia in 1937 continued fighting with only one sound lung. He won the British featherweight title in 1931, lost it twice but regained it, and finally gave it up after a successful defence in 1945. He was then 39 years old. He twice fought Freddie Miller for the world title, in 1934 and 1935, losing narrowly on points each time – on the second occasion the decision was far from popular. Tarleton died in 1956, two days before his 50th birthday, when he would have been the first to qualify for the £1 per week pension due to outright Lonsdale Belt winners.

Henry Armstrong (right) was for once forced to go the distance when challenged by Ernie Roderick for his welterweight title at Harringay Arena, London, in 1939.

Jack 'Kid' Berg, the 'Whitechapel Whirlwind', won and defended the world junior welterweight title 11 times in 14 months from 18 February 1930.

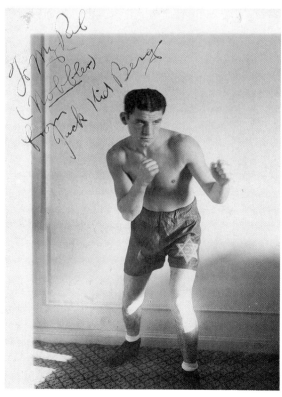

6 THE MODERN ERA

After the Second World War, boxing quickly got under way again. The reigning heavyweight champion, Joe Louis, was just past 32 years old when he resumed in 1946 with a defence against Billy Conn, who had given him his hardest challenge five years earlier. The years of war service seemed to have had more effect on Conn, who this time was comfortably knocked out in the eighth round.

Louis then knocked out Tami Mauriello in the first round, and in 1947 beat Jersey Joe Walcott on points in a match that everybody but two of the three men who mattered thought he'd lost. Louis knocked out Walcott in a return, and on 1 March 1949 announced his retirement.

The retirement of Louis marked a change in the overt control of boxing in the United States. Since early in his career Louis had been 'controlled' by Mike Jacobs, a speculator who sold tickets for Tex Rickard promotions, and who, on Rickard's death, moved into promotion himself. In 1933 his Twentieth Century Sporting Club was formed with three 'undercover' members of the Hearst newspaper group, with the laudable objective of promoting in aid of Mrs William Randolph Hearst's Free Milk Fund for babies. Jacobs, with the aid of the Hearst papers, challenged the position of the Madison Square Garden Corporation, which had a hold on boxing promotion.

With Louis under his wing, Jacobs took over the sole ownership of the Twentieth Century Sporting Club. As related in the previous chapter, Jacobs matched Louis with the champion

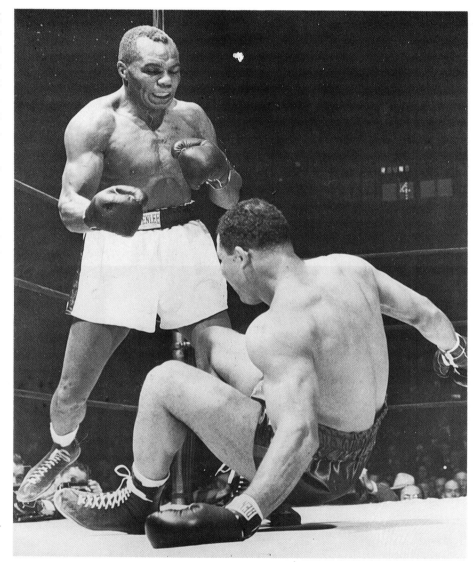

Braddock, although Braddock was under contract to Madison Square Garden, and 'acquired' the heavyweight title. It was also said that Jacobs, through loan deals, had a share in Braddock, as did Owney Madden, a notorious underworld character.

Joe Louis down in the first round of his fight with Jersey Joe Walcott in 1947. Louis got up to retain his title on points over 15 rounds.

In the years in which Louis held the championship, Jacobs promoted over 60 world title contests. He secured a lease on boxing promotions at the Garden, and had a near-monopoly of the big matches. During this time his name was frequently coupled with underworld figures.

Jacobs was ill when Louis retired and Louis joined forces with James Norris and others who owned or had shares in stadiums up and down the country, to form the International Boxing Club (IBC). This organization had signed up exclusively the leading contenders to Louis' title prior to his retirement, and announced that two of them, Ezzard Charles and Jersey Joe Walcott, would fight for the vacant championship, a move authorized by the National Boxing Association (NBA), but not by the New York State Athletic Commission (NYAC).

The NYAC's opposition was futile. The IBC assumed a monopoly of boxing even more marked than Jacobs' had been. Louis, who owed a fortune to the Inland Revenue, did not, in the end, emerge with much control or financial reward, but it transpired that several underworld figures had a continuing influence on the sport, its contracts and its finances. And the finances were considerable, as the era of world-wide broadcasting and television developed.

Among gangsters eventually charged with conspiracy and extortion in relation to boxing were Frank Carbo and Frank Palermo, found guilty with others and sentenced to long prison terms in 1961.

In the ring, Ezzard Charles beat Jersey Joe Walcott on points on 22 June 1949 in Chicago to become the champion. Charles, born on 7 July 1921 in Lawrenceville, Georgia, was a very skilful boxer, but at 6ft (1.83m) and 13st 3lb (185lb – 84kg) one of the smaller of the heavyweight champions. He was universally recognized as champion on 27 September 1950 when he was challenged by Joe Louis, making a come-back, and beat him on points. Charles successfully defended eight times in all, Lee Oma, Walcott again, and light-heavyweight champion Joey Maxim being among his victims, until Jersey Joe Walcott surprisingly knocked him out in the seventh round at Pittsburgh on 18 July 1951. It was their third title fight, and Walcott confirmed the form with a points victory at Philadelphia on 5 June 1952. This was even more surprising, since Walcott was 37 years and five months old at the time of winning the title, and should not have been improving. Walcott was born Arnold Raymond Cream, in Merchantville, New Jersey, and took his boxing name from the old Barbados-born welterweight champion, adding the 'Jersey' after his own birth-state. Like former champion Braddock, Walcott had retired once, thinking that the ultimate honour had passed him by.

Jersey Joe was not to reign for long, for coming along was the next really great champion in heavyweight boxing, Rocky Marciano. Marciano was of Italian descent (his real name was Rocco Marchegiano) and he came from Brockton, Massachusetts. He had had 42 wins, most by the knock-out route, when given a title shot with Walcott, his most notable scalps being Joe Louis, whom he dispatched in eight rounds, persuading Louis to end his come-back campaign, and Lee Savold. Marciano took the title in an absorbing contest which is described in Chapter 8, and having estab-

Ezzard Charles (left) beat Jersey Joe Walcott in Chicago in 1949 to win the world heavyweight championship vacated by Joe Louis.

On a comeback trail in 1951 Louis (left) was beaten by a technical knock-out in the eighth round by up-and-coming Rocky Marciano.

lished his superiority, lost no time in the return, knocking out Walcott in the first round.

Marciano defended six times, twice against the old champion Ezzard Charles, the only challenger to take him the full distance, although on his second attempt he went the way of all the others, knocked out in the eighth. Charles fought on until his 38th year, but suffered ill-health after his retirement and was confined to a wheel-chair before his death on 27 May 1970, in Chicago.

Marciano defeated a British challenger, Don Cockell, who put up a game show for nine rounds, then retired after knocking out light-heavyweight champion Archie Moore on 21 September 1955. Marciano did not attempt a comeback and remains the only heavyweight champion unbeaten in his entire career. Louis and Tunney, who both also relinquished the title, each suffered a defeat before becoming champion, and, of course, Louis suffered two more when he returned to the ring.

On Marciano's retirement, Floyd Patterson, from Waco, North Carolina, just beat Tommy 'Hurricane' Jackson in an eliminator for the chance to meet Archie Moore for the vacant title. Moore was favourite, but never had a light-heavyweight champion been able to add

the heavyweight crown to his laurels, and this tradition was maintained when Patterson recorded a fifth-round knock-out on 30 November 1956. At 21 years, 10 months and 26 days, Patterson became the youngest of all heavyweight champions.

Patterson was a 1952 Olympic gold medalist, whose asset was speed of punch. For a world champion he could be put down easily, as his second defence showed. This was against the reigning Olympic champion, Pete Rademacher, making his debut as a professional, at Sicks' Stadium, Seattle, Washington. The Washington commissioners were asked by authorities around the world to ban this one-sided match, but Rademacher actually shaded the first round and put Patterson down in the second. Thereafter he was down seven times himself before being knocked out in the sixth.

Patterson had a couple of easy wins, including a knock-out of Brian London, an Englishman from Blackpool, before taking on Ingemar Johansson, of Gothenburg, Sweden, at the Yankee Stadium, New York, on 26 June 1959.

Johansson was an interesting boxer, whose previous impact on the world at large had been a shaming one – he was disqualified for 'not trying' in the final of the Olympic heavyweight tournament in 1952, and was not awarded the silver medal (he was finally given it 30 years later). He was something of a singer and actor, was good at business, and arrived for the fight with a party of admirers which included his dazzling fiancée. In all, he gave the impression of the talented amateur rather than the dedicated professional.

Johansson was born on 22 September 1932. After turning professional he had 22 straight victories, 14 by the knock-out route, before challenging Patterson. He was the 4–1 underdog, but had a tremendous punch in his right fist, called by journalists 'the hammer of Thor', and affectionately referred to by Johansson as his 'toonder and lightning' right.

After two rounds of feeling out, this right caught Patterson early in the third, and the champion was down. He rose quickly, but was clearly unaware of what was going on, and Johansson knocked him down again. This pattern was repeated until on Patterson's seventh visit to the canvas, the referee moved in and awarded the championship to the Swede.

This fight marked a departure for boxing. The television audience now became more important than the live gate. Only about 20,000 were present in the 60,000-seater stadium, but the closed circuit television brought in over $1 million – Patterson himself was paid more than was taken at the gate.

The contract called for a return, and this took place at the Polo Grounds, New York, on 20 June 1960. If Patterson had under-estimated Johansson on the first meeting, the reverse might have been true for the second. The fun-loving Ingemar, now known in the press as 'Ingo', did not train too seriously, it seemed, believing that he had only to tap Patterson on the chin with his right – 'Ingo's Bingo' – to remain champion.

Patterson went into seclusion and trained hard – despite this he came into the ring at 13st 8lb (190lb – 86kg), 8lb heavier than for the first fight. Johansson, despite his carefree attitude, was slightly lighter than the first time at 13st 12lb (194lb – 88kg), so the two were much closer in weight.

In the second round, Johansson landed his right to Patterson's head – but the challenger remained upright. This gave him confidence, and he took the fight to Johansson. In the fifth round a

hard right, followed by one of his leaping lefts, saw the champion hit the canvas. He was up at 'nine' but Patterson rained a succession of hooks on him, the last crumpling up Johansson, who was out for the count.

Patterson was the first heavyweight champion to regain his crown. The 32,000 spectators paid less than $1 million; the closed circuit TV audience nearly $2 million.

The rubber match, at the Miami Beach Convention Hall, on 13 March 1961, proved the most exciting of the three contests. Both men were at the heaviest of their careers, but Johansson,

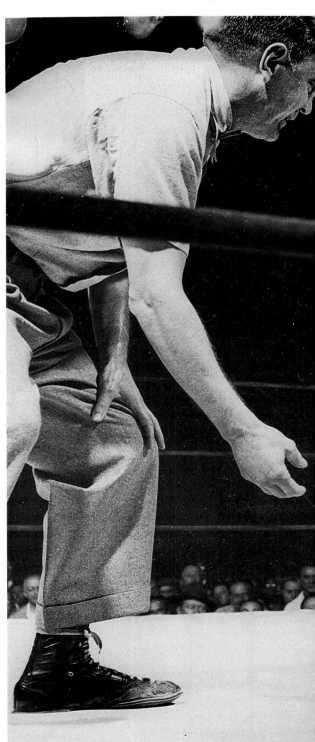

at 14st 10½lb (206½lb − 93.5kg) carried some of his extra weight as fat. He was 4–1 outsider again.

After an exchange of blows in the first round, a Johansson right cross put Patterson down. This was the first heavyweight championship fight in which a new convention was used – that of the mandatory eight count. So, although Patterson rose at 'three', the referee continued counting to 'eight' before the action was resumed. Johansson then rushed Patterson, and put him down again. The champion was hurt.

However, as Ingo rushed in to finish it after another 'eight' count, Patterson found some reserves to flash a right and left to his face, and Johansson was down. For the next four rounds each man manoeuvred to get the heavy blow in first. Both succeeded in landing big punches, without being able to put the other down. The end came in the sixth. Patterson was clearly the fitter, and absorbed some of Johansson's best rights before launching an assault which put the Swede on the canvas. Ingemar lost his balance as he tried to rise at 'nine', and was still getting up when counted out.

While Patterson was champion, a lurking shadow was Sonny Liston, a man

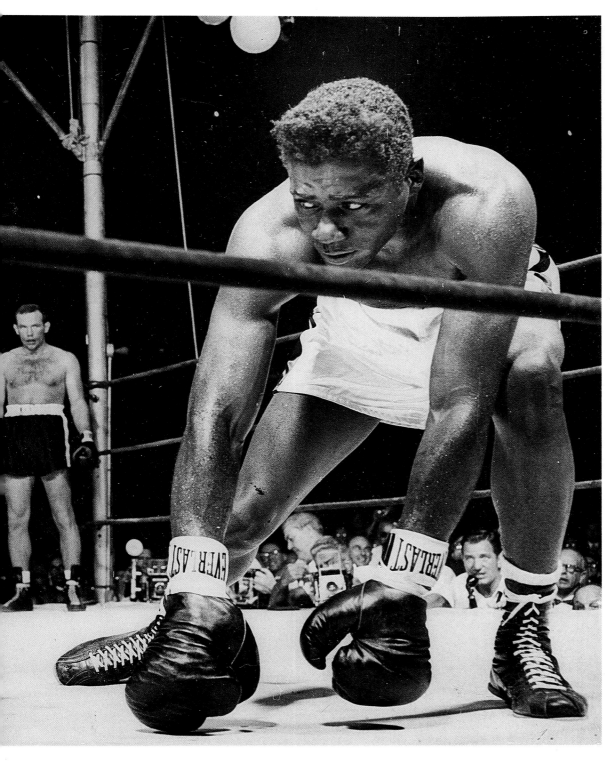

Ingemar Johansson waits in a neutral corner in the rain-soaked Yankee Stadium as referee Ruby Goldstein counts over the champion Floyd Patterson, down for one of seven counts in the third round, in which he was knocked out.

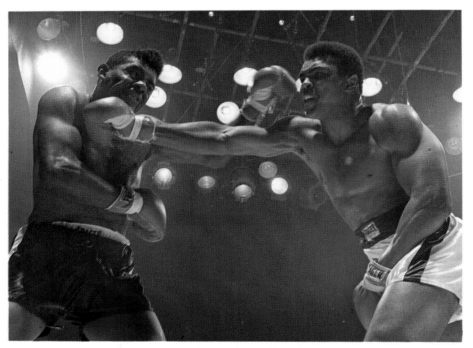

Muhammad Ali (right) lands a right on former champion Floyd Patterson's chin in their 1965 contest. Patterson was stopped in the 12th round.

who could hardly read or write and was grudging with speech. From a large family (his father had 25 children) he had run away from home at 13 and been constantly in trouble, even having his boxing career interrupted by assaulting a policeman and serving nine months in prison. He had had underworld connections for most of his life, and the mobster Frank Palermo had guided his career.

Liston was of fearsome aspect, with 15-inch (38cm) fists. At one time it was thought that, despite eliminating all contenders, he would not be allowed a shot at the heavyweight championship because of his police record. Patterson found, however, that he could not avoid him for ever, and on 25 September 1962, the two met at Comiskey Park, Chicago.

Liston, at 15st 4lb (214lb – 97kg) outweighed Patterson by 25lb (11kg), and he outreached him by 13 inches (33cm). He was the slight favourite. It is possible that the thought of the glowering Liston waiting for him in the wings for so long, and then the press build-up of the stone-faced 'baddie', had got to Patterson. He was clearly lacking confidence, and Sonny merely stalked him for a while and then knocked him out with three powerful left hooks. It took two minutes and six seconds of the first round.

When the two met again, on 22 July 1963 at the Convention Hall in Las Vegas, Liston was 5–1 on. The fight took a similar course to the first, except that this time Patterson got up twice and took two mandatory counts of 'eight'. This

prolonged the fight to two minutes, ten seconds – four seconds longer than the first encounter. Patterson did not get up a third time.

Liston, who had won two title-fights by boxing little more than four minutes, which included standing around while his opponent was counted over, was thought by now to be invincible. He was also the most disliked champion since Jack Johnson. There was even newspaper talk of a search for a 'white hope'. But it was another black man who came to dethrone the 'Ugly Bear' – one of the most remarkable figures in the history of boxing, Cassius Clay.

Clay himself was unpopular at this stage of his career. A braggart, he took to composing verses about his fights, predicting the round in which he would win, often with remarkable accuracy. He usually put on a ranting, non-stop display at weigh-ins to discomfort his opponent and his performance at the Liston weigh-in was weird, as he heckled the champion continuously and gave every indication of a man in a state of hyper-active excitement. He was called the 'Louisville Lip' or, sometimes, 'Gaseous Cassius'.

The two fights which Clay had with Liston are described in Chapter 8. Both left questions unanswered, particularly about Liston, who succumbed unexpectedly each time.

Between taking the title and his first defence against Liston, Clay embraced the Islamic religion and assumed a new name, Muhammad Ali. He was also classified 1Y by the US armed forces draft board after failing its intelligence tests. The World Boxing Association (WBA) deprived Ali of his title and installed Ernie Terrell as champion instead.

The WBA was formed at Tacoma, Washington, in August 1962, and succeeded the NBA, which, since 1927, had nominated world champions in opposition to the NYAC. At its inauguration, the WBA comprised most of the state and city boxing commissions outside New York, and federations from other parts of America.

In February 1963, the World Boxing Council (WBC) was founded in Mexico to counter the claims of the WBA to be the world authority regarding world championships. It comprised the British Boxing Board of Control, the European Boxing Union, the authorities of the

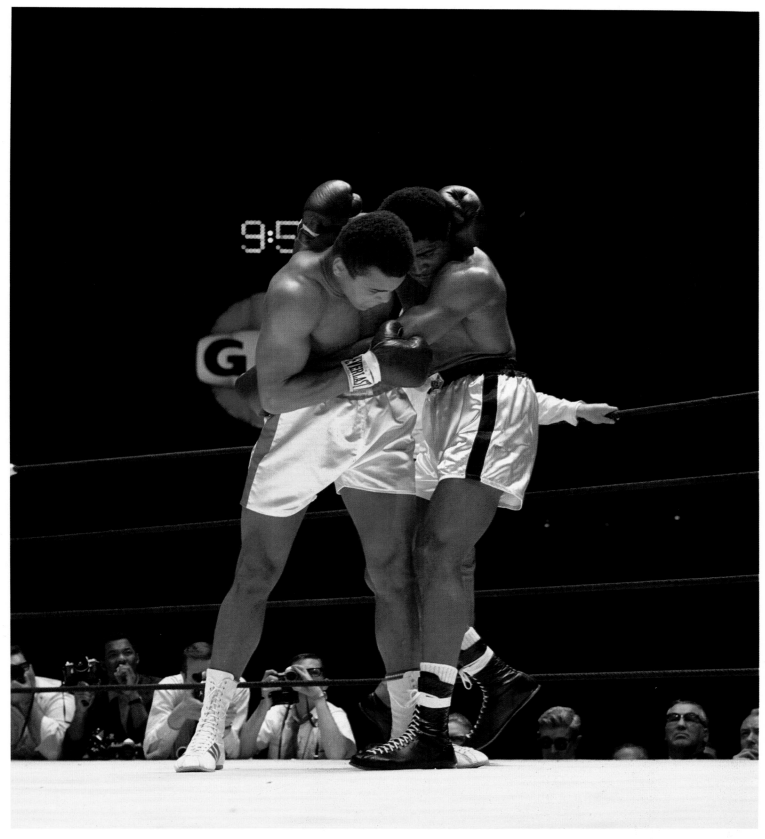

Commonwealth, Asian and Carribbean countries, South Africa, those American states and North, Central and South American countries not affiliated to the WBA and the Mexican Federation of Boxing Commissions. It also has support from the NYAC.

The WBA and WBC therefore represent the old NBA and NYAC respectively, but whereas disagreements over world champions before the 1960s were the exception rather than the rule, the situation since has worsened until now there are usually two world champions for each weight. This means that recently there have been approaching 30 world champions in the 15 weight divisions, where there used to be only eight.

With Ernie Terrell the WBA champion, Ali remained WBC champion, and defended against Patterson. Then, in

Ernie Terrell (right) was made champion by the WBA, and refused to recognize the new name assumed by Cassius Clay, Muhammad Ali. Ali taunted him throughout their fight in 1967, asking 'What's my name?' as he punished him for 15 rounds.

Opposite: Ali, deprived
of his titles in 1967,
finally obtained a
comeback fight in 1970
against Jerry Quarry
(right) and knocked him
out in the third round.

Below: Joe Frazier was
down six times in a
round and a half in
Kingston, Jamaica,
when he defended his
title against George
Foreman in 1973.
Foreman walks away,
the new champion, as
the referee spreads his
arms over Frazier.

February, 1966, Ali's draft board re-classified him A1, which meant he was eligible for service in the Vietnam war. Ali's reaction was: 'I got no quarrel with the Vietcong'.

This remark received wide publicity, and Ali was forced to cancel a contest with Ernie Terrell and to campaign overseas. He won in Canada, London and West Germany in 1966 before returning to the States to beat, among others, Ernie Terrell, and become un-disputed champion again.

Ali had attempted to get deferment from service by claiming first to be a conscientious objector and then a Mus-lim minister. These appeals were re-jected and Ali was ordered to report to be inducted; he refused, and on 9 May 1967 a federal grand jury indicted him on a charge of failing to submit to the draft. Soon afterwards both the WBA and WBC stripped him of his titles, and he was banned from boxing in the United States.

Nothing indicated more the confused state that the divided rule of the WBA and WBC would lead to than the situation which arose after Ali's removal from the title. The WBA organized an eight-man tournament to find a new champion from among Joe Frazier, Thad Spencer, Ernie Terrell, Oscar Bonavena, Karl Mildenberger, Jimmy Ellis, Floyd Patterson and Jerry Quarry. Frazier, however, refused to join the group, and was replaced by Leotis Martin. Jimmy Ellis eventually tri-umphed, beating Jerry Quarry in the final to become the WBA champion, but in the meantime Frazier had beaten Buster Mathis and was named as the WBC champion.

Both Frazier and Ellis beat off challen-gers until they met on 16 February 1970 in New York. Frazier won when Ellis was unable to come out for the fifth round. For the first time for three years there was an undisputed world heavy-weight champion.

Meanwhile Ali, found guilty of violat-ing the United States Selective Service laws, was sentenced on 20 June 1967 to five years imprisonment and a $10,000 fine. He was released on bail and appealed, but his passport was con-fiscated. While the appeal was being heard, Ali obtained a licence to fight in Georgia, and in October 1970 in Atlanta knocked out Jerry Quarry in three rounds. It was his first fight for over three years. Indeed a few months earlier he had announced his retirement, think-ing that he would not get a chance of boxing professionally again. Another breakthrough for Ali occurred when a judge nullified the refusal of the NYAC to grant Ali a licence to fight in New York. On 7 December 1970 Ali fought Oscar Bonavena there and stopped him in the 15th round.

On 8 March 1971 Ali fought Frazier at Madison Square Garden and tried to regain the title he had never lost in the ring. In the 15th and last round Frazier dropped Ali with a left hook. It was a tough, close fight, but Frazier won a unanimous points decision to remain champion.

After two further, easier defences, Frazier faced George Foreman in King-ston, Jamaica, on 22 January 1973. Foreman, like both Ali and Frazier, was a former Olympic champion. Born on 22 January 1948 in Marshall, Texas, he stood 6ft 3in (1.91m) and weighed 15st

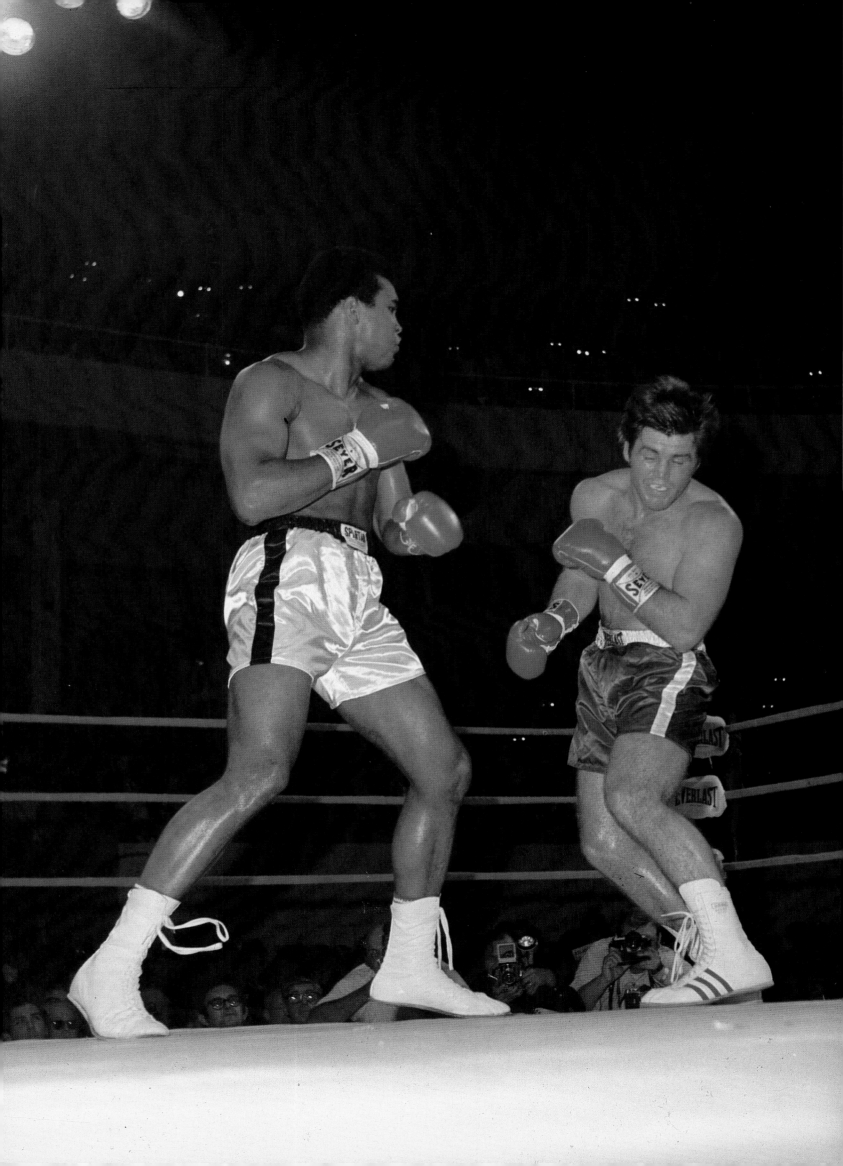

10lb (220lb – 100kg). Of his first 37 opponents, only three had taken him the distance. Even so, he was the underdog at 3–1.

Frazier attacked, but the 3½in (9cm) taller challenger stood his ground. Foreman's punches looked more solid than Frazier's and midway through the first a right to the jaw put the champion down. Twice more Frazier was put down in the first round. The second round went like the first. Frazier rushed in, but Foreman put him down. Foreman's blows were hard enough to knock Frazier clean off his feet, but Frazier kept getting up quickly. Finally, although Frazier got up for the sixth time midway through the second round, the referee allowed him to continue no further. There was a new champion.

While Foreman was defending against Joe Roman and Ken Norton, neither of whom lasted more than two rounds, Ali and Frazier met for a second time. The date was 28 January 1974, the place, Madison Square Garden. Such was Ali's drawing power, and his developing rivalry with Frazier, that the non-title fight grossed over $20 million, including the television and film rights. It was a second gruelling fight between the two, and again went the distance. This time Ali obtained the unanimous verdict.

On 30 October 1974 Ali had the chance to make his comeback complete when he fought Foreman for the championship in Kinshasa, Zaire. Foreman was 3–1 favourite, and started in his usual style, piling into Ali with both hands. Ali defended his head, and allowed Foreman to pin him on the ropes and punch away at his body. After two rounds, Ali, unlike most opponents Foreman had fought, was still standing up, and in the third he began to poke his fists into Foreman's face as the champion came in. Foreman was nonplussed and could not adjust his tactics. He kept pushing forwards and as he failed to put Ali down he became exhausted and dispirited. In the eighth round a left, right, left combination deposited Foreman on the canvas, from where he could not rise and was counted out.

So Muhammad Ali regained the heavyweight title over seven years after it had been taken from him, a remarkable achievement. Foreman fought on for a while, and retired in 1977.

Ali, now 32 years old, proceeded to defend impressively, and had a third

Opposite: Larry Holmes (right) beat Ken Norton at Las Vegas to win the vacant WBA heavyweight championship in 1978.

meeting with Joe Frazier on 1 October 1975. This fight was even more exciting than the previous two, and is described in Chapter 8. It was a great surprise when Ali lost the title to Leon Spinks on 18 February 1978. Spinks, born at St Louis, Missouri, on 11 July 1953, had been the Olympic light-heavyweight champion only two years before, and had made only seven professional appearances. He fought at manic speed as if supercharged, and won a split points decision in Las Vegas.

The WBC stripped Spinks of the title almost immediately for refusing to meet Ken Norton and named Norton as champion, a decision which looked silly on 10 June 1978 when Norton was outpointed by Larry Holmes in Las Vegas, Holmes becoming champion. It looked even sillier when, on 15 September 1978, Ali met Spinks in the return fight guaranteed by the contract of the first, and won by a unanimous points verdict in New Orleans.

So Ali became the first man to regain a world heavyweight title twice, although, because of the WBC decision, it was only half a title.

Holmes, meanwhile, proved an impressive WBC champion, winning his first seven defences inside the distance. He then met Ali on 2 October 1980 at Caesar's Palace, Las Vegas, and forced him to retire at the end of the tenth round.

This should have meant an undisputed champion again, but unfortunately Ali had retired as WBA title-holder in 1979, and the WBA recognized

Ali covers up on the ropes as he loses his title to Leon Spinks in 1978. Spinks never defended the title, being stripped for refusing to meet Norton.

John Tate, from Knoxville, Tennessee, as champion when he beat Gerry Coetzee, of South Africa, in Johannesburg on 20 October 1979. While Holmes continued his sequence of wins into the 1980s, Mike Weaver, of Gatesville, Texas, took the WBA title from John Tate on 31 March 1980 and lost it to Michael Dokes on 10 December 1982 in Las Vegas, the referee stopping the fight in the first round.

On 23 September 1983, Gerry Coetzee won the WBA title by knocking out Dokes in the 10th round in Richfield, Ohio. He became the first South African to hold a version of a heavyweight title, and the first white man to do so for 24 years, since Ingemar Johansson.

In his first defence, Coetzee was beaten by Greg Page on 1 December 1984 in Sun City, South Africa. Controversy surrounded the fight, as Coetzee, who had been down twice in earlier rounds, was knocked out 49 seconds after the eighth round should have ended. The time-keeper's error was confirmed by the television video-recording. Coetzee immediately protested to the WBA that the decision should be void, and the heavyweight championship was in further confusion.

Larry Holmes announced in 1983 that he was relinquishing the WBC title to assume the championship of a new organization, the International Boxing Federation. In June 1984 he was set to meet the WBA champion Coetzee at Caesar's Palace, Las Vegas, but this failed to take place due to promotional difficulties. The WBA later threatened to

Ali, having retired as WBA champion in 1979, attempted to win the heavyweight title for the fourth time by challenging WBC holder Larry Holmes (left) in 1980s, but he was forced to retire in the 10th in Las Vegas.

Mike Weaver (right) knocked out champion John Tate in the last round at Knoxville to take the WBA title in 1980.

strip Coetzee of his title if he fought Holmes.

When Holmes relinquished his WBC title, Tim Witherspoon won a 12-round split decision over Greg Page to become champion. On 31 August 1984 he defended against fellow-American Pinklon Thomas, a former heroin addict. Thomas, a 26-year-old from Philadelphia, weighing 15st 6lb (216lb – 98kg), outpointed Witherspoon to become new champion.

Thus, at the end of 1984, there were four boxers claiming to be heavyweight champion of the world: Larry Holmes, Pinklon Thomas, Greg Page and Gerry Coetzee.

In 1979 a new division was introduced by the WBC: cruiserweight, with a maximum of 13st 13lb (195lb – 88kg). Marvin Camel, of Missoula, Montana, was the first holder, beating Mate Parlov,

of Yugoslavia, in Las Vegas, after a draw in Split, Yugoslavia. Carlos de Leon, of Puerto Rico, took it in 1981, and regained it in 1983 after dropping it to S. T. Gordon. Meanwhile, the WBA recognized Ossie Ocasio, also of Puerto Rico, as champion after he outpointed Robbie Williams, of South Africa, in 1982.

Among the post-war light-heavyweights, Freddie Mills, who was undisputed champion for the first time on 26 July 1948 when he beat Gus Lesnevich on points in the second of their two fights, defended on 24 January 1950 in London, and was knocked out in the 10th round by Joey Maxim.

During his reign, Maxim had a remarkable contest with Sugar Ray Robinson, the middleweight champion. When the two met at the Yankee Stadium on 25 June 1952 the tempera-

Above: Gerry Coetzee of South Africa (right) attacking Michael Dokes at Richfield, Ohio, in 1983. Coetzee knocked out Dokes in the 10th and became the first South African heavyweight title holder.

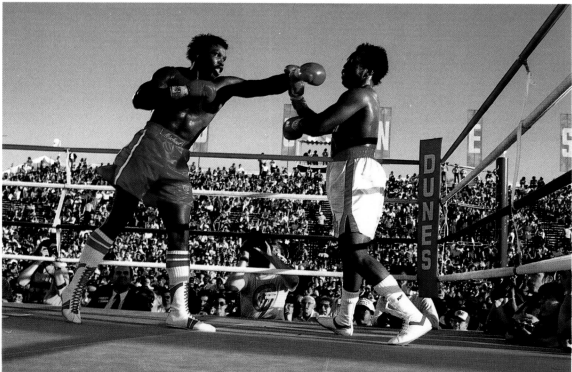

Left: Michael Dokes (right) took the WBA heavyweight title when he knocked out Mike Weaver in the first round in Las Vegas in 1982.

World light-heavyweight champion Gus Lesnevich, who won the title in 1941 and held it to 1948, when he lost the second of two great battles with Freddie Mills.

ture was the hottest for that day in New York history. Under the lights it was 104°F (40°C). The lighter Robinson easily outpointed Maxim for 13 rounds but was so exhausted by the heat that he could not come out for the 14th round of a fight he had virtually won.

Maxim then fought Archie Moore three times, in St. Louis, Ogden and Miami. Moore won on points each time. He was 36 years old (possibly 39) when he first took the championship in 1952, and he made some brilliant defences, notably against Yvon Durelle, a durable, tough Canadian, on 10 December 1958. Moore was down three times in the first round and again in the fifth, but fought back to floor Durelle four times; twice, including the knock-out, in the 11th round. It was Archie Moore's 127th knock-out victory, an all-time record.

Moore had his title taken away by the NBA for inactivity in 1960. They named Harold Johnson, who knocked out Jesse Bowdry in Miami on 7 February 1961, as champion. Moore continued to be recognised elsewhere, and defended for the last time on 10 June 1961, beating Italy's Guilio Rinaldi on points in New York. Moore retired as unbeaten champion in 1962, and the NBA champion Johnson was then universally accepted.

Johnson lost on 1 June 1963 to Wille Pastrano, who successfully defended in Manchester against Britain's former world middleweight champion Terry Downes, before being knocked out by Jose Torres, of Puerto Rico, on 30 March 1965. Torres was a former Olympic silver medalist, having been beaten in the 1956 featherweight final by Lazslo Papp, of Hungary.

Left: Freddie Mills won the British version of the world light-heavyweight championship in 1942, lost to Gus Lesnevich, who became undisputed champion in 1946, but became undisputed champion himself by beating Lesnevich in 1948.

Below: Joey Maxim (right) takes the world light-heavyweight title from Freddie Mills in London in 1950. Mills retired after this battle.

Dick Tiger, of Nigeria, the former middleweight champion, took the title from Torres in 1966. When Tiger lost it to Bob Foster on 24 May 1968 he was knocked out for the only time in his career.

Foster was a busy defender until 1974. Among those he defeated was Chris Finnegan, the British, European and Commonwealth champion, and Olympic gold medalist. During this run Foster challenged Joe Frazier for the heavyweight title in 1970, but was knocked out in the second round. In 1972 Foster stepped up a weight again to fight Muhammad Ali, and this time lasted until the eighth. Foster's final light-heavyweight defence, against Jorge Ahumada, of Argentina, on 17 June 1974 in Albuquerque, New Mexico, was given as a draw, although most ringsiders

thought Foster had been clearly outpointed. Three months later Foster retired.

There were then two light-heavyweight champions. John Conteh, from Liverpool, beat Ahumada on 1 October 1974 in London to become WBC champion, while Victor Galindez, of Argentina, beat Pierre Fourie, of South Africa, on points in Johannesburg a few weeks later to become WBA champion.

Conteh was stripped of his title in 1977 for declining a match against Miguel Cuello, of Argentina, who then became WBC champion. Later, when Cuello had lost the title to Mate Parlov, of Yugoslavia, Conteh attempted to regain it, but was adjudged a points loser in a hotly disputed decision in Belgrade.

Marvin Johnson and Matt Franklin then held the WBC title in turn, Franklin changing his name to Matthew Saad Muhammad. He finally lost the championship to Dwight Braxton on 19 December 1981 in Atlantic City, New Jersey. Braxton changed his name to Dwight Muhammad Qawi, and lost the title to WBA champion Michael Spinks in 1983.

Galindez, meanwhile, retained his WBA title until 1978 when he dropped it to Mike Rossman, but he regained it in 1979, only to lose it to Marvin Johnson, the former WBC title-holder. Johnson lost in 1980 to Eddie Gregory who changed his name (a common event in this division) to Eddie Mustapha Muhammad. Michael Spinks, a former Olympic champion and brother of the former heavyweight champion Leon Spinks, beat Muhammad on 18 July 1981, and in 1983 became undisputed champion when he beat Qawi.

The middleweight division since the Second World War has continued to

Below: Marcel Cerdan (right) cracks a right to the chin of middleweight champion Tony Zale in Jersey City in 1948. Cerdan won by a 12th round knock-out.

Right: Bob Foster, world light-heavyweight champion for six years, dumps challenger Chris Finnegan on the canvas in the 14th round of their fight in London in 1972.

produce outstanding performers. In 1946 Tony Zale was champion. He beat Rocky Graziano that year, but lost the title to him in 1947, only to regain it in 1948. These three tremendous fights are described in Chapter 8.

Zale lost his title to Marcel Cerdan, of France, the European champion, who knocked him out in the 12th round in Jersey City on 21 September 1948. Cerdan was one of the great middleweights. On 16 June 1949 he lost his title to Jake LaMotta, in Detroit, Michigan. The Frenchman injured his shoulder in the first round when thrown to the floor. He fought on under handicap but was forced to retire after ten rounds. He was flying to New York for the return when he died in an airliner crash in the Azores on 27 October 1949.

Jake (real name Giacobe) LaMotta was himself an aggressive, two-fisted fighter who was known as 'The Bronx Bull' or 'The Raging Bull'. LaMotta lost

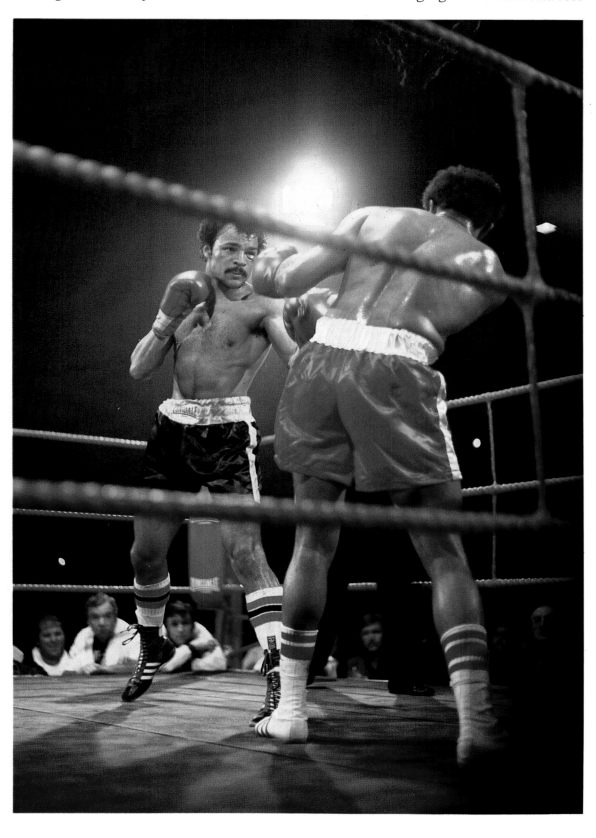

John Conteh, the world light-heavyweight champion from 1974 until stripped in 1977 for refusing a fight in Monte Carlo. He is in action against Joe Cokes.

Marcel Cerdan of France, one of the great middleweights, and champion in 1948, who was tragically killed in an air crash before he could show the world his full talents.

his title to Sugar Ray Robinson, one of the best middleweights of all time. That same year, 1951, Robinson lost and regained the championship in two fights with the British and European champion, Randolph Turpin.

On 18 December 1952, Robinson announced his retirement – but he was to come back to win the title three more times! Carl 'Bobo' Olsen beat Turpin to assume the championship, but Robinson knocked him out in the second round on 9 December 1955 to regain it. He lost it to Gene Fullmer on points on 2 January

1957 and on 1 May he won it back again with a fifth-round knock-out. On 23 September Robinson was beaten on points by Carmen Basilio in a great fight, notable for the way each man came back in turn after appearing to be on the receiving end. Basilio, the welterweight champion, was only 5ft 6½in (1.69m), five inches (12cm) shorter than Robinson, and at 11st (154lb – 70kg) was 6lb (2.7kg) lighter. Basilio's two-fisted attacking prevailed in a points victory, but in a return on 25 March 1958 Robinson won the title for the fifth time.

The NBA declared the championship vacant in 1958, and awarded it to Fullmer after he had beaten Basilio. On 22 January 1960 Robinson lost all claims to the title when outpointed by Paul Pender in the latter's home town, Boston.

Pender lost and regained the title in two battles with Britain's Terry Downes but retired in 1962, angry at arguments with the boxing commissions. Meanwhile Robinson made attempts to win a version of the title for the sixth time by twice challenging Fullmer. On the first occasion, on 3 December 1960, he held Fullmer to a draw – three months later he lost on points.

On 23 October 1962 Dick Tiger, of Nigeria, outpointed Fullmer in San Francisco to become the first undisputed world champion for three years. He lost and regained the title in contests with Joey Giardello before losing on points to Emile Griffith, from the Virgin Islands, on 25 April 1966. Tiger later won the light-heavyweight title as related, but three years after losing that, in 1968, he died in Nigeria, of cancer.

Left: Jake LaMotta, the 'Bronx Bull', took the middleweight championship from Marcel Cerdan in 1949 and kept it for nearly two years.

Below: Sugar Ray Robinson (right) and Randolph Turpin threaten each other in the second of their great fights in which they exchanged the world middleweight championship.

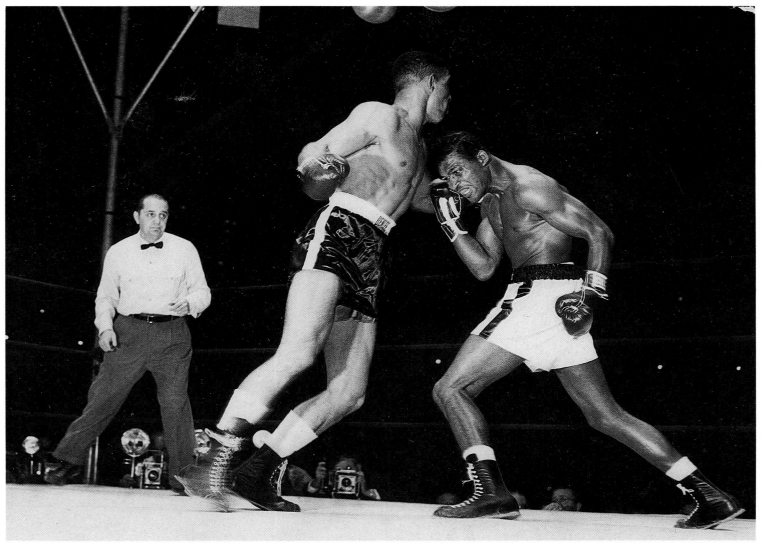

97

The new champion, Emile Griffith, had been welterweight champion from 1961 to 1965 and was a top-liner for nearly 20 years. He lost his crown, finally, on 4 March 1968 to Nino Benvenuti, of Italy, in the third of three fights in which the title changed hands each time.

Benvenuti, another former Olympic gold medalist, was a very polished boxer who also possessed a hard punch. He might have held the title longer, but on 7 November 1970 had the misfortune to meet Carlos Monzon, of Argentina, one of the best and most successful boxers of the 1970s and 1980s. From 1970 to his retirement, in 1977, Monzon ran up a string of successful defences, mostly by knock-outs. Emile Griffith, in 1973, gave him one of his hardest challenges. In 1974 Monzon failed to defend his title against the official WBC challenger, Rodrigo Valdes, of Colombia, and the WBC announced Valdes as champion after he'd beaten Bennie Briscoe at Monte Carlo on 25 May 1974. Thereafter Valdes defended four times before meeting Monzon, still WBA champion, twice, in 1976 and 1977. Monzon won on points each time and then retired.

Carmen Basilio, a small middleweight, facing camera, had two tremendous fights with Sugar Ray Robinson, winning and losing the world title. His opponent here is Art Araglion.

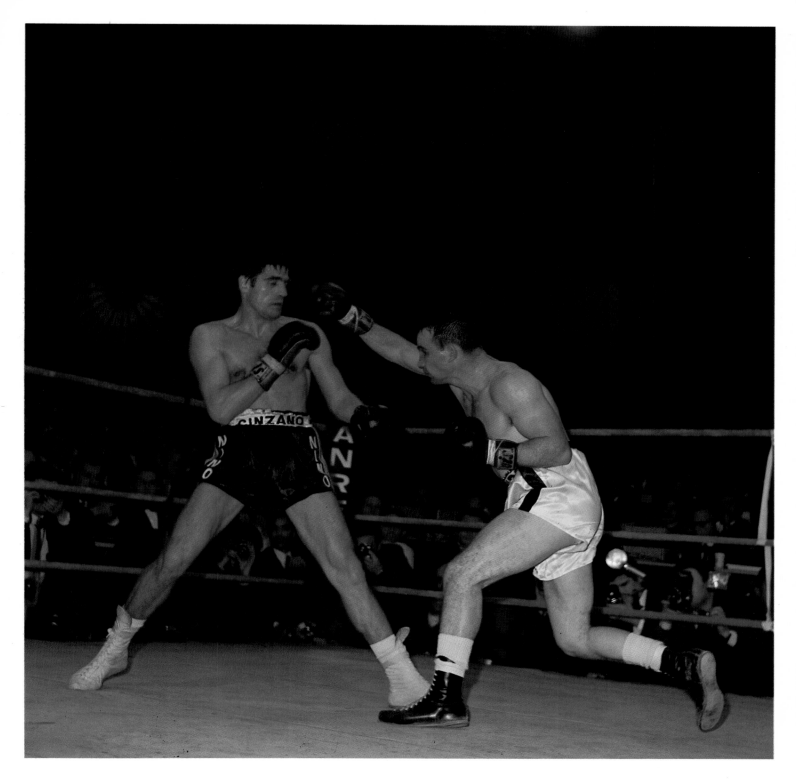

Valdez beat Briscoe again on 5 November 1977, this time to become undisputed champion, but soon lost to Hugo Corro, of Argentina. Corro lost to Vito Antuofermo, of Italy, who drew with Marvin Hagler before losing to Alan Minter, of Crawley, England, at Las Vegas on 16 March 1980. Minter knocked out Antuofermo in a return, but was himself despatched in the third round by Hagler in London on 27 September 1980. Hagler continued to beat all-comers in the 1980s.

In 1962 a light-middleweight class was formed. The limit was 11st (154lb – 70kg). Among the more successful champions were Sandro Mazzinghi, of Italy, in the 1960s, Koichi Wajima, of Japan, in the 1970s, and more recently Maurice Hope, of Britain, Wilfred Benitez, of Puerto Rico, Sugar Ray Leonard and Thomas Hearns.

The welterweight class immediately after the Second World War was dominated from 1947 to 1951 by Sugar Ray Robinson, who then moved up to middleweight. Kid Gavilan held the title till 1953, then Johnny Saxton, Johnny De Marco and Carmen Basilio were champions in quick succession. Basilio

Nino Benvenuti (left) the world middleweight champion from Italy, who was the best boxer of the 1960 Olympic Games (Cassius Clay included), defending his crown against Don Fullmer at San Remo in 1968.

Above: Marvin Hagler (right) in action against Juan Roldan of Argentina. Hagler extended his reign as middleweight champion from 1980 to 1985.

Far right: John Mugabi of Uganda (left) in action against Mike Gonzales of the USA, who was knocked out in the first round in 1984. Mugabi is among the leading middleweight contenders.

Right: Alan Minter (left) went to Las Vegas in 1980 to take the world middleweight title from Italy's Vito Antuofermo, and later in the year repeated the victory in London.

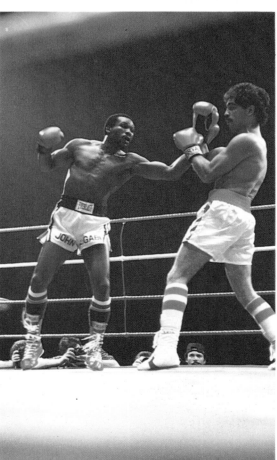

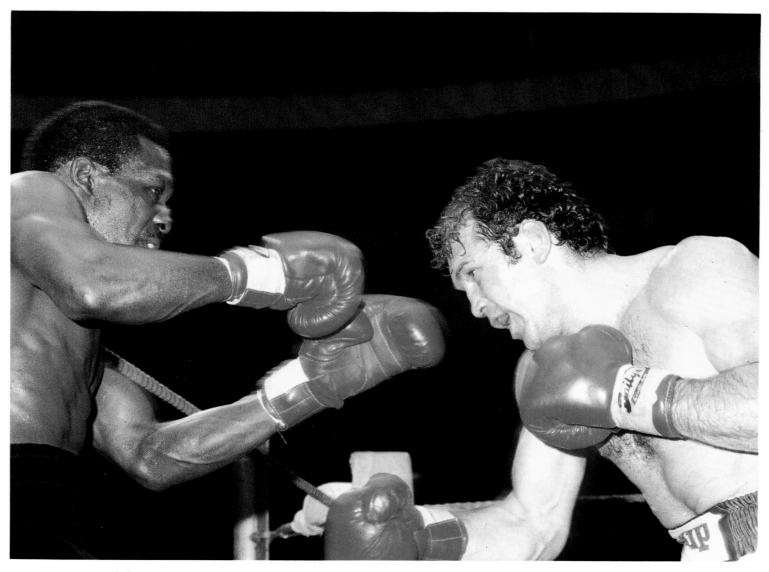

moved up to win the middleweight crown, then Virgil Atkins, Don Jordan, Benny 'Kid' Paret and Emile Griffith were title holders. When Griffith moved up a division, Curtis Cokes was champion from 1966 to 1969, when Jose Napoles deposed him.

Jose Napoles was born in Oriente, Cuba, and settled in Mexico City to pursue a professional boxing career. He was welterweight champion from 18 April 1969 to 12 December 1975. He challenged for the middleweight championship in 1974 but found Carlos Monzon too good. Napoles finally lost his welterweight title to Britain's John H. Stracey, and retired. He was 36 years old.

Stracey lost the crown to Carlos Palomino, of Mexico, who beat off a challenge from another Briton, Dave 'Boy' Green. His tenure as WBC champion ran parallel to the WBA reign of another Mexican, Jose Pipino Cuevas.

Wilfred Benitez, of Puerto Rico, beat Palomino on points and might have expected a long career as the champion,

but one of the great modern boxers, Sugar Ray Leonard, was lurking in the wings and on 30 November 1979 Leonard knocked out Benitez in the last round in Las Vegas.

Leonard was surprisingly deposed by Roberto Duran, of Panama, the long-time lightweight champion, who won on points on 20 June 1980, but he reversed the result on 26 November 1980 when Duran retired in the eighth round. Meanwhile Thomas Hearms, from Memphis, Tennessee, won the WBA version of the title, and his meeting with Leonard on 16 September 1981 at Las Vegas for the undisputed title was eagerly awaited. Leonard won when the referee intervened in the 14th round.

Leonard retired in November, 1982, because of eye problems. Milton McCrory assumed the WBC title on 13 August 1983 when narrowly beating Colin Jones, of Wales, on points in Las Vegas – five months previously the two had fought a draw in Reno for the vacant title. Don Curry, from Fort Worth, Texas, took the WBA version of the title

Maurice Hope of Great Britain (left) won the world light-middleweight title from Rocky Mattioli of Italy at San Remo in 1979 and repeated his win in London in 1980.

Right: A young John H. Stracey (red shorts) in action against Brian Lewis in 1969, the year Jose Napoles won the world welterweight championship. Six years later Stracey deposed him.

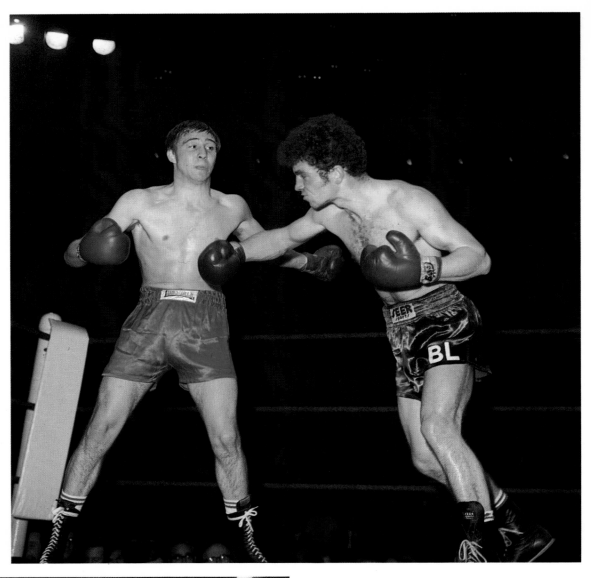

Below: The world welterweight champion Jose Napoles stands over his challenger Ralph Charles in the sixth round of their title fight at Wembley in 1972. Napoles won in the following round.

by outpointing Jun Sok Hwang, of South Korea.

The light-welterweight division, which had lapsed when Barney Ross relinquished the title in 1935, was revived when boxing resumed in 1946 after the war. Bruno Arcari, of Italy, was one of the longest-reigning champions, from 31 January 1970 until he relinquished the title in August, 1974. That was the WBC version. Antonio Cervantes, of Colombia, held the WBA version from 29 October 1972 to 6 March 1976, when he was beaten by Wilfred Benitez, but he regained the vacant title on 25 June 1977 when Benitez moved up in class. Cervantes did not lose the title again until 2 August 1980 when Aaron Pryor took it from him in Cincinatti, Ohio. Bruce Curry, brother of welterweight champion Don Curry, held the WBC version briefly in 1983 and 1984. Billy Costello and Gene Hatcher were the champions as 1984 ended.

The lightweight champion after the Second World War, Ike Williams, lost his crown in 1951 to James Carter, who then lost and regained it twice. Joe Brown won the title in 1959 and defended it 12 times against all-comers, including twice against Britain's Dave Charnley, before losing it in 1962 to Carlos Ortiz, of Puerto Rico.

Ken Buchanan, of Scotland, took the title from Ismael Laguna, of Panama, on 26 September 1970 in San Juan, Puerto Rico. A brilliant boxer, Buchanan defended successfully twice before Roberto Duran, a rough, tough, all-action fighter from Guarare, Panama, won a battle of slugger versus artist in New York on 26 June 1972. Duran was champion until 1979, when he gave up the title to challenge for the welterweight crown.

Jim Watt, another Scottish boxer, won the WBC version of the championship on 17 April 1979 when the referee stopped his fight with Alfredo Pitalua, of Colombia, in the 12th round in Glasgow. Ernesto Espana, of Venezuela, won the

Above: Wilfred Benitez (left) was world champion at light-welter, welter and light-middleweight in the 1970s and 1980s. Here he is fighting Randy Shields, who was stopped in the sixth.

Left: The first fight between Roberto Duran and Sugar Ray Leonard in 1980. Duran has Leonard on the ropes and went on to a points win. He captured Leonard's welterweight crown.

Right: Sugar Ray Leonard fought Thomas Hearns (facing camera) for the undisputed welterweight title in 1981, Leonard becoming champion when the referee stopped the fight in the 12th.

Below: Leonard taunting Duran and inviting him to come forward in their second fight in 1980. Duran gave up in the eighth round and Leonard regained his title.

Bottom: Don Curry (right) proved himself one of the best of the 1980s' champions with an easy victory over Colin Jones in their world title fight in 1985.

WBA version two months later by knocking out Claude Noel, of Trinidad, who himself became champion in 1981.

Watt made four successful defences before losing on points to Alexis Arguello, of Nicaragua, on 20 June 1981. Arguello relinquished the title to move up a division. Livingstone Bramble and Jose Luis Ramirez, of Mexico, were WBA and WBC champions respectively at the end of 1984.

The junior lightweight division, which lapsed in 1933, was not revived until 1959. Alexis Arguello was WBA champion from 1974 to 1977, moving unbeaten up to lightweight. Rafael Limon was twice WBC champion, losing once to Cornelius Boza-Edwards, the British-based Ugandan, and once to Bobby Chacon, whom Boza-Edwards had beaten.

The featherweight division was quick to provide excitement after the Second World War. The champion, Willie Pep, had four tremendous fights with Sandy Saddler – remembered almost as much for their doubtful methods as for the skill which the boxers displayed. In the first bout, on 29 October 1948 at Madison Square Garden, Saddler surprised Pep and knocked him out in the fourth round. Saddler was a tall man for a featherweight with a very long reach, who might have outboxed his rivals, but he was also a devastating puncher and most of his

Left: Ken Buchanan winning the world lightweight title from Ismael Laguna of Panama at San Juan, Puerto Rico, in 1970.

Below: Two world champions of the 1980s, Aaron Pryor (left) light-welterweight champion, and Sugar Ray Leonard, welter and light-middleweight champion.

Bottom: Joe Brown (right), a tall lightweight champion, ducks low against a left swing from Dave Charnley, in the second of two narrow victories over the British champion in 1961.

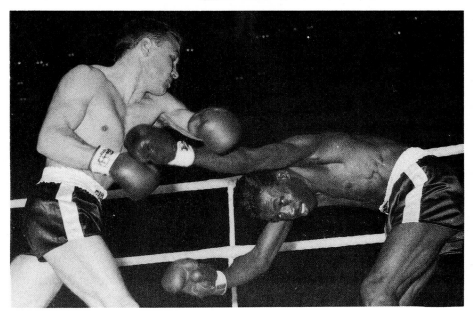

fights ended inside the distance. If an outsider for the first meeting, he was a firm favourite for the second. But this time, on 11 February 1949, again at the Garden, Pep, a brilliant boxer called 'Willie the Wisp', used all his skill and won an overwhelming points victory.

The third fight, on 8 September 1950, had to be at the Yankee Stadium to accomodate the numbers who wanted to see it. The fighter this time beat the boxer. Saddler had Pep down in the third round and, although Pep recovered and was beginning to get his blows to tell, he failed to come up for the eighth round, claiming a shoulder injury.

The fight had been one in which each man accused the other of dirty tactics: Saddler of holding, Pep of tripping.

The fourth fight, on 26 September 1951, was the worst, with both men committing fouls as often as they could: hitting in the clinches, thumbing and twice wrestling each other to the canvas. Saddler was best at this, and retained the title when Pep retired with a cut eye after the eighth round, which he claimed was caused by Saddler's thumb. Both boxers were given a six-months suspension by the NYAC.

Saddler was inducted in the army in 1952 and the championship was kept on ice for a while, but in 1956 he was badly injured in an automobile accident and gave up the title.

Above: The referee
steps in with Buchanan
helpless against the
ropes as Roberto Duran
takes the lightweight
title in New York in
1972.

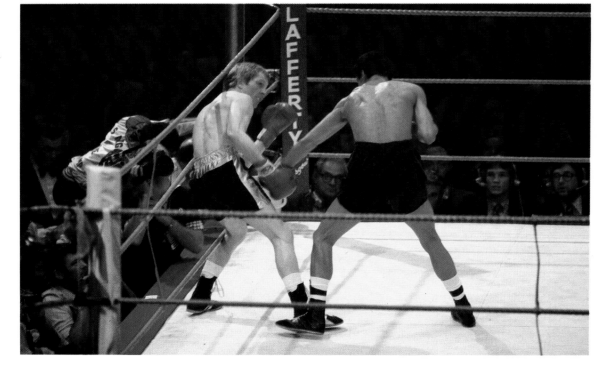

Right: Scotland's Jim
Watt (left) loses his
lightweight title on his
fifth defence, as Alexis
Arguello of Nicaragua
beats him on points in
London in 1981.

Hogan Bassey, of Nigeria, won an eliminating tournament to become champion, but lost the title to Davey Moore in 1959. Four years later Moore lost his life as well as his title when he died after being knocked out by Sugar Ramos, of Cuba. Vicente Saldivar, of Mexico, was an impressive champion, taking the crown from Ramos in 1964 and holding it until 1967, when he retired unbeaten. He had three times defended against Howard Winstone, of Wales, a brilliant boxer who went the distance with Saldivar twice but was not strong enough to beat him. When Saldivar retired, Winstone beat Mitsunori Seki, of Japan, to win the WBC title. The next two WBC champions were Jose Legra of Cuba and Johnny Famechon of Australia. Saldivar made a comeback and beat both to regain his title

on 9 May 1970 in Rome, but he reigned only seven months this time.

Eder Jofre, of Brazil, and Ruben Olivares, of Mexico, were two great bantamweights who moved up to hold a version of the featherweight title briefly in the 1970s, while Alexis Arguello also was champion before winning titles at two heavier weights. Eusebio Pedroza, of Panama, from 1978, and Salvador Sanchez, of Mexico, from 1980, were busy WBA and WBC featherweight champions respectively. Sanchez died in an accident in 1982 after beating Pat Cowdell, of Essex, on points in Houston, while Pedroza was still champion at the end of 1984, having ruled for nearly seven years. Azumah Nelson, of Guam, was WBC champion as 1984 ended, having taken the title from Wilfredo Gomez, of Puerto Rico, in December.

Above left: Vincente Saldivar of Mexico. He won the title in 1964, defended it eight times, retired unbeaten, and then came back in 1970 to win it again.

Top: Willie Pep (left) and Sandy Saddler in their fourth fight in 1951. Pep was beaten through cut eyes.

Above: Jules Touan, paying a fifth visit to the canvas in two minutes as he challenges world featherweight champion Hogan Bassey in London in 1958.

A super bantamweight class was formed by the WBC in 1976 at 8st 10lb (122lb – 55kg), Rigoberto Riasco, of Panama, becoming the first champion. Wilfredo Gomez became champion from 1977 to 1983 before moving up unbeaten to featherweight. In 1977 the WBA named Soo Hwan Hong, of South Korea, as their first champion. Juan 'Kid' Meza, of Los Angeles, won the WBC championship in December, 1984, his fight with Jaime Garza being stopped in the first round, while Victor Callejar, of Puerto Rico, was WBA king.

Manuel Ortiz, the world bantamweight champion during the Second World War, lost his title to Vic Toweel, one of a famous South African family of boxers. Four of his brothers fought, one, Willie, becoming Commonwealth lightweight champion. Vic Toweel was the first South African to be a world titleholder. He lost the crown in sensational fashion on 15 November 1952, being knocked out in the first round by Jimmy Carruthers, of Australia. An excellent champion, Carruthers retired after defending successfully in a remarkable fight in Bangkok, Thailand, against the local Chamrern Songkitrat. Boxing was new in Thailand and this was the first time a native boxer had fought for a world title. A record 60,000 were in attendance, but the contest became known as 'The Battle of the Typhoon' as a tropical rainstorm flooded the ring and shattered the light bulbs. Twice the fight was stopped to clear debris from the ring, and the boxers fought in bare feet as the raindrops bounced knee high. They lasted the 15 rounds, with Carruthers getting the nod.

Howard Winstone having his arm held aloft by manager Eddie Thomas after winning the world featherweight championship in 1968.

Johnny Famechon (right) had two tremendous battles with 'Fighting' Harada of Japan in Sydney and Tokyo, for the world featherweight championship. Famechon won each time.

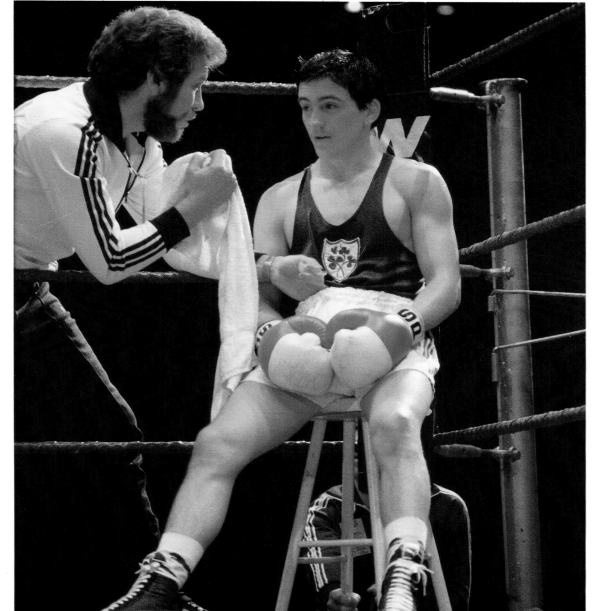

Ireland's Barry McGuigan as an amateur. His victory over former featherweight champion Juan Laporte in 1985 put him in the forefront of title challengers.

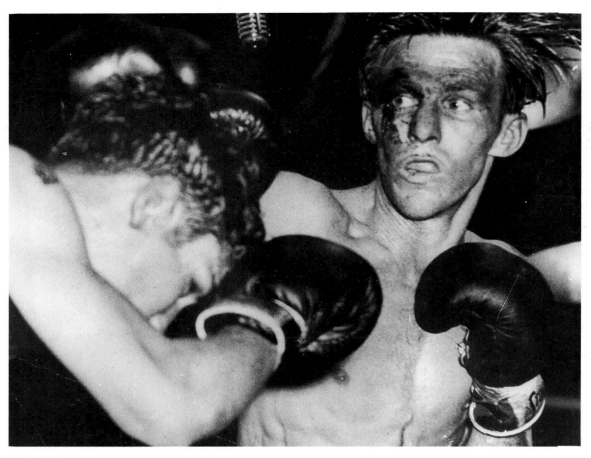

Right: Australia's Jimmy Carruthers, with a mass of blood from a cut over his eye, beat Pappy Gault to retain his world bantamweight title in Sydney in 1953.

Above: Lionel Rose, of Australia, raises his arms in triumph after a successful defence of his world bantamweight title in Melbourne in 1969. Britain's Alan Rudkin moves to congratulate his points conqueror.

The 1960s were vintage years for the bantamweight division. Johnny Caldwell, of Belfast, and Eder Jofre, of Brazil, were good champions, and Fighting Harada, of Japan, an excellent one. Alan Rudkin, of Liverpool, tried to take the title from Harada, then from two other great champions, Lionel Rose, an Aborigine of Australia, and Ruben Olivares, of Mexico.

Lupe Pintor, of Mexico, reigned for four years from 1979, relinquishing the WBC title undefeated in 1983, and Jeff Chandler, of the USA, was WBA champion from 1980 to 1984. Two Californians, Richard Sandoval and Albert Davila, were the WBA and WBC champions respectively at the end of 1984.

The newest weight division in world championship boxing is the super flyweight, maximum 8st 3lb (115lb – 52kg). It was launched, as usual, by the WBC in 1980. The first champion was Rafael Orono, of Venezuela. In 1981 the WBA recognized Gustavo Ballas, of Argentina, as their champion. Payo Pooltarat, of Thailand, and Jiro Watanabe, of Japan, were the respective champions in 1984.

The British domination of the flyweight class continued for a while after the Second World War. When Jackie Paterson, of Scotland, eventually lost the championship it was to Rinty (real name John) Monaghan, of Belfast. The name Rinty came from the famous dog of the films, Rin Tin Tin, Monaghan's footwork being considered as good. He was a popular fighter, who led the crowds in song after a win. He died in 1984 as this book was being written. Monaghan lost the title on 5 April 1950 to Terry Allen of Islington, London.

Allen was champion for only 98 days, losing his crown on 1 August 1950 to Dado Marino, of Honolulu. Marino was 34 years old, but more remarkable for being a grandfather when he became world champion.

110

Left: Jackie Paterson standing over Peter Kane in Glasgow in 1943 after Paterson had knocked out Kane in 61 seconds to become world flyweight champion.

Yoshio Shirai, of Japan, Pascual Perez, a brilliant Argentinian boxer who was champion from November 1954 to April 1960, Pone Kingpetch, of Thailand, who regained the title twice after losing it to Fighting Harada and Hiroyuki Ebihara, both of Japan, and Salvatore Burruni, of Italy, were worthy champions.

Walter McGowan, of Scotland, won the title back for Britain at last in 1966, but lost it the same year to Chartchai Chionoi, of Thailand, who lost and regained it from Efren Torres, of Mexico. Erbito Salavarria, of the Philip-

pines, and Venice Borkorsor, of Thailand, were then champions, but Borkorsor relinquished the title when he unfortunately became overweight in 1973.

From then on, WBC and WBA champions changed rapidly, often twice a year. Charlie Magri, of Stepney, London, held the WBC title in 1983, then Frank Cedeno (Philippines), Koji Koboyashi (Japan), Gabriel Bernal (Mexico) and Sot Chitalada (Thailand) all held it in 1984. The WBA champion from 1982 to 1984 was Santos Laciar, of Argentina.

Above: Yoshio Shirai lost his flyweight title to Pascual Perez, right, who knocked out the champion in the fifth round in Japan in 1957.

Above left: Yoshio Shirai of Japan (right) and Dado Marino of Honolulu after Shirai had taken the world flyweight title from the grandfather champion in 1952.

Right: Walter McGowan, a brilliant flyweight champion in 1966, was plagued with cuts around the eyes.

Below: Charlie Magri on the canvas and on his way to losing his world flyweight title to Frank Cedeno of the Philippines in 1983.

In 1975 a world light-flyweight class was introduced for very small men, the limit being 7st 10lb (108lb – 49kg). Franco Udello, of Italy, was the first WBC champion while the WBA quickly followed suit and named Jaime Rios (Panama) as their champion. So far no boxers have campaigned for long at the top level of this weight except Yoko Gushiken, of Japan, WBA champion from 1976 to 1984.

The proliferation of weight classes (there are now 15) and of ruling bodies is spoiling boxing in the 1980s. It is now usual for 25 or so boxers to claim world titles at the same time. There might be over 50 world champions in one year. Of course the championships are devalued. A boxer who claims to be world champion is usually only half a world champion these days. It is remarkable how the WBA and WBC ratings differ, which makes things incomprehensible for the man in the street.

If boxing is to maintain its position as a great sport, a world authority must

Left: Mark Breland, one of the hottest favourites at the 1984 Olympic Games, winning the gold medal against South Korea's Young-Su An and creating opportunities for a money-making professional career.

Below: Paul Gonzales, the 1984 Olympic flyweight champion, another of the brilliant boxers who could make a big impression on the professional ranks.

evolve to give some credibility to the championships. Such a body is unlikely to happen, as there is so much money to be made by independent promoters and managers who have a vested interest in the confusion and the ballyhoo.

Sad to say, it might all be too late anyway. The report of a working party to the British Medical Association conference in 1984 suggested that x-ray scans showed conclusively that boxers suffered brain damage. A campaign against boxing was expected to get under way, and there was talk of it being banned in Britain within ten years.

In December, 1984, the American Medical Association at a delegate conference in Honolulu added its weight to the argument and called for the banning of both professional and amateur boxing. The president mentioned increasing evidence of acute and long-term brain injury to boxers; it may be that the great fistic heroes, from Jack Broughton to Marvelous Marvin Hagler, will form an episode in history, like those Roman gladiators of long ago.

Meanwhile, the professional careers of several of the fine boxers who won gold medals for the United States at the 1984 Olympic Games have got under way in extremely lucrative fashion. There will be plenty of battles both inside and outside the ring in the next few years.

113

7 GREAT BOXERS

James Figg

James Figg (or Fig) is known as the 'Father of Boxing'. He was born at Thame, Oxfordshire, in 1695, and became adept at all forms of man-to-man combat popular in his day, including pugilism. He went to London, gave exhibitions of his skill, and acquired enough money to open an amphitheatre, where he taught gentlemen the noble science of defence.

He had made friends with the artist William Hogarth, who put him in his famous picture of Southwark Fair, and designed a business card for him. The young bloods of the day came to Figg's amphitheatre, and he became popular with the aristocracy, including the Prince of Wales. All this attention, and a string of victories with backsword, cudgels and fists, led to Figg claiming the championship of England. This was disputed by a pipe-maker from Graves-

James Figg, who was a scientific man with sword or stick but 'more of a slaughterer than a neat, finished pugilist'.

Jack Broughton faced all-comers for 17 or 18 years without being beaten, and according to Captain Godfrey was 'captain of the boxers'.

end, Ned Sutton, but Figg beat him three times and was recognized as champion.

Figg was, in fact, more proficient with sword and staff than with his fists. Strength and courage won him more victories than skill. When he moved his academy, his old premises were taken over by a pupil, George Taylor, who claimed the championship when Figg retired around 1730.

Several other academies of pugilism were founded after the success of Figg's, ensuring the progress of prizefighting in England. Figg died on 8 December 1734.

Jack Broughton

Jack Broughton went to London from Cirencester, Gloucestershire, where he was born around 1703, to become a Thames waterman. A muscular 5ft 11in (1.80m) he took up pugilism, polished his technique at Figg's and Taylor's academies and was good enough to beat Taylor in 20 minutes and claim the championship of England in the 1730s. Broughton then opened his own academy, sponsored with a £300 loan by the Duke of Cumberland.

In 1741, one of his challengers, George Stevenson, a coachman from Yorkshire, died from the bad beating Broughton gave him. Broughton thereupon drew up his rules, which were published in 1743 and governed prizefights for nearly 100 years. He also invented 'mufflers' – lightweight boxing gloves to prevent his patrons from being injured when sparring.

Broughton brought skill to the ring; he was athletic, blocked blows, and punched with precision rather than abandon. He, too, in his turn, was called the

'Father of Boxing', and might well have been the best of all the prizefighters.

He was undisputed champion till 1750, when he fought Jack Slack – a challenge he had acquired by accident and did not take seriously enough. Undertrained, he was blinded and beaten by the younger man, to the disgust of the Duke of Cumberland, who lost £50,000 in bets, and turned his back on Broughton, having his establishment closed.

Broughton never fought again, but sold antiques, and became a rich man. When he died in Lambeth on 8 January 1789 he was a Yeoman of the Guard. He is commemorated by a stone in the floor of Westminser Abbey which says he was aged 86 when he died.

Tom Cribb

Tom Cribb (or Crib) came from Hanham about five miles (8km) from Bristol, where he was born on 8 July 1781. He went to London when only 13, then worked on the wharves where he built up a muscular frame.

Cribb began a run of success in pugilism with a method of boxing on the retreat, which was not always appreciated by the Fancy. He had a setback against the otherwise undistinguished George Nicholls, however, in 1805. Nicholls considerably upset the gambling fraternity by rumbling Cribb's style and beating him in 52 rounds. Cribb then easily beat Bill Richmond, a black fighter from America.

Tom Cribb, known during his career as 'The Black Diamond' because at one time he was a coal merchant, was champion from 1808 until he retired in 1812.

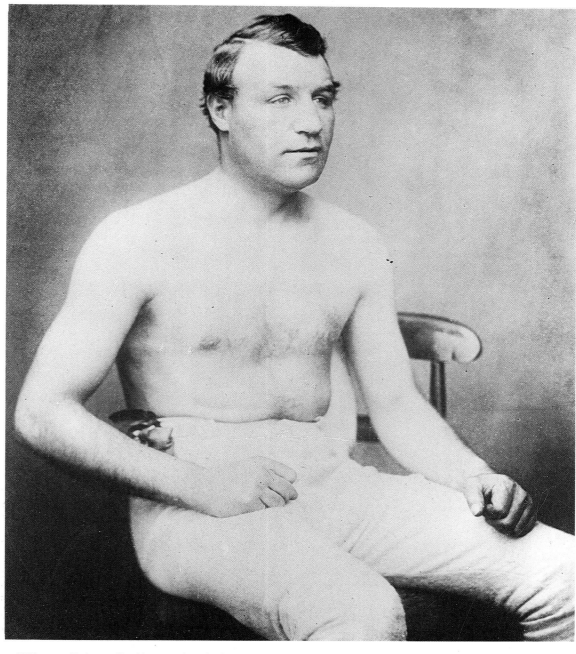

Champion of England Tom Sayers lost only once, despite the fact that he was little more than a welterweight.

When John Gully retired in 1808, Cribb beat Bob Gregson and former champion Jem Belcher to be acknowledged champion of England himself, but really captured the notice of the whole country with his defeat of another, much tougher, black American, Tom Molineaux, although, as explained in Chapter 8, it was a win not without its dubious aspect. A second encounter, however, Cribb won more fairly.

The fighting fraternity, in their gratitude for Cribb's repulsion of the foreign challenger, presented him with a magnificent silver cup at a dinner at the Castle Tavern, Holborn, on 2 December 1811, inscribed with the motto: 'And Damn'd be him that first cries Hold, Enough'.

Cribb fought once more, in 1820, then gave up the title and ran 'The Union Arms' pub in Piccadilly. He died on 11 May 1848.

Tom Sayers

At 5ft 8½in (1.74m) and around 10st 12lb (152lb – 68.5kg), Tom Sayers would be classed today as a light-middleweight, but in the 1850s he was *the* prize ring champion of England.

Sayers was born in Brighton, Sussex, on 25 May 1826, and began work as a bricklayer. He spent so much time sparring, however, that he was sacked and advised to go to London and take up pugilism. He was then 22, and in the next few years scored impressive wins: Abe Couch in 13 minutes, Don Collins in 84 minutes (after a draw spread over two hours 19 minutes at two locations – one being invaded by the police), Jack Grant in two hours 30 minutes, and Jack Martin in 55 minutes were all stopped.

Then Sayers met with his only defeat. Nat Langham forced him to give best

Jem Mace, the 'Swaffham Gipsy', was prize ring champion from 1861 and did more than any man to spread boxing skill round the world.

after 122 minutes at Lakenheath, Suffolk, in 1853. He was defeated because Langham managed to close both his eyes, but Sayers was soon back on the winning trail, beating Harry Poulson in three hours eight minutes (109 rounds) and Aaron Jones in two hours (85 rounds).

Sayers won the championship when he beat Bill Perry, 'The Tipton Slasher' over ten rounds (102 minutes) at the Isle of Grain, Kent, although the 'Slasher' was 4in (10cm) the taller and over 2st (28lb – 12.6kg) heavier. He defended against Bob Brett, Aaron Jones, Bill Benjamin (twice) and Tom Paddock before, in 1860, his historic draw with John Camel Heenan for the 'Champion-

ship of the World', which is described in Chapter 8. Each fighter was awarded a silver belt, and they became friends.

Sayers did not fight again. He became ill with tuberculosis, and admirers subscribed £3,000 on condition that he did not re-enter the ring. He went to live in Camden Town, where he died on 8 November 1865. He is buried at Highgate Cemetery, where he has a large memorial.

Jem Mace

Jem Mace, the last British prize ring champion, was another boxer who was really no more than a middleweight. He was born in Beeston, Norfolk, on 18 April 1831, and built up his physique on his blacksmith father's anvil, although he was never taller than 5ft 9½in (1.77m). After turning 20, he began to travel the coUntry with the fairs, boxing in the booths and playing the violin, an accomplishment which earned him the title of 'The Swaffham Gipsy'.

Mace won the championship of England when he beat Sam Hurst, 'The Stalybridge Infant' on 13 June 1861. Mace was giving away five inches (13cm) and over three stone (42lb – 19kg) and won in eight rounds. He followed this with two terrific battles with Tom King, winning the first but losing the second.

Mace reclaimed the title when King refused a third match. He then went to America and fought Joe Coburn, who was claiming the American championship, but after three hours and 48 minutes of Mace superiority the referee announced a draw. A disgusted Mace moved on to Australasia. In Timaru, New Zealand, he 'discovered' and coached Bob Fitzsimmons, and in Australia trained many notable boxers, including Peter Jackson, Frank Slavin and Dan Creedon.

Mace had effectively retired when he returned to England, but in 1890, aged 59, he fought the 30-years-younger Charlie Mitchell for the British championship under Queensberry rules, losing when the referee stopped the fight in the third round. When he was 64, Mace gave an exhibition at the National Sporting Club, sparring with the British lightweight champion, Dick Burge.

Jem Mace went back to his travelling life, taking a boxing booth round the country. He died in Newcastle on 3 March 1910, and is buried in Liverpool.

John L. Sullivan, the prize-ring champion of the world, in his prime, showing his muscular frame.

John L. Sullivan

John L. Sullivan (the L. is for Lawrence) was born in Roxbury, Massachusetts, on 15 October 1858. As a youth he enjoyed performing feats of strength, and when he began prizefighting he became known as 'The Boston Strong Boy'.

Sullivan was a braggart, who boasted he could 'lick any sonofabitch in the house'. He won the American championship when knocking out Paddy Ryan, from Tipperary, in nine rounds and ten minutes 30 seconds on 7 February 1882.

His larger-than-life roistering character (he loved drink and the company of women) endeared him to the fans. He decided to cash in by joining a theatrical troupe, giving exhibitions of boxing under Queensberry rules throughout the United States. When it was suggested that the opponents were paid to make him look good, he offered $100 to any man who could stand up to him for four rounds without being knocked out. This daring move packed the theatres, and Sullivan increased the prize to $500. Only once did Sullivan pay out – to an English boxer, Tug Wilson, who avoided Sullivan's best punches by taking a count at the least provocation.

Richard K. Fox, proprietor of the *Police Gazette*, presented a belt for the world heavyweight championship which Sullivan scorned, so Fox promoted a campaign to find a man to beat him, without success. In 1887 Sullivan's Boston admirers presented him with a finer belt, worth $5,000 and including nearly 400 diamonds.

Sullivan went to England, but fought the English champion, Charlie Mitchell, in France – the match was drawn after 39 rounds. His girl-friend (he was married), buxom burlesque queen Ann Livingston, watched the fight dressed as a boy.

After a famous knockout of Jake Kilrain over 75 rounds (two hours and 16 minutes) in 1889, Sullivan played on tour in a melodrama 'Honest Hearts and Willing Hands'.

He became out of condition, and lost his title in 1892 to James J. Corbett, a younger and more skilful boxer. They fought in gloves in a fight that has gone into the records as the first heavyweight championship of the world.

Although Sullivan's only defeat was a tragedy for his fans, he did not lose their esteem. He turned against liquor and became an evangelist, touring the United States preaching against the evils of 'John Barleycorn'. He died on 2 February 1918 in Abingdon, Massachusetts.

Jack Dempsey, 'The Nonpareil'

Two great boxers fought under the name Jack Dempsey – it was the real name of neither. The first was named John Kelly and was born in County Kildare, Ireland, on 15 December 1862.

He was taken to New York as a boy, and became a cooper. He attended a boxing show in 1883, and volunteered as a substitute when a contestant failed to appear, giving his name as Jack Dempsey. He won.

Weighing no more than about 10st 10lb (150lb – 67.5kg), he then proved unbeatable by men of his weight and earned the title 'The Nonpareil'. On 30 July 1884, Dempsey knocked out George Fulljames in New York in 22 rounds and was acclaimed by Americans as the first world middleweight champion.

He met his first defeat in 1889, when George LaBlanche, a Canadian whom he had previously beaten, knocked him out in 32 rounds. LaBlanche, however, used a 'pivot punch', pivoting completely round with his arm stuck straight out like

John L. Sullivan (right) in his famous fight with Jake Kilrain. Left are Kilrain's corner men, British boxer Charlie Mitchell, Mike Donovan and bottle-holder Johnny Murphy. The referee, in the outer ring, is John Fitzpatrick. The timekeeper, with watch, is Tom Costello. The men with rifles are Mississippi Rangers, to keep order. Perched in the tree is a photographer.

a bar. The punch was immediatley banned, and Dempsey was adjudged not to have lost the title.

However, 'The Nonpareil' lost his edge after this and forfeited his title when Bob Fitzsimmons knocked him out in 1891. Dempsey also lost his last fight, with future middleweight champion Tommy Ryan, in January 1895. He fell sick, went to the West, but died on 2 November of the same year in Portland, Oregon.

In 1899, his attorney, M. J. McMahon, found his neglected grave in lonely woods and wrote a famous poem, printed anonymously in the *Portland Oregonian*. The last two verses run:

> Forgotten by ten thousand
>   throats,
> That thundered his acclaim,
> Forgotten by his friends and foes,
> Who cheered his very name.
> Oblivion wraps his faded form,
> But ages hence shall save
> The memory of that Irish lad
> That fills poor Dempsey's grave.
>
> Oh, Fame, why sleeps thy
>   favoured son
> In wilds, in woods, in weeds,
> And shall he ever thus sleep on,
> Interred his valiant deeds,
> 'Tis strange New York should
>   thus forget
> Its "bravest of the brave"
> And in the fields of Oregon,
> Unmarked, leave Dempsey's
>   grave.

The poem received worldwide circulation, and is now inscribed on a tombstone erected with the funds the poem inspired his friends to subscribe.

James J. Corbett

The first heavyweight champion of the world was a different kind of boxer to the prizefighters who had gone before.

James J. (for John) Corbett, of Irish descent, started life as a bank clerk before becoming a professional boxer. He was well-spoken, had polished manners, and did not rely on strength and aggression, but on a scientific technique. He was known as 'Gentleman Jim'.

Born in San Francisco on 1 September 1866, Corbett was a professional at 19, stood 6ft 1in (1.86m) and weighed 13st 2lb (194lb – 87.3kg). He beat Joe Choynski, whom he met four times, and

Jake Kilrain, and drew with the West Indian Peter Jackson over 61 rounds before being the first to find a $10,000 side-stake necessary to meet John L. Sullivan for the championship.

Corbett outspeeded his heavier rival and won by a knockout in the 21st round. Corbett then beat veteran Englishman Charlie Mitchell, in the third round, and 'retired', but he accepted a challenge from another Englishman, Bob Fitzsimmons, in 1897. Fitzsimmons took the title with his solar plexus punch.

Jack Dempsey, 'The Nonpareil', one of the first boxers to claim a world championship under Queensberry Rules. He was recognized in America as middleweight champion in 1884.

Corbett's fights with Sullivan and Fitzsimmons are described in Chapter 8.

Corbett tried twice to regain the title, nearly succeeding in his first fight with the then new champion, Jeffries, in 1900, when he was winning easily until trapped and knocked out in the 23rd round of a 25-round bout. He tried again against the same opponent in 1903 but was knocked out in ten rounds, and then retired for good.

Gentleman Jim was never a popular champion, having deposed the rough-tough Sullivan, the idol of the fans. He died in New York on 18 February 1933.

'Gentleman Jim' Corbett, a scientific boxer who gave thought to defence and became the first heavyweight champion under Queensberry Rules.

Bob Fitzsimmons

Born in Helston, Cornwall, on 26 May 1863, Bob Fitzsimmons was taken to New Zealand as a boy and helped his father in his blacksmith's business at Timaru. He developed his chest and shoulders, won novice boxing competitions organized by his fellow Englishman, Jem Mace, on a visit, and became a pugilist in Australia, where he won the middleweight championship.

In 1890 he went to America, and in his fourth fight knocked out Nonpareil Jack Dempsey to become middleweight champion of the world. After a few more wins and two title defences, he knocked out Peter Maher in the first round in Lantry, Texas, on 21 February 1896 in a fight advertized as for the heavyweight championship of the world, Corbett having announced his retirement. His claim was not taken seriously, however, until he faced Corbett himself. He knocked out Corbett in 14 rounds on 17 March 1897 in Carson City, Nevada. The fight is described in Chapter 8.

Fitzsimmons as heavyweight champion was freakish. With legs so spindly that he sometimes padded out his tights to give him 'calves', he was balding and freckled. He was 35 years old, and never weighed much more than 12st 2lb (170lb – 76.5kg). But he had a tremendous punch.

Fitzsimmons lost his title to the giant Jeffries on 9 June 1899. After some quick wins he took on Jeffries again in 1902, but was knocked out in eight rounds.

Next year, however, on 25 November 1903 in San Francisco, Fitzsimmons beat George Gardner on points over 20 rounds to become light-heavyweight champion of the world. He thus became the first man to win world championships at three weights, and remains the only heavyweight champion to do so.

Fitzsimmons was 40 years old when he won his last title, which he lost to Philadelphia Jack O'Brien on 20 December 1905. Two years later Fitzsimmons was knocked out in the second round by Jack Johnson, one of the greatest heavyweights ever, and then in his prime. In 1909 Fitz fought for the heavyweight championship of Australia, but lost to Bill Lang by a 12th round knockout, after doing well earlier.

Fitzsimmons had his last fight on 20 February 1914, aged 50, and was only prevented from further matches by

Cornishman Bob Fitzsimmons, with red hair and freckles, was known as 'Ruby Robert'. He won world titles at three weights.

boxing commissioners refusing to licence a man of his age. He died in Chicago on 22 October 1917.

James J. Jeffries

James J. (for Jackson) Jeffries might have been remembered, like Rocky Marciano, as the heavyweight champion who won all his fights, but sadly he was persuaded into a fatal last one.

Born in Carroll, Ohio, on 15 April 1875, Jeffries became apprenticed to a boilermaker, work which developed his already strong frame. At 6ft 2in (1.88m) and 15st 10lb (220lb – 99kg) he began boxing and was chosen as a sparring partner to Jim Corbett, the champion.

After Corbett lost his title to Fitzsimmons, Jeffries surprised the boxing world by winning it back for America by a knockout in the 11th round.

With no pretensions to science, Jeffries merely belted his opponents with his strong arms, usually to the body. He usually took as much punishment himself, and adopted a crouching technique to make himself a more difficult target.

been even better, but as a black fighter at the turn of the century he had to obey orders and lose a fight or two.

Born in Baltimore, Maryland, on 25 November 1874, he began earning money in the boxing clubs from an early age. He graduated into contender class as a lightweight and met Frank Erne for the title in 1900, but retired in the twelfth round, ostensibly because of an eye injury, but probably under orders. It was almost certainly a 'fix' when Gans was knocked out by Terry McGovern in the second round in Chicago, a scandal that killed boxing in Illinois for over 20 years.

Gans won the lightweight championship on 12 May 1902, however, when he knocked out Erne with the first punch of the fight in Fort Erie, Canada, another result that caused comment.

Gans marked his victories by letting his family know they could now afford to

Above: James J. Jeffries, the immensely strong boilermaker from Carroll, Ohio, had little science, but his strength allowed him to retire undefeated as world heavyweight champion.

With his huge, hairy chest he was like a bear boring in.

Jeffries broke two of Tom Sharkey's ribs in a bruising defence (only won on points over 25 rounds), beat Fitzsimmons again and twice beat his old master Corbett, although once he was in danger of being outpointed and got in his knockout with only two rounds left.

Having beaten all the contenders, Jeffries retired to his California farm in 1905 unbeaten. In 1910, however, he was persuaded out of retirement because Jack Johnson, a disliked black fighter, had become champion. Alas, it was a mistake, and Jeffries was well beaten (the fight is described in Chapter 8). Jeffries went back to his farm, and died in Burbank, California, on 3 March 1953.

Joe Gans

Joe Gans (real name Joseph Gaines) is acknowledged as one of the cleverest of all boxers. He was called the 'Old Master'. His great record might have

Right: One of the cleverest lightweights in the world, Joe Gans had to wait for his title chance, but held the championship for six years.

eat a luxury food, bacon. He sent his mother telegrams 'I am bringing home the bacon'. Gans' best victory was against Battling Nelson in 1906, a fight he won on a disqualification, but he took severe punishment from low blows, and was never quite the same again. Nelson took his title on 4 July 1908 in San Francisco, and later beat him again. Gans was possibly already suffering from tuberculosis. He died on 10 August 1910 in Baltimore.

Jack Johnson

At least two full-length feature films have been made of the life of Jack Johnson, one of the best but most controversial of champions at any weight.

Born in Galveston, Texas, on 31 March 1878, John Arthur Johnson (he liked to call himself 'Little Arthur'), began boxing professionally at 19, and for many years fought fellow-blacks and top whites like Joe Choynski, who stopped him 1901. It was a thorough training and Johnson developed those defensive skills and counter-punching techniques which were to stand him in good stead later. By about 1906 he was ready to challenge for the championship, and was lucky enough to find Tommy Burns in possession in 1908, and willing to fight him in Australia. It was unlikely that Johnson would have got a chance against the previous champions.

Johnson fought Burns on 26 December 1908, and did as he liked with the smaller man, the police finally stopping the fight in the 14th round. From this moment until he was beaten there was a desperate campaign in America to find a 'white hope' capable of winning back the title for the white race.

Johnson returned to America, where he was now the most hated man in the country. Not only was he the first black heavyweight champion, which to many whites was painful to contemplate, but he was a boastful champion, arrogant and smiling, and he had a succession of affairs with white women – behaviour utterly unacceptable at the time.

Johnson fought six times in 1909, the first a no-decision bout against Victor McLaglen, the Irish film star, the last a defence of the title against Stanley Ketchel, the middleweight champion. Ketchel put Johnson down in the 12th round but Johnson rose to knock out

Jack Johnson was the first black heavyweight champion of the world, and stirred more emotions than any champion before or since.

Ketchel immediately. Johnson then beat Jeffries, brought out of retirement to try to stop him. The fight, and the race riots which Johnson's win provoked, are described in Chapter 8.

Johnson did not fight for two years, then had no difficulty in beating Jim Flynn in Las Vegas, Nevada. It was his preference for white women that finally stopped Johnson.

A Senator Mann introduced a bill into the US Senate making it a federal offence for anyone to cross a state line with a woman for immoral purposes. The mother of one of Johnson's girl friends made trouble for him, and in 1913 he was convicted under the Mann Act and sentenced to a year and a day in jail.

Johnson jumped his bail and went to Europe.

In Paris, Johnson twice defended his title. On the second occasion, against Frank Moran on 27 June 1914, he fought for nothing, as the promoter disappeared and war broke out before anything could be done.

Johnson eventually agreed to fight Jess Willard and later claimed that part of the deal for the fight was that he would forgo serving his prison sentence. The fight, and its controversial ending, which Johnson alleged was fixed, are described in Chapter 8. Johnson lost his title in Havana, Cuba, but on his return to the United States was imprisoned for nine months.

Johnson was not given a chance to regain the title. He continued boxing till 1928, when he was 50 years old, and gave exhibitions till 1945. After his retirement he ran a gym in Harlem, New York, lectured, and managed a flea circus, generally keeping himself fit and in funds. Gradually, the animosity against him subsided, and he was recognized as the great boxer he had been. A black fighter did not win the world champion-ship again until Joe Louis in 1937 – sadly Louis and his connections could not admit Johnson to their circle.

Johnson loved fast cars and was killed when he crashed one in Raleigh, North Carolina, on 10 June 1946. His grave, marked just JOHNSON, is in Graceland Cemetery, 200yd (183m) from that of Bob Fitzsimmons, whom he fought in 1907.

Stanley Ketchel

Stanley Ketchel was born in Grand Rapids, Michigan, on 14 September 1886. His father was a Polish immigrant farmer, and his real name was Stanislaus Kiecel. At 17 years old he tried on the gloves at a boxing booth, knocked out the resident pugilist, and decided to earn his living as a boxer.

Ketchel had little science, but less need of it, as his non-stop aggression and punching power ran up a string of knock-out victories. When Tommy Ryan retired as middleweight champion, Ketchel assumed the crown with two victories over Joe Thomas, who had claimed it, and a knockout of Jack 'Twin' Sullivan.

Ketchel, who became known as the 'Michigan Assassin', fought Billy Papke, the 'Illinois Thunderbolt', three times in 1908. In the second Papke took the title by ignoring Ketchel's proffered glove at the start and flooring him with a terrific punch. Ketchel was down four times in the first round, and had one eye closed, but fought on, taking severe punish-ment, to the 12th, when he was knocked out. In a return less than three months later Ketchel battered Papke from the bell and knocked him out in the 11th.

In March 1909, Ketchel fought the light-heavyweight champion, Philadel-phia Jack O'Brien, in a ten-round no-decision bout in New York. In a grandstand final round, Ketchel caught O'Brien a terrific punch on the jaw, and as the bell sounded O'Brien was com-pletely out, with his head laying in the resin box in his own corner. Ketchel knocked out O'Brien in three rounds in a second match in Philadelphia, and beat Papke again over 20 rounds fought in a storm in Colma, California.

Later in the year Ketchel took on Jack Johnson, the heavyweight champion, giving away three stone (48lb), and actually put Johnson down in the 12th round, but the champion rose and

Stanley Ketchel (left), the outstanding middleweight of his day, takes a huge swing at heavyweight Jack Johnson.

knocked out not only Ketchel but some of his teeth.

After defending his title with more knock-out wins in 1910 Ketchel took a rest at a ranch in Conway, Missouri. There a jealous ranch hand, believing Ketchel to be paying attention to his girl friend, shot him in the back with both barrels of his shotgun as the 24-year-old middleweight champion was having breakfast.

Jim Driscoll

One of the greatest of ring artists, who boxed in the upright style with a straight left, Driscoll earned himself the ring epithet 'Peerless Jim'.

He was born in Cardiff on 15 December 1881. As a printing apprentice on a local paper, he would scrap with the other apprentices, using old newspapers wrapped round the fists. He graduated to boxing booths, and then turned professional in 1899.

With his style, looks and personality, Driscoll was in demand at the London National Sporting Club, where he won the British featherweight title in 1906 by outpointing Joe Bowker, and in 1911 won outright the first Lonsdale Belt in that class.

His only defeat in his prime came when he fought Freddie Welsh, the lightweight champion in 1910. This was a scrappy, needle contest, and the normally cool and composed Driscoll was disqualified for butting.

On 19 February 1909 Driscoll fought the world champion, Abe Attell, but Attell insisted that the contest be held in New York, where it would have to be a 'no-decision' affair. Driscoll won every round, and became the uncrowned featherweight king.

Driscoll knocked out Jean Posey, of France, on 3 June 1912 to win the European championship and in 1913 defended both his titles against Owen Moran, boxing a draw over 20 rounds in London.

Driscoll retired and served in the Army in the First World War but was persuaded to fight again in 1919. Already a sick man, he met Charles Ledoux, of France, for the European bantamweight title. For 14 rounds Driscoll outboxed his 11-years-younger opponent, but a punch to the stomach finished him and his corner threw in the towel in the 16th round. It was Driscoll's second defeat

and his last fight. He retired again and was given £25,000, the result of a testimonial fund organized by the National Sporting Club, but he lived only until 31 January 1925, dying of pneumonia in Cardiff.

Ted 'Kid' Lewis

Ted 'Kid' Lewis was a professional boxer before his 15th birthday. By the time he was 19 he was British featherweight champion.

Born Gershon Mendeloff, in Aldgate on 24 October 1894, he joined the nearby Judaens Club where he enjoyed boxing. Turning professional he fought at

Jim, or Jem, Driscoll, one of the great boxers of all time, who earned the adjective 'Peerless' because there was none better.

Wonderland, and when he beat Alec Lambert at the National Sporting Club just before his 19th birthday, he became British and European featherweight champion, Driscoll having retired.

In 1914 he went to Australia, where he kept as active as ever before going on to the United States. Lewis' all-action non-stop style was very popular, and he was called the 'Crashing, Dashing Kid'. On his arrival in America he was a welterweight, and on 31 August 1915 he beat Jack Britton on points in Boston to become world champion, having already beaten another claimant, Mike Glover. Lewis and Britton then began a great rivalry. They fought each other 20 times in all, Lewis winning three and Britton four, with one draw and 14 no-decisions.

They shared the welter title for over seven years, Lewis' spells being August 1915 to April 1916, and June 1917 to March 1919.

Lewis returned home at the end of 1919 and won the British, European and Empire welterweight titles by beating Johnny Basham on 9 June 1920. Basham was a second great rival to Lewis, but, unlike Britton, he could never master the Kid. Lewis added the British and European middleweight titles in 1921, beating Basham, and the Empire middleweight title in 1922, beating Frankie Burns of Australia.

Lewis went back to New York in 1921 to try to regain the world welter title from Britton, but lost on points in their 20th meeting. In 1922 he challenged Georges Carpentier, then both the world light-heavy and European heavyweight champion, in a fight that ended in a sensation in the first round, when Lewis turned his head to the referee, who had spoken to him, and Carpentier knocked him out while he wasn't looking.

On 15 February 1923 Lewis lost his middleweight titles to Roland Todd, and on 26 November 1924 his welterweight titles to Tommy Milligan. He fought on till he was 35 years old, by which time he had had 280 fights, winning 170 and losing 13. He died in London on 20 October 1970.

Jimmy Wilde

Jimmy Wilde was born in Tylorstown, Wales, on 15 May 1892, and grew up to stand all of 5ft 2½in (1.59m). At his heaviest he tipped the scales at 7st 10lb (108lb – 48.6kg).

He worked in the mines at 14, using the muscular strength this developed to box in the local clubs and in the booths. He claimed to have had some 700 fights in these circumstances before attracting national attention.

Wilde was a popular and unique boxer. With thin arms and legs and a young, pale face, he looked an unlikely fighter. With his hands held low he came in hitting at all angles and looking open to a counter. But he was, in fact, difficult to hit, and his blows were as hard as those of most lightweights. He was called 'The Ghost with a Hammer in his Hand'.

When Wilde came to London and continued his winning ways, he was given a shot at the British flyweight title at the National Sporting Club, but he

Ted 'Kid' Lewis, an all-action fighter who was one of the busiest and most successful champions of his day.

lost to the crafty 'Tancy' Lee, when the referee stepped in in the 17th round on 25 January 1915. But Wilde became champion a year later, when the referee stopped his fight with Joe Symonds on 14 February 1916. Wilde avenged his defeat by Lee in June, this time the ref coming to Lee's assistance in the 11th round.

Wilde forced Johnny Rosner, of America, to retire in 11 rounds at Liverpool in 1916 and became undisputed world flyweight champion by knocking out Young Zulu Kid, also of America, later in the year. The fight is described in Chapter 8.

Wilde was forced to meet men from higher divisions. He beat featherweight Joe Conn and, in 1919, two top American bantamweights, Joe Lynch and Pal Moore – the former became world bantamweight champion the following year. Wilde went to the United States himself in 1919–20, and remained unbeaten in 12 fights.

Wilde agreed to meet Pete Herman of the United States for the world bantamweight title in London in 1921, but Herman came without the title, having just lost it to Wilde's victim, Lynch. Herman was also over the bantam limit, and refused to weigh-in, at which Wilde refused to go on. However, on being told that the Prince of Wales was waiting, Wilde went out to fight, and was beaten by the heavier man, the referee stopping the contest in the 17th round.

With nobody around to challenge him for his flyweight title, Wilde retired, aged 29. Sadly, he was persuaded to go to the Polo Grounds, New York, to fight Pancho Villa on 18 June 1923. Against advice, he felt obliged, as champion, to defend, despite being inactive for 30 months. A large crowd came to see the legendary Wilde. He put up a tremendous show against the nine-years-younger Villa, and refused to quit until knocked out in the seventh round.

Wilde died in Cardiff on 10 March 1969. In the view of most followers of the sport, he was the greatest of all flyweights.

One of the greatest boxers for his weight the world has ever seen, Jimmy Wilde, wearing the Lonsdale belt which he won outright.

After two defeats as a novice, Leonard's career was for a long time one of interrupted success. He fought the world lightweight champion, Freddie Welsh, three times under the 'no-decision' Frawley Law in New York. After getting the newspaper nod in the first two fights, Leonard knocked out Welsh in the ninth round on 28 May 1917 to take the title.

In six years of defences, Leonard had more than once to fight back to keep the crown. His fight with Charlie White, when he was knocked out of the ring, is described in Chapter 8. Richie Mitchell had Leonard down and dazed but stood back when Leonard invited him to come on. A similar ploy worked against Lew Tendler. 'Is that your best punch?' Leonard asked in a clinch when Tendler had him severely hurt – and Tendler was sufficiently discouraged.

Leonard stepped up a division in 1922 to challenge the welterweight champion Jack Britton. Leonard dropped Britton in the 13th round at the Velodrome, New York, but hit him again while he was on one knee and was disqualified. It was an inexplicable lapse in the cool Leonard's career.

Leonard retired as unbeaten lightweight champion in 1924 after seven years as the king. He claimed it was to please his mother. Everybody was surprised when he made a comeback seven years later as a welterweight. He won 18 fights but on 7 October 1932 was beaten by Jimmy McLarnin, soon to be champion, and retired again.

In 1943 Leonard became a referee, but on 17 April 1947 he collapsed and died during a round while refereeing at the St Nicholas Arena, New York.

Benny Leonard was regarded as one of the best boxer-fighters, who could win with skill or punching power, and usually both.

Benny Leonard

Benny Leonard was the complete boxer, clever, scientific, correct, of good temperament, with a good punch and the ability to take one himself.

He was born Benjamin Leiner, in New York on 7 April 1896. He modelled himself on his boyhood hero, Joe Gans, and by coincidence he also grew to be a lightweight. Leonard's mother encouraged him to be a boxer, and when he first fought away from New York he remembered Gans' telegrams home and sent his own mother the same message: 'I am bringing home the bacon'.

Georges Carpentier

Georges Carpentier was a champion at *la boxe Francaise*, in which the feet were used. When *la boxe Anglaise* became popular in France, he rapidly became adept. He had his first fight aged 14, weighing little more than 7 stone (98lb – 44.5kg). Before he was 16 he won the French lightweight championship and continued winning national and European titles from middleweight up to heavyweight.

Carpentier was born in Lievin-les-Lens, in the Pas de Calais on 12 January 1894, the son of a miner. His youthful talent was spotted by a man who was an itinerant one-man show, an acrobat and hypnotist, Francois Descamps. He became Carpentier's manager, and together they made a fortune from boxing.

The handsome, elegant French champion was known as the 'Orchid Man' and his career was followed with interest by women in Paris and London. Carpentier was particularly severe on British champions. On 23 October 1911 he beat Young Joseph in London to become European welterweight champion. He was 17 years old. On 29 February 1912 he knocked out Jim Sullivan in the second round in Monaco to win the European middleweight crown. On 12 February 1913 he knocked out Bandsman Rice in the second round in Paris to become European light-heavyweight champion. On 1 June 1913 he knocked out Bombardier Billy Wells in the fourth round in Ghent, Belgium, to become European heavyweight champion. He was still only 19 years old. Six months later he knocked out Wells again in London. This time in only 73 seconds.

Nineteen days before the First World War began Carpentier beat the American, Ed 'Gunboat' Smith, on a disqualification in London to become the 'white heavyweight champion of the world'. During the war Carpentier

Georges Carpentier in 1926. He was a champion from the age of 14, and one of the ring's outstanding personalities.

served in the Air Force and was awarded the *Croix de Guerre* and the *Médaille Militaire*. In 1919 he defended his European light-heavy and heavyweight titles against British champions, knocking out Dick Smith in eight rounds and Joe Beckett in 74 seconds.

Carpentier was never more than a light-heavyweight. He was a good boxer who also carried a knock-out punch as his record proves. His main strength was his speed of punch, and a lightning right accounted for many of his opponents.

In 1920 Carpentier went to the United States to win the world light-heavyweight championship with a fourth round knock-out of Battling Levinsky, and he then fought Jack Dempsey for the world heavyweight title in the first million-dollar boxing match. Although Carpentier got his lightning right to connect early on, it broke his thumb, and he could not resist the heavier man.

The punishment he took in this fight had its effect and next year he lost his world championship to Battling Siki in one of boxing's biggest upsets. But he did knock out Ted 'Kid' Lewis in the first round in controversial manner in 1922 and Beckett again in 48 seconds in 1923. In 1924 he went back to America to challenge Gene Tunney for the world light-heavyweight title, but was stopped in the last round by what his manager claimed was a low blow.

He did not fight in 1925, but tried a come-back with four fights in 1926 before finally calling it a day and opening a celebrity bar in Paris, where he died on 28 October 1975 – France's greatest boxer.

Harry Greb

Harry Greb was a natural fighter – a rough, tough battler who stepped into the ring 294 times in 13 years. Outside the ring he eschewed training and lived life to the full. As a fighter he also got on with it – a boxer who ignored defence and went straight into non-stop attack. Delivering punches from all directions with flailing arms, he earned himself the name 'The Human Windmill'. He was not too fussy about where some of his blows landed, and was frequently booed as a villain.

Greb was born in Pittsburgh, Pennsylvania, on 6 June 1894. He loved scrapping from an early age, and was a professional boxer before his 19th birthday. Although only a middleweight, he challenged Gene Tunney for the light-heavyweight championship of America, and gave Tunney a stone (14lb – 6.3kg) and a battering, breaking Tunney's nose in the first round and putting him in bed for a week. Tunney later beat Greb four times – half the total defeats Greb suffered in the ring. Greb also fought heavyweights, and earned a victory over Bill Brennan, who challenged Dempsey for the world title.

Greb won the world middleweight title on 31 August 1923 when he beat southpaw Johnny Wilson on points. He

One of the greatest of all crowding fighters, who never gave his opponents the slightest rest, Harry Greb was the only boxer to defeat Gene Tunney.

Jack Dempsey was lucky enough to be around when boxing boomed in the 1920s, and his style pleased the fans.

defended the title six times, the best win coming against Mickey Walker in 1925. After this fight, Greb and Walker met in a New York restaurant, and words outside on the pavement led to blows, the police stopping the rematch.

Greb finally lost his title to Tiger Flowers in 1926, and failed to regain it in a return. He was then 32 years old and had been fighting for some time with the sight of only one eye. Later in the year he entered hospital for an operation on the other, and the man who was so seldom stopped in the ring died under the anaesthetic.

Jack Dempsey

Unpopular early in his career, when he was considered a 'draft-dodger', Jack Dempsey ended his life as one of the most respected of all boxers.

He was born William Harrison Dempsey in Manassa, Colorado, on 24 June 1895. He built up a reputation as a boxer while working in mines and timber camps in the west, and came to the attention of manager Jack Kearns, known as 'Doc'. His elder brother also boxed, and first took the name 'Jack' Dempsey from the old middleweight,

'The Nonpareil'. When his brother gave up, the younger Dempsey became Jack.

Kearns managed Dempsey well, and it was on his directions that the young boxer went to work in the shipyards rather than join the army during the First World War. A whole string of well-known heavyweights were dispatched until Dempsey was the obvious challenger for champion Jess Willard. They met in 1919 in Toledo, Ohio, and Dempsey beat Willard in three rounds.

Dempsey was an aggressive boxer who could knock out an opponent with either fist. He was called 'The Manassa Mauler', and usually came into the ring with his body suntanned and with a growth of black beard on his face, which helped to make him look fearsome. His dashing style became popular with the fans, and Dempsey was involved in five fights which grossed over a million dollars at the gate.

The first was the meeting with Georges Carpentier at Boyles Thirty Acres, New Jersey, in 1921, the second the knock-out of Luis Firpo at the Polo Grounds, New York, in 1923. That was Dempsey's fifth defence, after which he married Estelle Taylor, a film star – a match which did not meet with Kearns' approval. He disliked the softening influence on Dempsey of his wife (Dempsey had his nose remodelled), and the boxer and manager parted company.

When Dempsey faced Gene Tunney in 1926 he had not fought for three years – years of bitter quarrels with Kearns. Tunney beat Dempsey on points with over 120,000 spectators present. Dempsey then beat Jack Sharkey (his fourth million-dollar gate) to earn a rematch with Tunney for the title. This time the gate receipts were a record $2,658,660. The fight is described in Chapter 8. Dempsey lost on points, and retired. He made a short comeback in 1931–32, but it came to nothing.

Jack Dempsey became proprietor of a restaurant in New York, a feature of which was a huge mural of the fight with Willard. He died on 31 May 1983, a few years after his restaurant was pulled down. He was 88 years old, and still nearly as famous as when he was boxing.

Gene Tunney

Gene Tunney had an exemplary career, but rarely features in arguments about the best-ever heavyweight champion, perhaps because he followed the colourful Dempsey, and retired after defending his title only twice.

He was born James Joseph Tunney on 25 May 1897 in New York, and determined to become a boxer as a boy, soon asking for a pair of gloves. At 18 he turned professional, but after a few wins he was drafted into the US Marine Corps, where he was posted overseas and obtained plenty of boxing practice.

Back in America, in 1919, he continued his winning ways right up to taking the US light-heavyweight title from Battling Levinsky in 1922. Four months later he lost it, to Harry Greb, taking a calculated beating from the Human Windmill for 15 rounds. But Tunney worked out how to beat Greb, and did so on four future occasions, Greb entering Tunney's dressing room after the last and saying: 'I never want to fight you again'.

Tunney became a heavyweight, beat an ageing Carpentier, and was then matched to meet Dempsey for the world title in 1926. He practised boxing on the retreat, and outpointed the Manassa Mauler over ten rounds. In a return a year later, which produced record receipts and a record pre-television payout to Tunney of $990,445, he again beat Dempsey after being down for a controversial long count – as described in Chapter 8.

Tunney defended once more, then retired without losing his title in the ring. He married an heiress, became a wealthy businessman, studied literature, becoming friendly with Bernard Shaw, and resisted all suggestions of a comeback. He was beaten only that once by Greb in a career of 77 fights. His life might have been planned as carefully as he planned his fights. He lived to be 81, dying in Greenwich, Connecticut, on 7 November 1978.

Mickey Walker

Edward Patrick Walker was born on 13 July 1901 in the tough, Irish part of Elizabeth, New Jersey. He liked scrapping as a boy, and had a boxer's pug nose, so was called Mickey rather than the grander Edward.

He was trained to become an architect but instead became a professional boxer, and started knocking out his rivals. He was a welterweight, and after a couple of years went 12 rounds with world

Gene Tunney was the first world heavyweight champion to retire while still champion and not attempt a comeback.

champion Jack Britton in a no-decision contest. But on 1 November 1922 he beat Britton on points in New York to become champion. On 2 July 1925, while still welter champion, he challenged Harry Greb for the middleweight title, but lost on points after a brilliant battle. Walker and Greb, with respective dates, met later that night in a restaurant, and enjoyed discussing the fight. As they were leaving, Walker upset Greb with a remark, and another fight developed outside. Walker's version was that as

Greb was peeling off his jacket and it was down round his elbows, he knocked the Human Windmill four feet in the air. Walker thus claimed the second decision, but admitted that in the ring Greb was the greatest fighter he ever met.

After a few defences of his welter crown, Walker, whose hard punching and tenacious style had by now earned him the title 'The Toy Bulldog', lost on points to Pete Latzo. But already he was thinking of the middleweights again and on 3 December 1926 he beat Tiger

Flowers on points in Chicago to become world champion. Now managed by Jack Kearns, who had broken with Dempsey, Walker went to London and beat the British champion, Tommy Milligan. Finding he was not favourite for this event, he and Kearns bet their purse on the outcome and cleaned up.

Between two successful defences against Ace 'Nebraska Wildcat' Hudkins, Walker took on Tommy Loughran for the world light-heavyweight title but lost on points in Chicago.

Walker then relinquished his middleweight crown to campaign amongst the heavyweights. Surprisingly, he did well, eventually holding Jack Sharkey, the leading contender, to a draw over 15 rounds. More wins followed, and then Walker took on Max Schmeling, who had just lost the world title to Sharkey. Down in the first, Walker fought back to be perhaps just ahead by the eighth, but then Schmeling battered Walker, and when he put him down with his right, the referee agreed with Schmeling's request to save the cut and bleeding Walker from further punishment.

Walker made one more attempt at the light-heavyweight title, losing on points to 'Slapsie' Maxie Rosenbloom, on 3 November 1933. He later avenged this defeat, but by then Maxie wasn't champion.

At 34 years old, Walker finally retired. In 163 fights he had lost 19 times, but that does not do him justice. He was never more than a middleweight at 11st 6lb (160lb – 73kg), and against Schmeling was giving away two stone (28lb – 13kg). When he fought Bearcat Wright he was outweighed by about 8½ stone (120lb – 54kg). He won world titles at welter and middleweight, and mixed it with the best at light-heavy and heavyweight. It was a glittering career.

The Toy Bulldog took up painting. He died in Freehold, New Jersey, on 28 April 1981, just failing to reach his 80th birthday.

Mickey Walker, a great middleweight champion, liked to fight heavyweights and almost became a contender for the title.

Len Harvey

Len Harvey was a master boxer in every respect – such a brilliant defensive exponent of the art that he ended over 20 years in the professional ring without a mark.

Harvey was born in Stoke Climsland, Cornwall, on 11 July 1907. His elder brothers boxed, and Len began when a boy. He had his first paid fight in 1920, when just 12½ years old. His idol was fellow-Cornishman Bob Fitzsimmons, who was ending his career when Harvey was born.

Harvey was a small flyweight as a boy, and he had the rare distinction of fighting in every weight division in his professional career. It was not until he was 18 that he reached championship class when he boxed a draw with Harry Mason over 20 rounds on 29 April 1926 for the British welterweight title. His first British championship came three years later; he knocked out Alex Ireland in the seventh round on 16 May 1929 for the middleweight crown.

After six defences, Harvey lost his middleweight title to Jock McAvoy, the 'Rochdale Thunderbolt', in Manchester on 10 April 1933, but two months later, on 13 June, he beat Eddie Phillips on points to become British light-heavyweight champion. This fight was scheduled for 12 June, but didn't actually start till after midnight.

On 4 July 1932 Harvey challenged Marcel Thil of France for the world middleweight title but was narrowly outpointed. Then, on 30 November 1933, he inflicted the first defeat on Jack Petersen, giving the British heavyweight champion nearly two stone (28lb – 13kg) and taking his title. He beat Larry Gains, of Canada, for the British Empire heavyweight title two months later, but lost both titles to Petersen on 4 June 1934, with a cut eye in the 12th round.

Harvey tried for the world light-heavyweight title on 9 November 1936 but was again just beaten on points in London by John Henry Lewis. He regained the British heavyweight title on 1 December 1938, on the disqualification of Eddie Phillips, and when John Henry Lewis retired, fought Jock McAvoy on 10 July 1939 for the British version of the world light-heavyweight title. Harvey won on points.

At the outbreak of war he joined the RAF, but was persuaded to put his titles

up against Freddie Mills on 20 June 1942. At 35 years old, and after three years out of the ring, his legs couldn't keep him out of trouble, and Mills knocked him through the ropes in the second round to take his world and British titles. Apart from the cut eye against Petersen, this last fight of 133 was the first in which he had been stopped. He was a champion for over 13 years. He died in Holloway, London, on 20 November 1976.

Len Harvey, a Cornishman like Fitzsimmons, fought as a professional at all the weights. A brilliant defensive boxer, he was world light-heavyweight champion from 1939 to 1942.

The Clown Prince of Boxing, Max Baer, won the world heavyweight championship but did not care for it enough to train sufficiently.

Max Baer

Max Baer was in the tradition of John L. Sullivan. He had the physique to be a great champion. He stood 6ft 2½in (1.89m) and was a perfectly-proportioned, muscular 14st 7lb (203lb – 92kg). He was well able to take a punch, and his right fist carried a blow capable of knocking over any boxer on whose chin it should land. Unfortunately for his career he had another of Sullivan's traits – he enjoyed life too much to take training seriously. Even in the ring he could not resist joking and clowning.

He was born on 11 February 1909 in Omaha, Nebraska, the son of a cattle dealer, and built up his muscles in the cattle business in Livermore, California. Attracted to the boxing booths, he soon discovered he could lay flat most of his rivals, turned professional and found his way to New York. He was known as 'The Livermore Larruper'.

His powerful punching caused him to be connected with two tragedies on his way to the top. Frankie Campbell was found to be dead after a battering by Baer, and Ernie Schaaf, who died after being beaten by Primo Carnera, had previously taken a terrific beating from Baer. Eventually he knocked out Schmeling to earn a world title shot against Carnera.

Baer and Carnera had made a film together, *Every Woman's Man*, during which the quick-witted, outgoing Baer had established a psychological superiority over the gentler, retiring Carnera. In the championship match, Baer treated the over-awed Carnera lightly. He could not keep the Ambling Alp on the canvas, but Carnera had been put down 11 times in 11 rounds when the referee stepped in.

Baer then fought exhibitions for a year, appeared on stage and screen, and had a radio series. He interrupted his schedule to take on James J. Braddock on 13 June 1935, with his title at stake. There appeared no danger. The 30-year-old Braddock, 'The Cinderella Man', had practically given up, having been

Henry Armstrong, perpetual motion, the only boxer to hold three world titles simultaneously.

beaten by most of the top men around. Baer did not take him seriously, but Braddock fought well, dodged all Baer's swings, and won on points.

Baer began a comeback campaign by taking on the young Joe Louis, and was knocked out for the first time in his career in the fourth round, counted out on one knee. He fought on till 1941, and was always a great draw, but did not regain his challenger status. He retired after two defeats by Lou Nova. Baer was only 50 when he died, at Hollywood on 21 November 1959.

Henry Armstrong

The secret of Henry Armstrong was a slow heart-beat. He would warm up by shadow-boxing in the dressing room before a contest to get into the groove, box 15 rounds of perpetual motion and end without showing much signs of distress.

Armstrong's style was all-out aggression, in which he would hit his opponent with blows from all angles, sometimes with such abandon that not all were fair. He was known as 'Homicide Hank'.

He was born on 12 December 1912 in Columbus, Mississippi, as Henry Jackson, and was brought up in St Louis, where he fought as an amateur – although as the family was poor he was often paid. He went to Los Angeles when 19 years old and fought professionally, but was exploited until noticed by the singer Al Jolson, a boxing fan. Jolson bought his contract and found the boxer a new manager, Eddie Mead, who took him to New York. Meanwhile he had begun using the name Henry Armstrong, taking a friend's surname so that he could get fights as an 'amateur' again.

Armstrong worked his way through the featherweights and was having his 30th fight in little more than a year when, on 29 October 1937, he knocked out Petey Sarron in the sixth round in New York to become undisputed world featherweight champion – he had held the NBA version for about a year.

By 31 May 1938, Armstrong had won around a dozen more victories, all but one by the quick route. On that day he moved up two divisions to challenge the great Barney Ross for the world welterweight championship. Ross stayed the distance, but did not fight again after taking a bad beating and losing his title.

On 17 August 1938, at the Madison Square Garden, Armstrong took on Lou Ambers for the lightweight championship and won – again on points. He thus held three world titles simultaneously – a unique record, and an amazing performance considering that the 'in-between' titles of light-welter and junior lightweight were in abeyance. Had they not been, Armstrong would no doubt have held five titles.

Armstrong relinquished the featherweight title to concentrate on the welter division. In the two years and four months of his reign he defended no fewer than 19 times. During this run he dropped down to lightweight to give Lou Ambers a return shot at that title, and lost on points. Seven months afterwards he ventured into the middleweights to try to win a world title at a fourth weight, but was held to a draw over ten rounds by Ceferino Garcia, of the Philippines.

Armstrong's almost continuous campaign could not last for ever, and on 4 October 1940 he lost his last, welterweight title, when outpointed by Fritzie Zivic, a fighter as rough as himself. Fifteen weeks later Zivic stopped Armstrong in 12 rounds in a return.

Homicide Hank rested for 18 months and then began again, having nearly 50 fights between June 1942 and February 1945, winning most, before finally calling it a day. He was not rich after his 175 recorded fights. In 1951 he became a Baptist minister, and director of a boy's club.

Benny Lynch

Scotland has produced some brilliant flyweights. Benny Lynch, Jackie Paterson and Walter McGowan were all world champions. The best of these, and the most tragic, was Benny Lynch, rated not far behind Jimmy Wilde as the greatest flyweight of all.

He was born in Clydesdale, Scotland, on 2 April 1913, and was brought up in the Gorbals, the poor district of Glasgow, where he sold newspapers as a boy. He boxed in an amateur club and in the booths, and became a professional when he was 18 years old.

Lynch rapidly became Scottish flyweight champion and in 1935 boxed a draw with Jackie Brown, the world champion, in Glasgow. On 9 September 1935 he got a title shot in Brown's home town, Manchester, and won in the second round after putting Brown down ten times.

Lynch defended against Pat Palmer, then beat Small Montana, who held the NYAC version of the world title, to be undisputed champion.

Lynch was a fast, perfectly balanced boxer, with an excellent defence and a knock-out punch which reminded fans of Wilde. On 13 October 1937 he knocked out future world champion Peter Kane in the 13th round of a tremendous fight.

The pressures of making the weight now began to tell on Lynch. He began to drink. He forfeited his titles when he was matched with Jackie Jurich, of the USA, and came in 6.5lb (3kg) overweight. He knocked out Jurich in 12 rounds, but rapidly went downhill. Three months later he was knocked out for the first time by Aurel Toma, of Romania, the European featherweight champion. Lynch retired, just one year after his great fight with Kane. He was 25 years old.

Eight years later the drink had destroyed him completely. He died of malnutrition in Glasgow on 6 August 1946.

Joe Louis

When arguments about the greatest heavyweight champions take place, one name is always on the short list: Joe Louis.

Louis was born Joseph Louis Barrow, in Lafayette, Alabama, on 13 May 1914, the seventh child of a poor family which later moved to Detroit. His mother intended him to be a violinist, but Joe used the lesson money to learn to box in the local gymnasium.

A good amateur, he turned professional in 1934, and began a rapid rise to championship class. Within 15 months he had knocked out both Primo Carnera and Max Baer, recent world champions.

He was managed by John Roxborough, a black business man, and trained by Jack Blackburn, a retired black boxer, until he was spotted by the ticket-speculator Mike Jacobs, who persuaded his handlers he could develop Louis into a champion. Blackburn's contribution had been vital. He had trained Louis to attack in a methodical, shuffling manner which was effective, and had also taught him to keep a poker face, so Louis did not arouse the racial hatred that Johnson had 25 years earlier.

Louis had his first setback (the only one of his prime) when he fought a third ex-champion, Max Schmeling. Schmeling knocked him out in the 12th round. Louis, who was still only 22, neverthe-

Benny Lynch (right) in action against Aurel Toma of Romania at the Empress Hall, London, in 1938, near the end of his career.

less bypassed Schmeling for the first crack at James J. Braddock's world title. After Louis had knocked out another ex-champion Jack Sharkey, Jacobs got the title fight for Louis with a deal that guaranteed Braddock a percentage of Louis's championship earnings. That Louis would win was almost a formality, although the 'Cinderalla Man' put up a surprisingly good defence.

Joe Louis, the 'Brown Bomber' who was world heavyweight champion for 11 years.

Louis was only 23 years old when he became the second non-white heavyweight champion of the world – he was known as the 'Brown Bomber'. He began a series of 21 defences which lasted until he went into the army in 1942. It was known as his 'bum of the month' campaign. Not all were bums, and there were some interesting contests.

Tommy Farr, for instance, the British champion, was one of only three challengers to go the distance with Louis, and some thought he should have got the verdict. Arturo Godoy, of Chile, was the next to go the distance – when stopped by the referee in the return, he tried desperately to fight on. Two-ton Tony Galento floored Louis in the first round, but lasted only three more. Louis' revenge over Schmeling and his great fight with Billy Conn are described in Chapter 8.

In 1946, the 32-year-old Louis resumed his career by knocking out Conn and Tami Mauriello, and then scored a points victory over Jersey Joe Walcott, only the third challenger to take him the distance. This was a bad decision, even an apologetic Louis thinking Walcott should have had the verdict. Louis knocked out Walcott in a return on 25 June 1948, however, and on 1 March 1949 retired. He was champion for 11 years and nearly eight months.

Unfortunately, he was forced to make a comeback to pay income tax demands. He challenged Ezzard Charles for the championship, but was beaten on points, and then was knocked out by an up-and-coming Rocky Marciano. That was the end for Louis, whose comeback had increased his number of bouts to 70, and his defeats to three.

Later Louis took part in wrestling matches to try to pay his debts, and after that the man who earned over 4.5 million dollars became a 'greeter' at a Las Vegas casino. He died at Las Vegas on 12 April 1981.

Archie Moore

Archie Moore was one of the most permanent of ring fixtures. He was born in Benoit, Mississippi, on 13 December 1916, or, if you believe his mother, 1913. Archibald Lee Wright was his real name.

He learned to box at a reform school, turned professional as a middleweight in 1935 and began a long career. Early on he was exploited (as were many black

boxers) by managers, and it took him 17 years to get a world title shot. He was then a light-heavyweight, and he won on points from Joey Maxim to become champion. That was on 17 December 1952, and Moore's first two defences were both against Maxim, with the same result. Thereafter Moore, having been kept waiting himself, took on all-comers.

While champion, he challenged Marciano for the heavyweight title and always claimed that only the referee giving Marciano an inappropriate mandatory eight count saved him from a second round knock-out. He also fought Floyd Patterson for the vacant title after Marciano's retirement, but the combination of weight and speed (plus giving away 18 or 21 years) proved too much for him that time. The emerging Ali was another heavyweight Moore gave away years to (at least 25!) and failed to beat.

In 1960 the NBA stripped Moore of his title for inactivity, and made Harold Johnson, whom Moore had beaten six years earlier, the champion. But Moore was recognized elsewhere, and picked an Italian for his last successful defence, against Giulio Rinaldi, on 10 June 1961.

Moore's success was built on the skill acquired by experience, fitness, and the strength he developed in his arms, which made him a knock-out specialist, with over 140 in his career. In 1962 other bodies withdrew championship recognition from the 46-year-old, and he retired in 1963.

Sugar Ray Robinson

A popular newspaper description for Sugar Ray Robinson over the years has been 'the best pound-for-pound boxer of all'. His record suggests it is a claim which is at least arguable.

He was born as Walker Smith in Detroit, Michigan, on 3 May 1921. He carried Joe Louis' kit when a youth, was a brilliant amateur, and turned professional in 1940. He substituted for a boxer called Ray Robinson, who was unfit, and continued using the name. When his manager referred to his prospect as 'sweet as sugar', he acquired another part of his ring name.

Robinson suffered his first defeat after 40 wins at the hands of Jake LaMotta. Thereafter he fought for eight years

The ageless Archie Moore (right) in a title defence against Yolande Pompey of Trinidad at Harringay in 1956. The 40-year-old Moore won when the referee stopped the fight in the tenth round.

Right: Sugar Ray Robinson attacking the punchball in a training session in 1951.

Below: The only world heavyweight champion to complete a career undefeated, Rocky Marciano.

without another, in the course of which he relieved LaMotta of the world middleweight title. That was in 1951, Robinson having already relinquished the welterweight title. Sugar Ray then toured Europe and dropped his new title to Randolph Turpin in London. However, 64 days later at the New York Polo Grounds he regained it in brave circumstances, fighting back when Turpin appeared to have him beaten again. A record crowd for non-heavyweights of 61,370 saw the fight.

In 1952, Robinson attempted to win a third world title by challenging Joey Maxim for the light-heavyweight crown. He was foiled only by a heat wave, having to give up exhausted with two rounds left when holding a big lead. Robinson retired at the end of that year but made a comeback in 1955 during which he actually won and lost the middleweight title three more times. He almost won the championship a sixth time, being held to a draw when challenging Gene Fullmer.

Sugar Ray boxed on, finally retiring at the end of 1965, aged 44. He took part in 22 world title fights at three weights. In 201 contests he was never knocked out.

Rocky Marciano

If boxing records were worked out like cricket or baseball batting averages Marciano would be top of the table. He had 49 professional fights and won the lot, 43 inside the distance.

He was born Rocco Francis Marchegiano, of Italian parents, on 1 September 1923 in Brockton, Massachusetts.

An all-round sportsman, his boxing talent blossomed when he served with the US Army in England. On discharge he went to Madison Square Garden for a trial, where he failed to impress. He was small for a heavyweight at 5ft 10½in (1.79m) and at 13st 2lb (194lb – 88kg) was only a cruiserweight by today's standards. He completely lacked science, but luckily nobody tried to coach him and he built up a winning streak with his own bruising methods. Of his first 12 fights, two lasted three rounds and two two rounds. The other eight were first-round knock-outs.

In 1951 Rocky, now being called 'The Brockton Blockbuster', began to fight possible title contenders. On 26 October he knocked out the ageing Joe Louis, the Brown Bomber's third and final defeat.

On 23 September 1952 Marciano got his title chance and took it by knocking out Jersey Joe Walcott. He defended six times and retired in April, 1956. He had earned more than $4 million, but it was difficult to discover where all this had gone when his affairs were put in order after his death in a private plane crash on the eve of his 46th birthday.

He stuck to his decision to retire, and was not to be persuaded back to meet new champion Floyd Patterson. Although his methods were rough and ready, in all other respects his was a model career.

Randolph Turpin

Randolph Turpin became world middle-weight champion by convincingly out-pointing the great Sugar Ray Robinson, but for one reason or another did not fulfil the expectations this performance aroused.

He was born on 7 June 1928 in Leamington, Warwickshire, into a boxing family. His eldest brother, Dick, was the first coloured boxer to win a British title, partly because their mother insisted he should have the first chance.

An amateur with a brilliant career, Randolph turned professional in 1946. He rapidly became British and European middleweight champion, and in 1951 world champion. The contract called for

Randolph Turpin at Waterloo Station, on his way to America to fight for the world middleweight championship in 1953. With him is the London promoter Jack Solomons.

a quick return bout, however, and Turpin lost his title only 64 days later at the New York Polo Grounds.

Turpin boxed on the retreat for the early part of that return, then stepped up his work and began to dominate the tiring Robinson. In the tenth, a right from Turpin split Robinson's eye, and as the blood began to flow the ex-champion realized that he had to win back his title quickly. In desperation he hurled blows at Turpin, and connected, and soon Turpin was ducking and bobbing on the ropes while Robinson piled in his best punches. Turpin's pride would not allow him to go down, but it lost him the fight.

Eventually the referee stopped the slaughter and Robinson had the title back. There were only eight seconds of the round left. If only Turpin had gone down for a rest he might have survived the round, and a tired Robinson with a badly cut eye would probably have not found another chance to win.

Turpin won the British and Empire light-heavyweight titles, and could have regained the world middleweight championship when matched with Carl 'Bobo' Olsen on Robinson's first retirement.

Alas, Turpin went to New York with domestic problems on his mind, and could not do himself justice. He lost on points, and then was knocked out in 65 seconds by Tiberio Mitri when defending his European title in Rome.

After a year he came back and regained the British and Empire light-heavyweight titles which he'd relinquished. He continued fighting until 1964 without giving the appearance of the zest which made him the best in the world. He had little left of the money he earned in the ring. On 17 May 1966 he shot himself dead at his home in Leamington.

Henry Cooper

Henry Cooper was British and Empire heavyweight champion for a record ten years. He also won three Lonsdale belts outright, another record. He came nearer than anybody to beating Muhammad Ali in his prime, and was perhaps only denied the highest honours by an unlucky tendency to cut easily around the eyes.

He was born on 3 May 1934 in Bellingham, Kent, one of identical twins who both boxed professionally. He turned professional in 1954 and had a disastrous spell, losing twice to Joe Erskine when trying to win the British title and being knocked out by Joe Bygraves and Ingemar Johansson in attempts on the Empire and European titles.

The tide turned in 1958 in a fight with Dick Richardson, a future European champion. With his eye pouring blood, Cooper recovered from the brink of defeat to win by a knock-out. He beat American Zora Folley and, on 12 January 1959, Brian London for the British and Empire titles.

In 1963 he fought Cassius Clay when Clay was about to become world champion. Cooper's left hook had Clay down and glassy-eyed when the bell rang to end the fourth round. In the interval Clay's glove mysteriously split. When it had been replaced, Clay had completely recovered his composure and cut eyes spoiled Cooper's chances in the delayed fifth round. Blood pouring from eye cuts also spoiled Cooper's attempt to win the world title in 1966, when the champion was now called Muhammad Ali, but he did win the European championship on three occasions.

In 1969 Cooper gave up his British, European and Empire titles in disgust when the British Boxing Board of Control would not sanction a proposed match between himself and Jimmy Ellis for the WBA heavyweight title. After a year he came back to regain them all.

The indestructible Cooper defended all his titles against Joe Bugner on 16 March 1971 at Wembley. After 15 rounds he offered his arm to the referee for it to be raised as victor, but the referee raised Bugner's instead. Few observers agreed with the verdict and 'our 'Enery' decided to retire. He was nearly 37 years old. Since then he has become a 'celebrity' and enjoys trading anecdotes and making advertisements more than he did trading punches.

Floyd Patterson

Floyd Patterson's career was a mixture of the brilliantly exciting and the disturbingly pathetic. He has a double place in boxing history becase at just under 22 years old he was the youngest man to win the world heavyweight championship,

and he was also the first champion to regain the crown.

Born at Waco, North Carolina, on 4 January 1935, Patterson was one of ten children in a poor family which soon moved to Brooklyn. He went to a school for retarded children and learned boxing, which he loved. He was an excellent amateur and won an Olympic gold medal in 1952, immediately turning professional.

A defeat by Joey Maxim in 1954 was the only blot on his record when he won the vacant world heavyweight title by beating Archie Moore in 1956.

Patterson was not a big heavyweight, and developed a style of his own, watching his man from between his gloves in a 'peek-a-boo' style and frequently throwing punches by leaping at his opponent with both feet off the floor. He was vulnerable to a counter punch, and often found himself on the floor, sometimes put there by quite inferior boxers.

His first contest with Ingemar Johansson showed his vulnerable aspect. He was completely helpless as he was put down seven times by the powerful Swede. Patterson's best aspects were seen in the subsequent two winning fights with Johansson, when he fought courageously and well.

It seemed confidence held the key with Patterson. He certainly lacked it against Liston who took his title and beat him twice in a single round. Patterson took a false beard with him to the stadium for the first fight and fled in his disguise after his defeat.

When he was 30 years old he challenged Ali for the title, but fought with a bad back and Ali tortured him for 12 rounds. He fought only seven times in the next five years, but made a comeback in late 1970, registering nine wins before meeting Ali, also on a comeback trail, on 20 September 1972. Patterson was knocked out and retired at 37 years old.

Terry Downes

Born in Paddington, London, on 9 May 1936, Terry Downes boxed as a junior and then went with his parents to America where he joined the US Marines and won the US All-Services boxing title before returning to England in 1957 to become a professional.

He was soon king of the British middleweights and on 14 January 1961

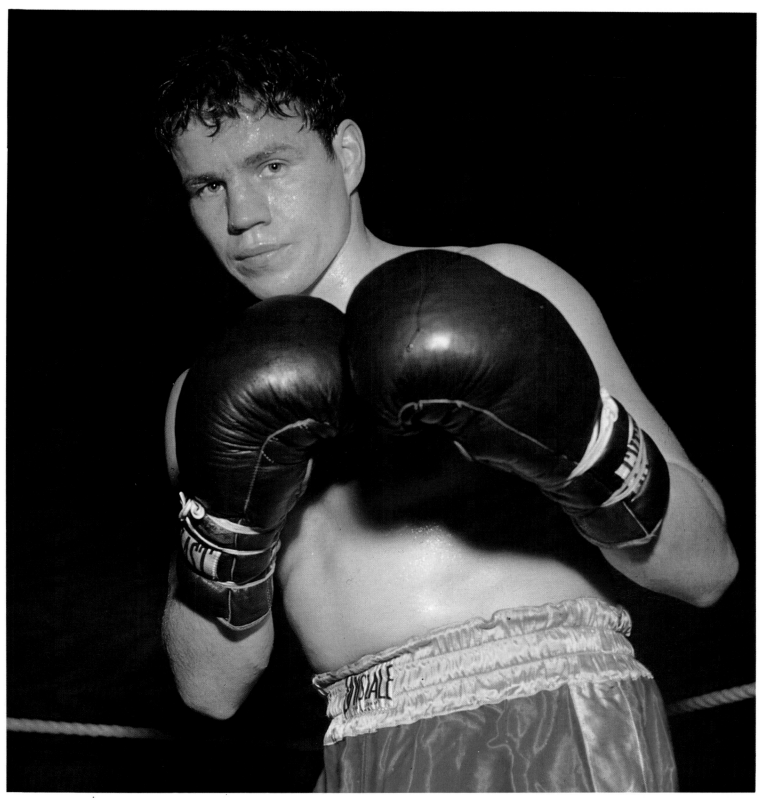

went to Boston to challenge world champion Paul Pender in his own den. A cut nose stopped Downes' effort in the seventh round. It was his tendency to cut, and the trouble he had with what he called his ''ooter' (nose) that prevented Downes being a long-reigning champion. He had all the attributes – strength, punching power and courage.

Downes took the title from Pender on his second attempt, Pender being forced to retire in the ninth round. The rubber match was lost in Boston, however.

Downes then took on the world light-heavyweight champion, Willie Pastrano, and was well in front until the 11th round in their fight in Manchester. A desperate Pastrano then caught Downes with a punch which put the challenger down, and tired by his exertions against the heavier man, Downes was stopped by the referee when he staggered to his feet.

Soon afterwards, Downes announced his retirement and became the owner of a demolition business and then a chain of betting shops.

Above: Terry Downes was one of the best and most entertaining world middleweight champions, and he nearly took the light-heavyweight title, too.

Opposite: Floyd Patterson, one of the fastest heavyweight champions, poses before the punchbag.

Muhammad Ali at a press conference. The articulate Ali became almost as famous for his interviews as for his boxing.

Muhammad Ali

Muhammad Ali was the most remarkable boxer of modern times – perhaps of any times.

He was born in Louisville, Kentucky, on 17 January 1942 as Cassius Marcellus Clay, the name he fought under until 1964. A distinguished amateur, he won a gold medal at the 1960 Olympics. The happy, talkative young man showed his fanaticism at this stage of his career. He was so proud of his medal that he refused to take it off. Later, in America, when a white motorcycle gang tried to take it from him, he threw it into a river.

He soon turned professional, began winning, and to get publicity began naming the round in which he would win. He was surprisingly accurate.

His progress continued right to the top. In 1964 he challenged Liston for the world heavyweight title and won. His two battles with Liston are described in Chapter 8.

Muhammad Ali, as he called himself after a conversion to the Muslim faith, made eight defences of his championship before being stripped of his titles in 1967 for refusing to be conscripted into the US Army. He actually retired in 1970, but late in the year obtained a couple of bouts, as described in Chapter 6.

The remarkable thing about Ali's career is that these three missing years were probably the ones at which he would have been at his peak. It is possible that the world never saw the best of Ali.

When his argument with the services was finally settled (he was vindicated and did not serve the prison sentence passed on him) he took some time to return to his earlier boxing standard. He was beaten by Joe Frazier when challenging for his old title on his third fight back. In 1973 he lost to Ken Norton on points after fighting for some of the time with a broken jaw. He soon avenged this defeat, and on 28 January 1974 also avenged his defeat by Frazier, although this was not for the world title. This came on 30 October, however, when Ali went to Zaire to beat George Foreman by a knock-out in the eighth round.

Ali then defended successfully ten times, giving both Frazier and Norton another chance to beat him, before he was surprisingly outpointed by Leon Spinks, a defeat he reversed later in the year. He had won the heavyweight title a record three times, and retired.

Two years later, however, in 1980, when he was 38, he tried to take the title a fourth time by meeting Larry Holmes, the new WBC champion. He was forced to give up in the 11th round however, and this time retired for good. He suffered four defeats in 60 fights, only the last not avenged.

Ali was a magnificent physical specimen, with great intelligence and confidence. He was able to fight in a number of styles. In some contests, particularly those title fights with George Chuvalo and George Foreman, he invited punches to the body in what he called a 'ropadope' technique, allowing these men to punch themselves out. Nobody could take a punch better than Ali.

He was 6ft 3in (1.91m) and weighed around 15st 5lb (215lb – 97.5kg). He was thus as heavy as any heavyweight since Carnera, although Foreman later outweighed him. But Ali was as fast on his feet as a middleweight. He even invented a 'shuffle', a fancy piece of footwork the value of which lay only in demoralising opponents. The description 'floats like a butterfly, stings like a bee' was applied to him.

Ali remained one of the most recognisable people on earth after his retirement, but there were fears for his health after a few years. His speech became slurred and he was lethargic, causing some enemies to claim he was punch-drunk. An explanation which gained currency was that he had Parkinson's disease. A happier report late in 1984 said that he was much brighter and talking more freely, and the signs were that he would make a good recovery.

Carlos Monzon

Carlos Monzon was one of the best fighters in a division noted for greats – the middleweights. Unlike many of them he was not a natural fighter. He saw the sport as a way of escaping the poverty which he shared with his ten brothers and sisters.

He was born in Santa Fe, Argentina, on 7 August 1942. He fought as an amateur and turned professional in 1963.

He learned the professional game entirely in Argentina, where he suffered three points defeats on his way up. He did not fight outside his native country until he challenged world champion Nino Benvenuti in Rome on 7 November 1970. Monzon's chance was not rated highly, but he caused a surprise by knocking out the champion in the 12th round.

That Carlos could still learn was shown when he won the return in only three rounds. Monzon, without a lot of publicity, went on to win 15 title fights in all. He beat off Emile Griffith, Jean-Claude Bouttier, Benny Briscoe, Tom Bogs, Jose Napoles and others, but was always disappointed that the WBC named Rodrigo Valdes as a rival champion in 1974, when Monzon declined a match with him. Monzon's career was rounded off on 26 June 1976 when he met Valdes to determine who would be undisputed champion. Monzon was approaching 34 years old, four years older than Valdes, but he took the points decision over 15 rounds. He repeated the feat 13 months later and retired. From the time he became champion in 1970 until he retired in 1977 nobody had been able to beat him, an excellent record.

Carlos Monzon of Argentina, undefeated world middleweight champion for seven years, training with the skipping rope.

151

Joe Frazier

Joe Frazier was born in Beaufort, South Carolina, on 12 January 1944, the seventh of 13 children. He worked on a vegetable plantation as a child, and dreamed of his hero, Joe Louis, and a boxing career. At 16 years old he married and went to Philadelphia.

The Police Athletic Club provided him with a place to train for his boxing. He got to the 1964 Olympics when Buster Mathis, who had beaten him, was forced to withdraw, and he won the heavyweight title. A year later he turned professional.

Frazier was short for a heavyweight at 5ft 11½in (1.72m), and a lot of his 14st 6lb (202lb – 92kg) was in his powerful legs – his thigh measurement of 26in (66cm) was the biggest of the heavyweight champions.

When Ali was stripped of his world title, Frazier beat Buster Mathis for the WBC version on 4 March 1968. After four defences Frazier beat Jimmy Ellis, the WBA champion, who was unable to continue after the fourth round, and so became undisputed champion. 'Undisputed' took on more meaning on 8 March 1971 when Frazier beat Muhammad Ali on points. Two years later, however, Frazier lost the title when he was annihilated in two rounds by George Foreman, who proved too big and far too strong a puncher.

The highlights of Frazier's career after that were his two further fights with Ali. Although he lost them both, he put up tremendous performances in each. He always gave Ali more trouble than most. He lost a return with Foreman on 15 June 1976 and retired. He had only 37 professional fights, but they were at an interesting time in the heavyweight division.

Larry Holmes

Larry Holmes complains that he does not receive the credit he deserves for being heavyweight champion of the world for over six years, and when his record is examined it must be conceded that he has a point.

Holmes was born in Cuthbert, Georgia, on 3 November 1949. He began professional boxing in 1973, and had 27 fights before he got a chance at the title, winning them all, 19 by knock-outs. On 9 June 1978 he fought and beat Ken Norton for the WBC version of the championship, after Leon Spinks had been stripped of it.

In the circumstances, with Ali about to regain the WBA version, it is not surprising that Holmes was not taken too

Joe Frazier (left), the WBC champion, becomes undisputed heavyweight champion by beating the WBA champion Jimmy Ellis (right).

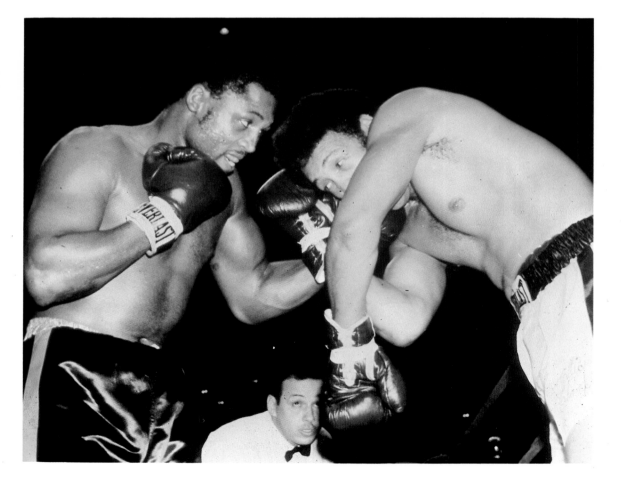

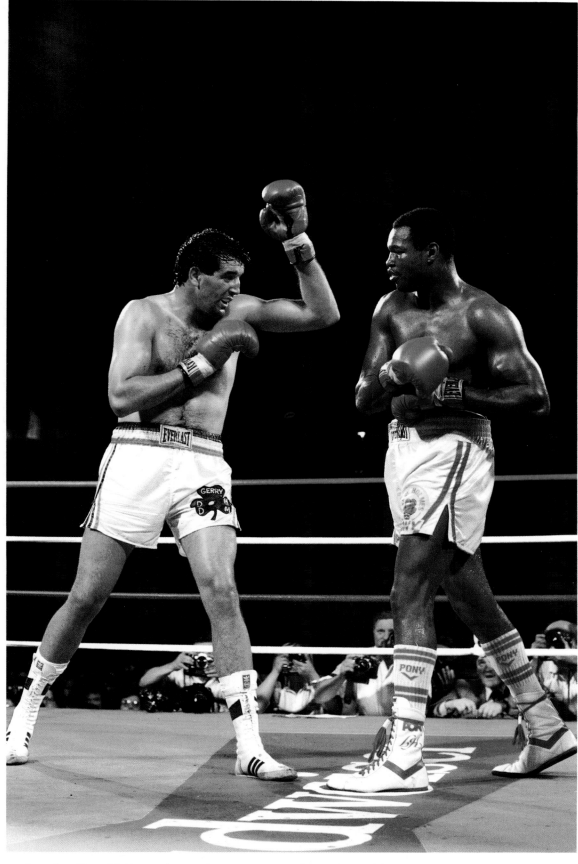

Larry Holmes (right) defeating Gerry Cooney, who was built up as a likely champion, at Las Vegas in 1982.

seriously. But Holmes beat all comers – including Ali, when Ali tried his final come-back on 2 October 1980. Gerry Cooney was built up as a big white hope in June 1982 but was well beaten in 13 rounds.

Holmes gave up the WBC title in 1983 to assume the International Boxing Federation title, but whatever com- bination of initials describes the version of the title he holds, Holmes ended 1984 as most people's world champion, and on the top of *The Ring* ratings.

Holmes has beaten all the contenders around, and no man can do more. To the end of 1984 he had a perfect record, like Marciano's. Perhaps his status will only be realized when he has retired.

Marvin Hagler

Three years after Carlos Monzon gave up the world middleweight title after a reign of nearly seven years, Marvin Hagler assumed the throne and began to look as if he could be king for as long.

Hagler was born on 23 May 1952 in Newark, New Jersey, and began his professional career in 1973. It took him a long time to get his first shot at the middleweight title, and he wasn't successful. The rugged Italian champion, Vito Antuofermo, forced a draw over 15 rounds and retained his crown.

Marvin showed his meanness and determination on his next attempt, however, going to London to stop Alan Minter in three rounds. There were some nasty scenes afterwards as the disappointed fans threw objects into the ring.

Hagler then boxed regularly, took on allcomers, and changed his name officially to 'Marvelous Marvin Hagler'; like his shaven head it was an aid to an 'image'. In the ring he is strong, well-muscled, and carries a lethal punch in both hands. He is also a clever boxer, and possibly the best of the 1984 champions.

Sugar Ray Leonard

Sugar Ray Leonard was hoped to be the great champion who would take over the role of the charismatic figure of boxing which was played by Muhammad Ali through most of the 1960s and 1970s.

Leonard was born in Wilmington, South Carolina, on 17 May 1956. He was a brilliant amateur, and won a gold medal in the 1976 Olympic games at light-welterweight, where he boxed with photographs of his girlfriend and their two-year-old son on his shoes.

He turned professional in 1977 and began his professional career impressively. He proved himself a brilliant boxer who also carried a knock-out punch. By the time he was ready to tackle Wilfred Benitez for the WBC world welterweight title he had had 25 fights, and won 16 of them inside the distance.

The fight with Benitez, himself a first-class champion, was a beauty, and Leonard won with a knock-out in the last round. He defended against Britain's Dave 'Boy' Green, who was outclassed and beaten by a knock-out in the fourth round, and then he tackled Roberto Duran, who had moved up from the lightweights. Leonard was a strong

Marvelous Marvin Hagler in action. After winning the middleweight title in 1980, Hagler forced the referee to come to the rescue of most of his opponents.

Sugar Ray Leonard, the outstanding world champion of the early 1980s, was forced to retire with eye trouble.

favourite, but suffered his first reverse when the crowding tactics of Duran were enough to get a points verdict. Sugar Ray put the record straight when he so bamboozled Duran in a return that Duran gave up in the eighth round.

Leonard won the WBA version of the light-middleweight title on 25 June 1981 when the referee halted the fight in the ninth round against Ayub Kalule, of Uganda, and then became undisputed world welterweight champion by stopping the WBA champion, Thomas Hearns, in the 14th round of a fight Leonard did not always look like win-

ning. After a defence against Bruce French, Leonard underwent an operation for a detached retina of his left eye, and retired on 9 November 1982.

Leonard tried a comeback in 1984. In Worcester, Massachusetts, he beat Kevin Howard, whom the referee rescued in the ninth round. But in the fourth round Leonard had been put on the canvas for the first time. He immediately retired for good. 'I wasn't there', he said, 'I was apprehensive of being hit'. His decision meant goodbye to an $11 million fight with Hagler, but it was the right one.

8 GREAT RING BATTLES

Tom Cribb v Tom Molineaux

10 December 1810, Copthall Common, Sussex

John Gully, champion of England, having retired in 1808 after beating Bob Gregson, Tom Cribb assumed the championship.

One of his first challengers was Tom Molineaux. Molineaux began life as a slave in Virginia, one of twin brothers. After beating a bully on a nearby plantation, his master gave him his freedom, and the means to go to England to make a living as a pugilist. He was not the first black American to fight in England. Bill Richmond, born in Sturton Islands, became servant to General Earl Percy when the island was taken by the English. He came to England with the Earl in 1777 and eventually became a leading pugilist. He fought Cribb in 1805, losing after 90 minutes.

Richmond was Molineaux's second in his first fight in England. Cribb helped his opponent, who was beaten soundly. Then Molineaux fought Tom Blake, a man known as Tom Tough, again with Richmond and Cribb in the corners. Molineaux dealt out so much punishment in the eight rounds of the contest that he was thought a match for Cribb, and this was made for 200 guineas a side, with 100 guineas purse subscribed for the winner.

The fight attracted attention from people not normally of the 'Fancy'. The honour of England and the supremacy of her pugilists was at stake. Cribb, at 5ft 10½in (1.79m) was taller than Molineaux by two inches (5cm), and, at 14st 3lb (199lb – 90.3kg) 1lb (0.5kg) heavier.

The betting was heavily in favour of Cribb, who was expected to win within 30 minutes. The Fancy and many followers arrived at Copthall Common, near East Grinstead, to see the battle in pouring rain. Gully and Joe Ward seconded Cribb, Richmond and Jones seconded Molineaux.

Cribb began impressively, and after three rounds, Molineaux having been down in each, the odds were 4–1 on Cribb. But Molineaux rallied, and Cribb was down in the sixth round. Both men showed signs of punishment, and Molineaux's chances were not to be denied in the ninth, when he put Cribb down with a blow to the face.

Cribb, having found his blows to Molineaux's head did not stop the challenger, began to box on the retreat, but was thrown in the 11th and 12th, when the odds were 6–4 on Molineaux, to the consternation of the betting fraternity. The 19th was an important round, Molineaux holding Cribb against the ropes while he rested his head on his chest. Many spectators got into the outer ring and tried to prize his fingers from the ropes. Cribb finally fell from exhaustion after Molineaux had got his head under his arm and punished him.

This round took the contest beyond 30 minutes, losing many bets for the Fancy who had supported Cribb to win within that time.

The faces of both men became unrecognizable as they fought evenly for several more rounds. In the 28th Cribb was knocked down by Molineaux and

The second fight between Tom Cribb and Tom Molineaux was Cribb's last competitive fight. The unlucky Molineaux continued to fight but died seven years later.

was in danger of not being able to resume. His second, Joe Ward, crossed the ring and accused Molineaux of holding bullets in his fist. The delay caused by this diversion enabled Cribb to recover, while Molineaux sat shivering in the December rain.

Cribb dealt a decisive blow in the 29th when he damaged Molineaux's right eye – Molineaux now could hardly see. However, he threw Cribb in the 30th, but in the 31st struck his head on a ring post in going down. Both men fell exhausted without a blow in the 32nd. Molineaux protested he could fight no more after the 39th. His seconds persuaded him to try another round, but he fell from weakness, and Cribb was the winner. The bout lasted 55 minutes.

Within three days Molineaux challenged Cribb by letter to a return, blaming the unfavourable weather for his defeat. The two met at Thistleton Gap, near Grantham, where three counties join, on 28 September 1811. Nearly 20,000 saw this battle, all the beds for 20 miles (35km) around being booked on the night before, and the fans being on the road at dawn.

The betting was once again on Cribb who, under the training of Captain Barclay, was fitter and lighter, but again Molineaux reduced the odds, from 3–1 to 7–4. But a terrific blow to the body by Cribb in the sixth round knocked the wind from Molineaux, and from then on he was a beaten man. Molineaux had not trained properly, and it was said that before the fight he had indulged in his favourite chicken pie and a tankard of porter.

He took a fearful beating over 11 rounds lasting just over 19 minutes. Twice Cribb's seconds could have claimed the match as Molineaux was late in coming up for the 10th and 11th rounds. In the ninth his jaw was broken, and he also ended with two broken ribs. But, the gallant Molineaux had knocked Cribb's head 'terribly out of shape'.

Molineaux, being black and a genuine threat to the champion, was never popular in England. He fought on until he died on 4 August 1818 in Galway, Ireland, aged 34. It had been a hard life.

Tom Sayers v John Camel Heenan

17 April 1860, Farnborough Common, Hampshire

Tom Sayers must have been one of the greatest fighters, pound-for-pound, ever. Only 5ft 8½in (1.72m) and 10st 12lb (152lb – 67.5kg), he was the champion of England in 1860.

John Camel Heenan, born in Troy, New York, of Irish parentage, was the champion of America. A machinist, he went to San Francisco and got a job in the workshops of the Pacific Mail Steamship Company at Benicia. He built up a reputation as a pugilist, and became known as 'The Benicia Boy'. He issued a challenge to Sayers for the 'world title', and the match was made for £200 (or $1,000) a side.

Tom Camel Heenan (left) and Tom Sayers in the great international battle of 1860.

The fight was the first to become front page news on both sides of the Atlantic. Reporters and artists travelled from New York and France, and all the English papers carried full accounts, with *The Times* issuing a special edition on the fight which proved extremely popular.

Discretion had to be shown in the preparations, as both men risked arrest. Heenan trained in a barn in Haram, Wiltshire, with a punchbag containing 30lb (13.5kg) of sand. Sayers trained in Newmarket, Cambridgeshire..

On the morning of the fight Sayers travelled to London in a horse-box. Heenan actually was arrested but was released on bail of £50. He was smuggled to London in disguise.

To get to the fight, fans paid £3 for return tickets, destination unknown. They began congregating at London Bridge Station around midnight – by 3.30 a.m. the first train of 33 carriages was full.

The Metropolitan Police, of course, were aware of the special trains. For the 16 miles (24km) of the track in their jurisdiction they kept watch to see they did not stop. Eventually the destination was reached – Farnborough, about 25 miles (37km) from London. The ring was pitched in a nearby meadow.

The spectators included the cream of society, parliament and the services. Lord Palmerston was there, as were the literary giants of the day, Dickens and Thackeray.

Heenan, at 6ft 2in (1.88m) was nearly 6 inches (17cm) taller, and at 13st 13lb (195lb – 88.4kg) just over 3st (43lb – 19.5kg) heavier. At 27 he was also seven years younger. Heenan clearly was physically superior, and he had a big punch. Sayers, however, was far more experienced in meeting top men, and the cleverer boxer.

The match commenced with Sayers connecting with punches but Heenan using his size and strength to grab Sayers and throw him. He threw Sayers to the ground in the first five rounds, and dealt a severe blow to Sayers' chances in the sixth when the Englishman blocked a punch with his right arm, which resulted in a broken bone.

Sayers decided that his best chance lay in concentrating on Heenan's eyes – the only defeat in his own career had come when Nat Langham had blinded him in both eyes seven years earlier and forced him to give best in 61 rounds.

Sayers was quickly successful, almost shutting one of Heenan's eyes in the seventh. Heenan himself had a similar setback to Sayers when, after a left to Sayers' head, he found his arm had suffered the more damage. The contest continued in this vein for round after round, Heenan continually throwing Sayers, Sayers constantly punching to the face until Heenan could hardly see.

The 37th round was critical. Heenan got Sayers by the throat and forced him back so that his neck was on the top rope. Sayers was in danger of being strangled, and the unruly crowd cut the rope. Sayers' seconds then interfered and the referee decided things had got out of

Before their battle for the heavyweight championship, John L. Sullivan and James J. Corbett fought an exhibition during Sullivan's theatrical tour. This is Sullivan in his corner on stage at the Opera House, San Francisco.

hand, and that he'd had enough. The fight continued without him in a riotous atmosphere for five more rounds, with Heenan so blind he knocked over his own second by mistake.

After 42 rounds, lasting two hours and 20 minutes, the police decided to intervene, and the crowd scattered. Heenan wanted to move the fight to a new site, but found himself chased to the train by an unfriendly mob. Sayers looked the better afterwards, owing to the dreadful punishment Heenan had taken around the face.

The decision rendered was a draw. The newspapers disagreed as to who was in front at the end – not surprisingly the English and American papers' opinions were coloured by patriotism. Sayers and Heenan became friends and gave exhibitions on tour together.

Sayers never fought again, and five years later he died of tuberculosis, aged 39. Heenan was given a great welcome on his return to New York, and after Sayers' retirement was considered there to be the world champion. He returned to Eng-

land in 1863 to fight Tom King and lost in 24 rounds. Thereupon The Benicia Boy retired. He died on 28 October 1873 at Green River Station, Wyoming Territory. So 14 years after the greatest prizefight ever fought, both principals had died.

John L. Sullivan v James J. Corbett

7 September 1892, New Orleans, Louisiana

John L. Sullivan, the 'Boston Strong Boy' was the last bare-knuckle champion of the world. A roistering man who could take a drink as well as a punch, he was in the mould of the old-timers, not too keen on training but confident his strength could see off any man.

James J. Corbett, 'Gentleman Jim', was of a more modern breed, a handsome, scientific boxer, a 'California Dandy', a man who preferred to fight with gloves, and thought defensive dodging and weaving as much a part of the manly art as knocking the other man's head off.

By 1892 Corbett had become the natural challenger for Sullivan, mainly on account of a 61-round draw he had fought with Peter Jackson, a coloured fighter whom John L. did not care to meet.

Sullivan, having seen off all logical contenders for his crown, had spent the previous three years on the stage, barnstorming in a melodrama called 'Honest Hearts and Willing Hands'. He was in no state for a big fight, but with challenges coming from Frank Slavin, Jackson and Charlie Mitchell, as well as Corbett, he agreed to fight, with gloves, for a $25,000 purse, anyone (except Jackson) who could put up a $10,000 side-stake. Corbett was first to find the money, and the bout was arranged for the Pelican Athletic Club, in New Orleans, as part of a three-day 'Carnival of Champions'. On 5 and 6 September 1892 Jack McAuliffe and George Dixon held on to their lightweight and featherweight titles respectively. On 7 September Sullivan defended his title, in the first bout for the heavyweight championship of the world under Queensberry Rules.

Sullivan, alas, was past tough training. No longer was William Muldoon, who had so effectively trained him for the 75-round battle with Jake Kilrain three years before, in his corner. He had boxed only in exhibitions since, one of them, in San Francisco in 1891, with Corbett, when Sullivan had worn evening dress.

Nevertheless he did his best, sweating the whisky from his pores and developing his temper. His train journey and arrival in New Orleans were majestic, with champagne flowing and his supporters, who thought him invincible, willing to shake any hand that had shaken the hand of John L. Sullivan. Corbett, by comparison, had a gymnasium fitted in his train, and crept into his hotel almost unnoticed. The city was packed with fans and the fight hangers-on – the pickpockets and petty criminals out to make a dishonest dollar.

Sullivan had got his weight down to 224lb (101.6kg) but it was not all the old muscle. The eight-years-younger Corbett was a fit, sleek 186lb (84.4kg). Such was the charisma of Sullivan, however, that the betting was 4–1 on him, and it was said that even Corbett's father had a substantial wager that the great John L. would beat his son.

With hindsight, nearly 100 years later, the result seems to be fairly predictable, and the odds against Corbett very attractive. He gained a psychological advantage at the start. Having made Sullivan agree that the boxers should enter the ring together, rather than the champion second as usual, he tricked Sullivan and climbed into the ring in the 'star' spot himself.

The fight followed a pattern. John L. rushed in in prize ring style trying to land his fearsome right to Corbett's body. Corbett just sidestepped, moving round the lumbering Sullivan and countering with hooks, or retreated, picking off Sullivan with counters as he bored in. Sullivan frequently almost lost his balance with his rushes, grabbing the ropes to steady himself as Corbett glided away.

This was something new in heavyweight boxing. The crowd jeered Cor-

An impression by the artist of the *Police Gazette* of James J. Corbett shaking hands with John L. Sullivan after the first heavyweight title fight.

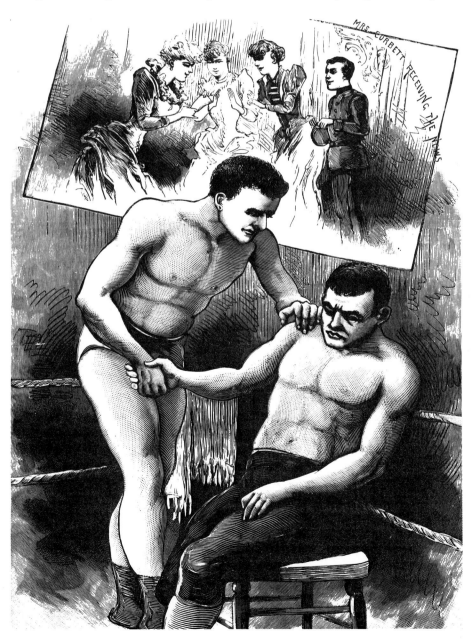

bett as he dodged and swayed, refusing to make a fight of it. All the time, however, his counter blows were catching Sullivan, and the champion's face began to be reduced to a pulp.

Sullivan had never fought a man like this before. He was being beaten not because he had lost his great punch, but because he could not find the man to hit. It must have seemed all rather unfair. Eventually, he had taken so much out of himself by his efforts to hit Corbett, and Corbett's blows had so worn him down, that he could not drag his great bulk from the canvas when Corbett put him down in the 21st round.

The great braggart took his defeat magnificently. Standing in the centre of the ring he asked for silence, got it, and told the crowd he was beaten fairly and he was glad the championship 'stays in our country'. Then he left, weeping, an example followed by many of his supporters. He never fought again, and remained the most popular of all American champions. As for Corbett, he had beaten a legend. Nobody would forgive him for that.

James J. Corbett v Bob Fitzsimmons

17 March 1897, Carson City, Nevada

There was no love lost between heavyweight champion James J. Corbett and challenger Bob Fitzsimmons. Once Corbett knew he had to fight Fitzsimmons he went out of his way to insult him whenever possible. The final insult came when the two met on the road when out training for the fight. As the parties shook hands, Corbett refused Fitzsimmons'. 'I'll shake after I've licked you' he said, and indicating Fitzsimmons' dog, who accompanied him on his runs, continued 'I'll see you next Wednesday, and you'd better bring your dog with you'. Fitzsimmons stored up each insult and resolved to make Corbett pay for them all on the day.

Carson City, Nevada, was chosen for the venue, and a large open-air arena was built on the racecourse. The stakes were $10,000 a side, with $15,000 purse added, plus moving picture rights. The crowd was around 4,000, stewarded by Bat Masterson, the Western marshal, and a gang of helpers who collected the six-shooters and knives at the gate.

Fitzsimmons, the balding spindly-legged Cornishman, was only a middleweight, and Corbett, with weight and superior skill on his side, was the favourite, but only at 10–6. Like Sullivan before him, he had been on the stage, but unlike Sullivan had trained hard and was in good condition.

Fitzsimmons, though, had an impressive record in the United States, and his punching power was greatly respected. Certainly the Cornish miners who arrived for the fight from Virginia City did not think he was without a chance.

Fitz got his own back on Corbett in the preliminaries, decling to shake Corbett's hand. The fight started in the sunshine just after noon.

Fitzsimmons attacked from the start, but Corbett easily avoided his punches and began to get in several blows himself. He made Fitzsimmons miss so easily at times that the challenger saw the funny side, and one photograph of the fight shows Fitzsimmons laughing as he grabbed Corbett in a clinch.

Fitzsimmons, like Sullivan, began to get a beating from Corbett, his face showing the attentions of Corbett's fists. But all the time he was confident that he could beat the champion.

His confidence looked misplaced in the sixth. A series of blows to the head had Fitz in trouble and hanging on, then a final left to his chin dropped him to one knee. He rose at nine, and managed to fight off Corbett for the rest of the round. But it looked as if his challenge was fading.

By now Fitz's wife, Rose, a great tactician, was visiting the corner between rounds. 'Hit him in the body Bob', she advised. She knew that her husband could not outbox Corbett, but that a few of his big punches in the right places would slow the champion down. The badly cut and bleeding Fitzsimmons told her not to worry. 'I've got him licked now', he said.

With Rose keeping up the advice to 'hit him in the body', both during and between rounds, the fight did, indeed, begin to turn. Corbett's blows came faster and more often, but it was noticeable that he looked as if Fitzsimmons' punches were now hurting him, whereas Fitz seemed less and less troubled by Corbett's hits.

Corbett began to tire in the tenth round, and the fight was decided in the

14th. After catching Corbett with punches to the head, Fitz suddenly shifted his stance. Stepping forward with his right foot, he shot a left with devastating force to the point just below Corbett's ribs.

Corbett went down gasping for breath. He did his best to rise but he was like a man paralyzed. With one glove and one knee on the canvas, he was forced to listen to the referee count him out.

The blow that won the fight was to the 'solar plexus', an area of the body that suddenly had a name for thousands, only just aware of its existence.

Corbett soon recovered, and belied his name 'Gentleman Jim', by rushing across to Fitzsimmons and aiming a right at his face. Fitz went into a clinch, while Corbett demanded that they must fight again. As Corbett was carried away struggling, and the crowd became excitable, Fitzsimmons found Wyatt Earp, with revolver at his side, offering protection. It was probably unnecessary, and Fitz did not forgive Earp for cheating him over the Sharkey fight three months earlier.

Sadly, Corbett's father went home and committed suicide after his son's defeat. Fitz began a roundabout journey back to New York and a huge reception, stopping to give exhibitions and face local challengers, who were paid $100 if they stayed four rounds with the new (lightweight) heavyweight champion.

Bob Fitzsimmons (left) and James J. Corbett hold their gloves high as they spar for an opening.

Terry McGovern v Young Corbett II

28 November 1901, Hartford, Connecticut

If ever psychology won a world title, it was in the first McGovern–Corbett fight.

Terry McGovern was one of the hardest hitting of the small men. He did not need science. Right from the start of his career his ferocious hitting was enough to smash the champions to pulp.

Born in Johnstown, Pennsylvania, in 1880, he moved to Brooklyn with his family when a child, and by the time he was 17 he was fighting in the local arena. At 19 he was world bantamweight champion, knocking out Britain's Pedlar Palmer in 75 seconds. Four months later he knocked out George Dixon, of Canada, and was world featherweight champion. He took on Frank Erne, the lightweight champion. No title was at stake, but Erne was to receive the loser's end of the purse if he could not knock out McGovern in ten rounds. McGovern knocked out Erne in three. Many other victims succumbed by the same quick route. He was not called 'Terrible Terry' for nothing.

Young Corbett II was born in the same year as McGovern, in Denver, Colorado, as William H. Rothwell. However, there resemblance ended. Corbett, who took his ring name from the former heavyweight champion, was by comparison unknown. He was tough, but was chosen as challenger mainly because he was likely to put up a good

fight. He was also confident. As he passed McGovern's dressing room on the way to the ring he banged on the door. 'Come on, McGovern. Come and take your licking, you Irish rat.'

McGovern was ready to fight in the corridor. By the time he had been restrained and had reached his corner he was in a fierce temper. It was exactly what Corbett had planned.

McGovern dashed from his corner at the bell throwing punches in all directions as he attempted to flatten this insulting upstart as quickly as possible. But this was just what Corbett expected. Remaining cool and in control, he dodged the wild punches and sank in heavy blows to the body himself. McGovern stood back.

Corbett resumed his provocation. 'Come on, you bum', he said, 'Come and fight'. Terry leapt in again, his Irish temper inflamed. But Corbett punched back, with cooler control. A short right found McGovern's chin, and the champion was knocked flat on his back. He was up at 'nine', but for the rest of the round Corbett was firmly in charge.

McGovern still hadn't recovered in the second round. A few more blows, another right to the chin, and McGovern was out to the world.

Young Corbett was the new champion, and he kept McGovern waiting for 16 months for a return, while he fought eight times and collected the purses.

On their second meeting, in San Francisco, both had become overweight and the featherweight title was not at stake. McGovern was favourite again, but the fight began like the first, with Terry's opening rush countered so effectively that he was down to an answering right to the chin. He was down again in the second, but this time fought back well. However, Corbett's punches were the better timed. Down again in the seventh, McGovern made a great rally in the 11th, but a flurry of blows fiercely exchanged found him in distress in a corner. A measured right and McGovern was on his back, this time failing to beat the count.

So 'Terrible Terry', invincible for so long, had finally met his match in an unknown. Both men fought thereafter as middleweights, without getting a title chance among the bigger men. McGovern died in 1918 aged 38. Corbett survived him by nine years, and died in his 47th year.

Terry McGovern (left) posing with his conqueror Young Corbett II before their title fight.

A French magazine cover picture of Jack Johnson destroying the white man's hope, James J. Jeffries.

Jack Johnson v James J. Jeffries

4 July 1910, Reno, Nevada

Never did a fight arouse so much interest, anticipation, passion and hatred than that between Jack Johnson, the heavyweight champion of the world, and James J. Jeffries, the ex-champion.

Johnson was the first black champion, winning the title in Australia when white American boxers could refuse to meet black boxers, 'drawing the colour line' as it was called. Many of them did, particularly if there was a chance they would lose their titles or rankings.

Johnson was also a black man who liked the company of white women, which was frowned upon – there were even 'immorality laws' prohibiting some liaisons. He had an arrogant manner. Some of his teeth were filled with gold. He liked to smile. The flashing golden smile and swagger of the 'upstart' champion were more than some whites could stand.

Jeffries was the champion who had retired unbeaten in 1905 because there was nobody around to test him. In 1910, when no new white hope had appeared to challenge Johnson, public opinion demanded that Jeffries come back to take on the task.

The fight was fixed for Reno on Independence Day, 4 July, 1910. The excitement during the preliminaries was intense. Both men were received with thunderous applause by their supporters – Johnson, in a black and white bathrobe smiling his golden smile from ear to ear; Jeffries, strangely, in a golf cap and grey business suit, which he took off to display purple tights.

The 36-year-old Jeffries got down to 16st 3lb (227lb–103kg), but after five years was hardly in condition. Johnson was fit at 14st 12lb (208lb–94.3kg). Nevertheless many expected Jeffries to win, and he was favourite at 10–6.

The fight began at 2.47 in the hot sun. Jeffries was more aggressive in the early rounds, but there was plenty of wrestling and few clean hits. The first really significant action was in the sixth, when Johnson gave Jeffries a terrific punch to the right eye, which closed it.

Johnson then started playing with Jeffries, laughing out loud when Jeffries hooked to his head in the seventh, and keeping up a commentary with Jeffries' second, Corbett, as Jeffries tried to blast him in the ninth. In the 10th and 11th Johnson began winking and laughing at friends at the ringside.

Johnson started to punish Jeffries in the next few rounds, but still taunted him, asking him in the 14th: 'How do you feel, Jim?', as they clinched.

In the 15th, Johnson put Jeffries down with a left and right to the chin; Jeffries got up, but was immediately put down again. When it became clear that Jeffries would not get up a second time, some of the crowd shouted for the fight to be stopped. 'Don't let him knock him out', they yelled, and by the time the count reached 'seven' people were climbing through the ropes and the timekeeper was forced away.

Johnson was undistressed at the end. Jeffries admitted: 'I couldn't come back, boys'. Later he rued the day he left his peaceful alfalfa farm to be the 'white man's hope'. Johnson gave Jeffries credit for a game battle, but claimed he was never in danger of losing.

The white population was bitterly disappointed by Johnson's decisive win. The black population was euphoric at this demonstration of superiority. Over the next couple of days the simmering racial tension of years turned to violence, rioting and killings all over the USA.

Johnson could smile his golden smile at his triumphs, but after this fight there was trouble in store for him, and tragedy for hundreds.

Jack Johnson v Jess Willard

5 April 1915, Havana, Cuba

After Jack Johnson had beaten Jeffries, he led an inactive life as a boxer, not fighting for two years, after which he was forced to flee from America to avoid a jail sentence for offences against the Mann Act. He defended his title twice in Paris, not very impressively – indeed against the black Battling Jim Johnson he broke his arm in an early round and was granted a draw by the kindness of the referee.

Finally, promoter Jack Curley turned up in London and proposed a fight with Jess Willard, who had proved best of the 'white hopes' to beat Johnson. It was put to Johnson that by fighting Willard he could re-enter the United States without being imprisoned.

Willard was not a great fighter. At 6ft 6¼in (1.99m) and up to 17st 12lb (250lb–112.5kg), with a reach of 83in (2.11m) and a strong punch at the end of it, he had all the physical advantages necessary but he lacked the mental one of a killer instinct.

The fight was intended for Mexico, but was finally put on in Havana, Cuba, on 5 April 1915.

Willard trained hard for the fight, and came in 13lb (5.9kg) heavier than Johnson, who was sadly out of condition. The fight was scheduled for 45 rounds (the last title fight of such a length), presumably in the hope that the longer it continued the more tired the 37-year-old Johnson would get. The ploy worked. Johnson would have won on points at all distances up to 25 rounds.

Johnson fought a similar fight to that against Jeffries. He outboxed Willard, losing no opportunity to show his different class, and he did plenty of talking. In the ninth round Willard was bleeding from the mouth and from a cut on the cheek. Johnson piled on the pressure and for the next ten rounds did his best, it seemed, to knock out Willard.

After about the 20th round, Johnson tired. In the 25th he was seen to make a sign to his wife, who left. In the 26th he allowed himself to be rushed into a corner by Willard, who, after a suc-

Left: The scene at the race track at Havana during the world title fight between Jess Willard and Jack Johnson.

cession of punches, knocked him out with a right-hand punch to the jaw.

The most famous aspect of the fight in subsequent years has been a photograph of Johnson being counted out. Johnson is holding his gloves above his face as if shielding his eyes from the sun.

Later, Nat Fleischer, editor of *The Ring* magazine, paid Johnson $250 for a confession that the fight was fixed and Johnson always maintained afterwards that he lost it deliberately. In his autobiography, written some years later, he explained that losing was part of the agreement he had made with the pro-moter. He said that he was also to be paid an additional percentage of the gate by Willard's managers. This money was to be given to his wife in $500 bills at the ringside when receipts were counted. According to Johnson, the end was arranged for the tenth, but he had not received a pre-arranged signal from his wife that the money had been paid. He received this signal before the 26th round. Hence his return signal to Mrs Johnson, her departure, and his lack of defence when Willard knocked him out in the next round.

The significance of the photograph mentioned is that a 37-year-old man knocked out after 26 gruelling rounds is hardly likely to bother to keep the sun out of his eyes, or, indeed, be in a

Above: The famous photograph of Johnson hiding his eyes from the sun as he was counted out in the 26th round.

position to. This makes a reasonable circumstantial case. Most experts, how-ever, including the respected Nat Fleischer, who named Johnson as the greatest-ever heavyweight, thought he was fairly beaten.

The truth will never be known for sure.

Certainly Willard would have been an easy victim for Johnson in his prime. But Johnson was 37 (at least), and had been living easy for a while. The 30-year-old Johnson of the Burns fight would have beaten Willard, as would the 32-year-old

Johnson of the Jeffries fight, but perhaps the comparatively fat and flabby 37-year-old Johnson really was beaten on merit.

No doubt Johnson, too, had considerable psychological reasons for not wanting to win. It would be easier for him to rehabilitate himself in the United States again, and see his mother (which he always maintained was a prime motivation) if he lost. The title may, in fact, have become a burden to him. And after the reaction to his defeat of Jeffries, he might even have wondered if his life would be safe if he won again.

So the answer may be not a calculated fix but an accumulation of pressures on Johnson that led him to accept that he was not going to win, which is not, after all, so very different. The outcome was a compromise, too. Johnson did not avoid a period in detention on his return to the United States, but on the other hand, without his title he was never again the object of such fierce hatred as he had been before.

Jimmy Wilde v Young Zulu Kid

18 December 1916, Holborn Stadium, London.

During the First World War, most boxers, being by necessity young and fit, served in the armed forces, many of them as physical training instructors. Jimmy Wilde, the hottest property in British boxing, was one of them.

Jimmy Wilde (right) knocked out Young Zulu Kid, the American pretender to the title in London in 1916, to establish his superiority among the world's flyweights.

In Britain, he was regarded as the world flyweight champion, after beating Joe Symonds, of Plymouth, and Johnny Rosner, of America. Wilde, never weighing more than 7st 10lb (108lb–49kg), was in his prime, having run up a string of knock-out victories, not only against flyweights. Bantams and feathers were also among his victims. His only defeat in 65 contests in a mere four years had been inflicted by Tancy Lee, when Wilde had first challenged for the flyweight title. Wilde had later avenged this blot on his record.

However, in America, a young Italian who was born Giuseppe di Melfi, but boxed out of Brooklyn under the name Young Zulu Kid, was claiming not only the American but also the world title.

A London promoter, Jack Callaghan, realized that a meeting between the two would be a great attraction. He made Young Zulu Kid an offer, it was accepted, and Callaghan set about arranging the match.

It being wartime, with building restrictions, he obtained permission to convert the derelict Central Hall, in Holborn, by promising it as a hostel to the government. Equipment could be stacked away to provide space for spectators.

Young Zulu Kid managed to get to Britain from America, and Wilde obtained leave to fight him. On the night of the battle, 18 December 1916, 4,000 fans made a capacity crowd for the new 'Holborn Stadium'. No doubt the exotic ring name of Young Zulu Kid attracted the customers – it was a change from the sort of names currently on the posters, such as Gunner James Moir and Bandsman Dick Rice.

Wilde himself, a mere 5ft 2½in (1.59m) with skinny arms and legs, had many sobriquets given to him by the press. 'The Mighty Atom' was one, the 'Ghost with a Hammer in his Hand' another.

Jimmy was astonished to find himself taller than his rival for a change. Young Zulu Kid was only 4ft 10in (1.47m). But at 7st 12lb (110lb–49.8kg) he was heavier than Wilde, and looked much more muscular. Wilde was a firm favourite, the home fans being unable to visualize anybody able to beat him.

But Young Zulu Kid began the fight in determined style, swarming over Wilde in an all-action display that took Wilde aback – he spent round one keeping his opponent at bay. It was the same in the

Charlie White (black shorts) has Benny Leonard helpless and about to crash through the ropes in the sixth round of their title fight.

second, until Wilde stopped the Kid's advance with an uppercut, following it up with more crashing blows to put him firmly on the canvas. Only the bell during the count saved the challenger from losing there and then.

He was a game fighter, though, and the third round saw him resume his rushing tactics. Wilde countered with the heavier punches, and soon the Zulu Kid began to show signs of strain. Few men stood up for long once Jimmy Wilde caught them with a clean punch, but Young Zulu Kid stood up and even, occasionally, tried to rally. He put everything he had into the ninth and tenth rounds, and Wilde knew that he had a worthy opponent before him. The spectators cheered as the two men piled punches into each other.

Wilde's punches were always the harder. Young Zulu Kid came out all right for the 11th, but Wilde's left hook immediately had him wobbling. A right effectively finished him off and more blows sent him crashing unconscious to the floor.

Young Zulu Kid was never the same fighter again after this beating, while Wilde was acknowledged on both sides of the Atlantic as the undoubted King of the flyweights.

Benny Leonard v Charlie White

5 July 1920, Benton Harbour, Michigan

Benny Leonard and Charlie White had something in common. Both fought at least three world championship contests that could have gone either way. But in another respect they were opposites. Leonard won his matches. White lost his.

Leonard was world lightweight champion, having won the title the hard way, knocking out Freddie Welsh in a 'no-decision' Frawley Law bout in New York in 1917. Before he gave up the title undefeated, he was to come back from the brink of defeat against Richie Mitchell and Lew Tendler, but Charlie White was his closest call.

White came from Liverpool, born as Charlie Anchowitz in 1891. His father was a Jewish tailor, who took the family to Chicago when Charlie was a boy. He was a tubercular boy, needing exercise to develop his lungs. At the gymnasium he discovered a liking for boxing, and proved so adept that by the time he was 23 he had won a title shot against the lightweight champion, Willie Ritchie. Ritchie insisted on a no-decision bout.

In the first round, White's left hook connected on Ritchie's chin and Ritchie was almost out. But White hesitated to finish off the champion, and Ritchie not only escaped that round but stayed on his feet for the remaining nine.

Two years later, Freddie Welsh was champion, and gave White a chance over 20 rounds. Welsh was a very clever boxer, and always likely to win on points, but White had 20 rounds in which to catch him with his favourite left hook. He did, twice. The first time he let Welsh escape. The second time, in the 12th round, a stand collapsed, and in the confusion Welsh was again allowed to recover. White lost on points.

So when White fought Leonard, a brilliant boxer and puncher five years his junior, he knew that any chance that came his way might be his last for a world title, and that he must take it.

It came in the sixth round. A left from White caught Leonard and had him retreating, another had him in trouble, a third left him tottering and a final succession of hooks ended with Leonard crashing through the ropes onto the apron, with his legs resting on one of the strands, practically out.

But where a crashing stand had spoilt White's chance before, this time Leonard's brother proved the villain of the piece. He lifted and pushed Benny back into the ring (illegally), and Leonard managed to get to his feet at 'nine'. Without the intervention of his brother, the title would have passed to White.

As it was, White tore in to take his opportunity – but this time he was over-anxious and Leonard managed to avoid his rushes to the end of the round.

Then the pattern of the Ritchie and Welsh fights began to repeat itself for White. Having caught his opponent with his left hook and nearly won, he now found it very difficult to nail him again. Gradually, Leonard recovered his wits, and three rounds after being knocked out of the ring he caught White with a right as he came in which dropped him to the canvas. White rose, was put down a second time, rose again, and then was himself put through the ropes. He climbed back, but Leonard made none of the mistakes White had. He kept cool, caught his man with a right, and White for the first time in his career was knocked out.

Jack Dempsey v Luis Firpo

14 September 1923, Polo Grounds, New York

Luis Angel Firpo was an Argentinian boxer who had only 35 professional fights in his whole career. One of them will never be forgotten.

He went to the United States in the early 1920s to make his fortune. His assets were a phenomenal build, and strength to match. He stood 6ft 3in (1.91m) and weighed 15st 10lb (220lb–100kg). He had no science, and he did not want any coached into him. Nor would he train very seriously. He was a fatalist. He believed that he would either connect with his bludgeoning right on his opponent's chin, which usually meant curtains, or he wouldn't. In his first six contests in the States he connected: six knock-out victories, including one over former world champion Jess Willard.

Tex Rickard, after his success in matching heavyweight champion Jack Dempsey with the foreigner, Georges Carpentier, and having noticed the box-office flop when Dempsey fought fellow-American Tommy Gibbons, decided Firpo was the likeliest contender around.

Firpo, reputed to be a man who liked making a dollar but not parting with one, overcame a desire to postpone meeting Dempsy till he had more experience when Rickard spelt out the finances. The match was made, and the fans scrambled to see 'The Manassa Mauler' against the 'The Wild Bull of the Pampas', as Firpo was called. Rickard had his second million-dollar gate, and although the fans saw only three minutes and 57 seconds of fighting, it was mayhem while it lasted and few were disappointed.

At the bell, both boxers came out in a crouch, Firpo scoring a clumsy right to the chin as Dempsey came forward, and the champion hit the deck in the first ten seconds.

Dempsey scrambled up, went into a clinch, the referee said 'break', Firpo glanced at the ref and dropped his hands, Dempsey swung a left hook, and Firpo was down. Twenty seconds had passed, and both men had been on the canvas.

Then it was Firpo's turn to connect again and he did, to Dempsey's jaw; but this time Dempsey did not go down. Instead he replied with an uppercut, and

Firpo crashed again, like a tree being felled. Dempsey stood over Firpo, and tried to apply the finisher when he rose, but the Argentinian withstood Dempsey's blows and began clubbing the champion's body with rights. Dempsey was the quicker puncher, though, and as Firpo wound up for another big right, Dempsey's left hook crashed him to the canvas again.

The champion again stood over Firpo, behaviour which was to have significance when he next defended, and when the groggy Firpo had half-risen he was quickly put down again. This time the referee tried to push Dempsey away, and was still trying when Firpo got up. Dempsey sprang, and a left and right sent Firpo back to the canvas. Once again Firpo was hardly upright when Dempsey crashed him down for the sixth time.

Instinct got Firpo to his feet, and even to attempting a punch, but the relentless Dempsey immediately put him down again. With his arms outstretched, Firpo looked to be almost out, but with a superhuman effort he got to his feet just before the count reached 'ten'.

As Dempsey came in again, the giant Firpo put everything into a last frantic effort. He charged at Dempsey, bulldozing him across the ring. When he had him on the ropes he threw a ponderous right to the head, and the champion went clean through the ropes, landing in the press seats with his feet in the air.

It was a scribe of the *New York Tribune* who determined that the championship would not change hands. By the count of 'seven' he had pushed Dempsey up onto the ring apron, and Dempsey clambered back and up just in time. He was ready to be knocked out, but Firpo could think of nothing but throwing his big right. Dempsey managed to avoid all the attempts to deliver the knock-out, and at the bell (and even after it) was landing punches on Firpo.

The second round began like the first. Firpo's right to the body caused Dempsey to clinch. At the 'break', he

A painting by George Bellows showing Dempsey going through the ropes onto the press seats in the first round.

piled half-a-dozen punches into Firpo's head and body, and the challenger once more slid to the canvas. He got up at 'five', flung his right again and caught Dempsey on the head. But Dempsey only sank in more punches, and a final right had Firpo crashing down yet again. He tried to haul himself up for the ninth time, but this time he failed. Dempsey was still champion of the world.

There is no doubt that Dempsey ignored the rules in this fight, and got away with it. He did not retire when Firpo was down; he hit him before he had got up; and he hit him after the bell. Some say, too, that he was out of the ring for more than ten seconds, the referee being slow to start the count. But the main reason that Firpo was not crowned the new champion was because he lacked science when Dempsey was ready to be taken. His bludgeoning right was not quite enough. Perhaps it was fate.

Gene Tunney v Jack Dempsey

22 September 1927, Soldier's Field, Chicago

When Gene Tunney relieved Jack Dempsey of the world heavyweight title by convincingly outpointing him in Philadelphia in September, 1926, both the boxing world and the general public were surprised. For years Dempsey had seemed indestructible. Although over 120,000 fans had paid nearly $2 million to see Dempsey's face battered to a jelly on that occasion, as soon as he retrieved his reputation with a knock-out of Sharkey, they were prepared once again to believe in his invincibility.

So when Tex Rickard made the rematch for Chicago in 1927, over 104,000 spectators paid more than has ever been paid before or since to be present at a fight: $2,658,660. Could the Manassa Mauler become the first champion in history to regain the crown, or would the methodical Tunney be able to avoid those fists for a second time?

There was plenty of controversy before the fight concerning the appointment of the referee, even to the extent of accusations about 'fixing'. Eventually Dave Barry was appointed. Tunney won an argument over the size of the ring: 20ft × 20ft (6.1m × 6.1m) rather than the 18ft × 18ft (5.5m × 5.5m) wanted by Dempsey. And the Tunney camp made much of the Dempsey habit of not allowing an opponent on the canvas to get to his feet; both boxers were instructed that, in the event of a knock-down, the standing boxer must retire to the furthest neutral corner.

The events of most of the fight have been forgotten due to the incident in the seventh round, the most famous in the history of boxing. Till then Tunney had outboxed Dempsey on the retreat, but at the start of that fateful seventh, Dempsey trapped Tunney against the ropes and hit him with four rapid punches to the chin, with Tunney already going down as the final blow landed.

It was then that Dempsey reverted to type. As referee Barry counted 'one', Dempsey took up a position menacingly close to the fallen champion. Barry stopped counting and waved him away. Even then Dempsey went to the nearer neutral corner. Only when he obeyed the referee and started to cross to the correct corner did Barry take up the count – back at 'one' again.

Tunney pulled himself up at 'ten' – by which time he had been down for at least 14 seconds – and, back-pedalling rapidly, avoided Dempsey's attempts at the kill for the rest of the round. After the interval, Tunney had recovered his composure. He even put Dempsey down in the eighth, and for the last three rounds he clearly outpointed Dempsey and easily retained his title.

Then the arguments began. Should Tunney have received the long count? And without it would he have been able to rise in time?

Certainly the answer to the first question is that the referee was right, and Dempsey spoiled his own chances. There are differences of opinion about whether Tunney would have been capable of rising. Some close to the ring say he was glassy-eyed, and would have been easy prey even if he had managed to drag himself up. On the other hand, photographs of Tunney watching the referee count suggest he was fully in control.

Tunney always maintained that he could have got up, and Dempsey, even 40 years later, said the same. In a way, nobody lost the 'Battle of the Long Count'. Tunney retained his title and was paid an amazing $990,445. Dempsey was cheered from the ring and became a legend. Rickard made another large profit. And boxing had one of its most enduring stories.

Barney Ross v Jimmy McLarnin

28 May 1935, Polo Grounds, New York

There was exactly a year between the first and third fights in which Barney Ross and Jimmy McLarnin disputed the welterweight championship of the world. Each was a violent encounter, and so close that the fans disagreed with the verdict each time.

Jimmy McLarnin was born in Belfast on 19 December 1906, his parents immediately taking him to Vancouver, Canada. He was spotted in a street fight by an ex-boxer who ran a gymnasium, Pop Foster, who 'adopted' him and groomed him to the world welterweight championship in 1933. McLarnin began professional boxing at 16 years old, and because of his young appearance was known as 'Babyface'.

Ross was born in New York on 23 December 1909, as Barnet Rosofsky. The family moved to Chicago, where his father, who had opened a grocery store, was shot by robbers. Ross turned professional when 19 years old, and won the lightweight and light-welterweight championships of the world in 1933 from Tony Canzoneri. He gave up the lightweight title because of weight problems, but was still light-welterweight champion when he challenged McLarnin for his welterweight crown on 28 May 1934.

The seventh round and Gene Tunney is down. Dempsey remains standing over Tunney and referee Dave Barry starts to push him away while getting ready to count.

Jimmy McLarnin (left) leads a long left but Barney Ross is out of range in the third and rubber fight in New York in 1935.

McLarnin was a great puncher who specialised in quick knock-out victories. Ross lacked a knock-out punch, but was so fast and skilful that he was never stopped himself throughout his career.

The first match was made at 10st 5lb (145lb–66kg), 2lb (0.9kg) below the welter limit, but McLarnin over-reduced to 10st 2lb (142lb–64kg). It weakened him. Forty thousand fans at an open-air arena on Long Island, New York, saw a tremendous battle, with the speedy Ross managing to evade McLarnin's blows for most of the fight. In the fifth round Ross was put down for the first time in his career, but he leapt up and soon afterwards dropped McLarnin. Neither took a count.

Ross fought cleverly, saving his all-out attacks for the last minute of each round to impress the judges. McLarnin, on the other hand, lost four rounds with warnings for low punches. At the bell, the judges were divided, and the referee cast his deciding vote for Ross. Many disagreed, particularly those who thought it wrong for a champion to lose his title on warnings.

A return was a natural, and took place on 17 September 1934 at Long Island. The fight was scheduled for 11 days earlier, but continuous rain kept nearly 20,000 fans waiting. McLarnin was fitter than in the earlier fight, and overcame a

shut eye in the third round to move ahead. But Ross took over half-way through the fight and was giving his opponent a beating until the last round, when a desperate McLarnin shook Ross with such a tremendous left hook that Ross could only stay on his feet by grabbing McLarnin and hanging on till the bell.

Once again the judges did not agree, and the referee decided – this time for McLarnin. The fans disliked this decision more than the first and the press agreed with them. McLarnin had his title back, but there had to be a third fight.

It took place on 28 May 1935, a year to the day since the first encounter. Again it was open air, and 31,000 packed the New York Polo Grounds for the grand decider.

This time the fight swayed two or three times. Ross made the early running; McLarnin came back with some big punches; Ross took over again. It was close going into the final round, and McLarnin made the first impression. Several hard punches had Ross in trouble, but the slippery Barney kept just out of the way of the pay-off one and in the middle of the round he started fighting back. Both men threw punches as hard as they could. It was the most exciting round of all, as each drew blood and tried, finally, to establish mastery over the other. With the fans in a frenzy, at the bell the two old enemies were still battling hammer and tongs.

This time the decision was unanimous – Ross was the winner. But the verdict was no better received than the other two. It seemed nobody could agree who was the better of these two great welterweights.

McLarnin shortly retired, invested wisely, and inherited a tidy sum when his trainer, Pop Foster, died in 1956. Ross carried on until losing his title to Henry Armstrong. He was awarded the Congressional Medal of Honor with the US Marines in the Second World War, fought drug addiction arising from the treatment for his wounds, but died of cancer on 17 June 1967.

Joe Louis v Max Schmeling

22 June 1938, Yankee Stadium, New York

When Joe Louis was progressing on his triumphant march to the heavyweight title, he received a nasty shock. He took on Max Schmeling, ex-world champion, at the Yankee Stadium in 1936. Schmeling was anxious to meet Louis, believing him susceptible to a short right. Interestingly, Jack Johnson had also spotted the same weakness in the Brown Bomber's defence.

So when the two met, Schmeling was not frightened by Louis' reputation, unlike many of the boxers who had contributed to his record of 27 straight wins, 23 by a knock-out. Max waited for his opportunity as Louis kept poking his left in his face, and it came in the fourth. Louis tried a left hook, and Schmeling crossed him with a right and the Brown Bomber hit the deck. Foolishly, he rose at 'two', and took more punishment. He could not get back into the fight, and in the twelfth round the Black Uhlan knocked him out with more hard rights.

A year later Louis was world champion, but he knew that Schmeling had been by-passed, and he himself could not regard himself truly as champion until he had defeated Schmeling. Now it was Louis who wanted the match. Two years and three days after his only defeat, he got it.

The fight doesn't take long to describe. Louis, a warm favourite, gave Schmeling no chance to throw his right. He swarmed over his opponent, hooking him and piling in lefts and rights until Schmeling went down after only 30 seconds. Three times more Louis forced

Handlers rush to help Max Schmeling after Joe Louis had comprehensively knocked him out in the first round.

Schmeling to the canvas, and only twice did Schmeling rise. The referee stopped it as a towel fluttered in after two minutes and four seconds of the first round. Schmeling was taken to hospital, and was still having treatment when he returned to Germany.

Unfortunately, the whole story became mixed with politics and revenge. Hitler had already insulted the black race at the Berlin Olympics in 1936. Naturally Hitler and his propaganda chief, Goebbels, were delighted with Schmeling's first success against Louis, and made the most of it. So when Schmeling came to New York he was built up as a representative of Nazism. And Louis' victory, and the devastating manner of it, were somehow seen as bringing honour to his race, and to America.

It was quite a turn-round for America, where, less than 20 years earlier, it had been impossible for a black boxer to get a title-shot in his own country. And the general rejoicing over Schmeling's humiliation was unfair to a good sportsman. After the Second World War the two became friends, and when Louis was in trouble with both the tax authorities and his health, it was Schmeling, a successful and rich business man, who came to his assistance.

Eric Boon v Arthur Danahar

23 February 1939, Harringay Arena, London.

The first fight ever to be televised 'live' on closed circuit cinema screens was one that has gone down in legend as a classic, as it should, for it had those two acknowledged ingredients – the tough fighter who would not be denied and the classic boxer.

Eric Boon, born in Chatteris, Cambridgeshire, three days before the end of 1919, had built up his muscles as a blacksmith's apprentice, and, it is said, was so keen on fighting that when 15 years old he would cycle over 70 miles (112km) to London on a Sunday, box a six-rounder and then cycle home again. He was not quite 19 when he knocked out Dave Crowley to become British lightweight champion.

Arthur Danahar was 18 months older than Boon, born on 2 June 1918. He had been a brilliant amateur champion, and

he boxed in the upright style with an educated straight left and a right that could do some damage.

The public clamoured for a meeting of the two young lions. When promoters disagreed on arrangements, there was even a proposal from rich sponsors to put the match on in private. Finally, the contest was arranged for 23 February 1939, little more than two months after Boon had won the title. All 12,000 seats at Harringay Arena were sold well before the big day, leading to the television 'overflow'.

The fight started as expected. Boon attacked, as he knew no other way of fighting. Danahar, taller, slimmer, noticeably less muscular, kept his left in Boon's face, whipped over an occasional right and began to build a points lead.

Boon's eye puffed up, but he kept boring in. Sometimes he got his heavy blows in to Danahar's body. More often, Danahar's clever counters picked him off. Soon Boon's eye was completely closed. Still he bored in. When he landed he clearly hurt Danahar.

The cumulative effect of Danahar's blows began to make a mess of Boon's face. If the fight went the distance Danahar must be an easy winner. But still Boon came on, banking everything on his getting one big punch home.

In the eighth round, half-way through the fight, Boon landed a cracking right on Danahar's chin. Down Arthur went, to scramble up at 'eight', when, still groggy, Boon crashed him down again for a count of 'seven'. It needed all Danahar's wits to last to the bell and reach the sanctuary of his corner.

The atmosphere was one of intense excitement as in the next round Boon marched forward again to try to finish it, but this time a lovely right counter from Danahar dropped Boon, and in a rush of blood Danahar struck Boon again as he sat on the bottom rope. The champion merely rose and tore into Danahar and the two men punched away for a spell while the crowd yelled their approval.

Then Danahar went back to his boxing, the knock-down and the flurry of toe-to-toe punching behind him, and he methodically punished Boon until the 11th round was about to end. Boon then caught him with another beauty, a left hook. Danahar sank down holding the middle rope, and then the bell saved him.

It appeared that Boon's plan had worked when, amid great excitement,

the twelfth started, for that blow seemed to have knocked the poise and resistance from Danahar. Boon began to punch him around the ring. He knew he must knock him out to win, and eventually a right sent Danahar to the canvas for 'nine'. But Arthur was game as well as clever. He had the crowd roaring as he now tried to steal the initiative by taking the fight to Boon. It was no good. Boon was best at that game, and soon Danahar was down again, and he was desperately hanging on at the bell.

Somehow Danahar came out for the 13th round. He was still well ahead, and even Boon, battered as he was and with one eye closed, was tired. But the champion drove himself across the ring and cracked Danahar with yet another right to the chin. Danahar collapsed, climbed painfully to his knees, and once more tottered to his feet at 'nine'. He was obviously helpless, however, and as Boon moved in again the referee called a halt.

Eric Boon and Arthur Danahar had given everything in a fight that all who saw it will remember. Both men were given a tremendous ovation as they left the ring. Soon they were both in the services fighting for their country. Seven years later, after the war, they met again in the welterweight division, but the fight was a disappointment. Danahar, did, however, get his revenge when the referee stopped the contest after Boon had been knocked down by a body blow in the fifth round.

The world's first televised fight. Fighter Eric Boon (right) tries to get inside boxer Arthur Danahar's guard.

Joe Louis v Billy Conn

18 June 1941, Polo Grounds, New York

Billy Conn was born in a poor district of Pittsburgh, Pennsylvania, on 8 October 1917. His family was Irish. As a boy he scrapped on the streets, and his fighting ability was obvious. He became a professional and began to beat the top boxers in the welter and middleweight divisions until, finally, he grew to light-heavyweight. In 1939 he won the NYAC version of the world title by beating Melio Bettina in New York. In 1940 he gave up this title and traded among the heavyweights, with great success.

On 18 June 1941 he attempted what four other light-heavyweight champions had failed to do before him: to take the heavyweight title.

Although this was to be Joe Louis' 22nd defence, and only two had previously gone the distance, Conn was thought to have a chance. He was a fast and skilful boxer, and he could ride a punch and take one when necessary. Only twice had he been on the floor, and he had never been stopped. Against that, Louis was in his prime, and he was 25lb (11kg) heavier. The gambling element made him 3–1 on.

Among the 54,487 present were about 6,000 from his home town of Pittsburgh hoping to see Conn win. They were not optimistic at first, as Louis shuffled forward and managed to get home on Conn's body. In the second round Conn looked troubled as two hard rights sank home.

In the third the fight began to take its predicted early course as Conn at last managed to bring his skill to bear, catching Louis repeatedly as he fought cleverly on the retreat. The fourth was even better for Conn, and after stopping the Louis advance with a straight left he took up the attack with some stinging rights which shook his rival. But Conn was given a warning here. A sudden left to his stomach followed by another to his head had him hanging on desperately.

Billy took a couple of rounds to recover from those blows, but in the eighth his speed suddenly seemed to bewilder Louis, who was punished as he stood in frustration like a bull before the matador.

Conn now went from strength to strength, boxing with confidence and continually poking his gloves into Louis' face. Apart from one slip to the canvas, he dodged the champion's blows, or tied him up close, every now and again exploding a flurry of rights and lefts to Louis' head which caused the Brown Bomber to grab Conn in a clinch.

The 12th round was Conn's best. Louis could find nowhere to hide as Conn caught him with a variety of shots. Suddenly their roles were reversed. Louis retreated and Billy Conn was close to being the champion of the world.

It was then that an aspect of Conn's temperament proved his undoing. In some earlier fights he had reacted to being hurt by mixing it rather than by collecting his wits. He had promised before the Louis fight that he would run away from trouble and beat Louis at long range.

He began the 13th with blows to Louis' head, but suddenly Louis, who realized he needed a knock-out, caught Conn as he came in with a right to the jaw. Before Conn could recover more rights caught him and stung him into retaliation. Suddenly his plans were forgotten and he was belting Louis, determined to finish a fight he was winning in style.

However, he was now playing at Louis' game. A right uppercut stopped Conn in his tracks. More blows rained in before a right to the head had Conn sinking to the canvas. Billy tried to rise, and staggered up, but the referee had already said 'ten'. There were two more seconds to go to the end of the round.

Billy Conn, handsome, talented, had had the crown held out to him. In the manner of the classical tragedies his own character was the reason he failed to grasp it – he loved a scrap too much.

Tony Zale v Rocky Graziano

27 September 1946, Yankee Stadium, New York

Tony Zale was Anthony Florian Zaleski when he was born in Gary, Indiana, on 29 May 1913. His parents were Polish immigrants. Working in the steel mills did something for his boxing character, for he was a man who could take a punch without flinching and he had a solid fist himself.

He first gave up professional boxing after fighting 28 times in his first year, but he began again in 1937, and by the time he joined the US Navy four years later he was world middleweight champion.

Rocky Graziano was nine years younger than Zale. He was born as Rocco Barbella on 1 January 1922. His father had been an Italian boxer. Rocky was a child gangster on New York's tough East Side. He went to reform school, to prison, where he assaulted a warder, and eventually into the Army, where he ran away after striking an officer. Boxing was to save him from a possible life of crime. He became a professional and ran up a string of knock-out wins.

Promoter Mike Jacobs saw Graziano as the chance to bring the title back to New York. He matched him with Zale at the Yankee Stadium on 27 September 1946. Over 30,000 came to see the action between the 'Man of Steel' and the 'Dead End Kid'. They were not disappointed.

Graziano, whose tactics in previous fights would not always have endeared him to the Marquis of Queensberry, was made favourite. They began piling into each other from the bell, but Zale's blows seemed the harder, and in less than a minute a left hook sent Graziano groping around the floor. Up at 'four' he took further punishment until just before the bell, when he finally buckled Zale with a desperate right to the chin in retaliation. As Rocky threw more rights to try to finish a groggy champion, the bell went.

In the second round Zale attempted to box off Graziano, and was successful until Rocky caught him with one of his tremendous right swings. With blood streaming from his nose Zale fought back but this time it was Graziano's blows that had more impact. Finally a succession of rights sent Zale to the canvas, one leg tucked under him while he hung with head and glove over the lowest rope. Graziano, his face a fury, ignored the referee and stood over Zale waiting to explode his fists on him when he rose. But again the bell saved Zale.

Billy Conn (left) and Joe Louis box an exhibition. In their world title fight in 1941, one judge and a referee had Conn well in front, while the other judge marked it even, when Louis delivered the knock-out in the 13th round.

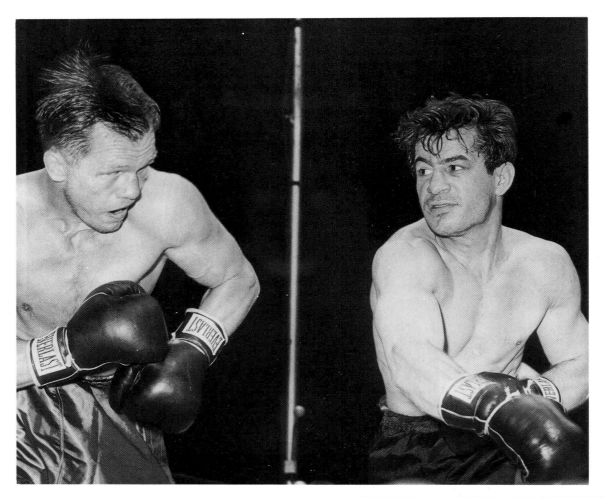

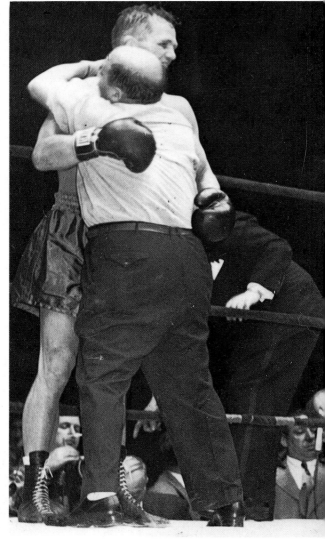

Tony Zale (left) and Rocky Graziano (right), the protagonists in one of the fiercest series of fights in the history of boxing.

Graziano tried again to nail his man in the third, but Zale had just enough strength in his arms to keep the challenger out as they traded punch for punch. Zale attempted to box in the fourth, but there was no boxing when Graziano, who ignored anything but the strongest punches, powered in swinging his huge blows. Once again they swopped punch for punch.

Graziano got on top in the fifth. Zale was having more and more difficulty keeping out this tormentor who would not be stopped and fought like a jungle animal. Swings to the ribs, digs in the body and rights which severely damaged his nose meant the Steel Man was almost beaten by the end of the round.

The weary Zale, breathing with difficulty through a bloody nose, forced his legs to carry him out for the sixth, but was soon set up with crashing rights to the body which left him stock-still as Graziano came in one more time for the kill. Zale then made his last, champion's, effort. As Rocky came in Zale threw a right into his solar plexus with all the strength he had left. Graziano stood paralyzed, and Zale sent him crashing with a left hook. Graziano just could not get up. Like Corbett when Fitzsimmons punched him in the solar plexus nearly

50 years earlier, Graziano's legs would not obey his orders.

Again like Corbett, when he recovered Graziano hurled himself at Zale, refusing to accept that he had been beaten. Police and his handlers pulled Graziano to his corner. The champion was battered, and after the fight it was discovered that his right hand had been broken in the second round. Graziano was indignant. 'The count crept up on me', he said, 'it went too fast'.

There had to be a return. It took place at the Chicago Stadium before 18,547 spectators, then an indoor record. The date, 16 July 1947, allowed ten months for the warriors to recover. And they provided another slugfest to rival the first.

Zale began by outboxing Graziano, punishing him with blows to head and body, and almost closing his left eye in the first round. In the second round Zale continued the treatment, attacking the eye, but Graziano at last connected with one of his sweeping rights near the end of the round causing a dazed Zale to go to the wrong corner.

In the third Zale split Graziano's left eye and floored him with a hook, but Graziano was up without a count, only to take further severe punishment. There was yet more in the fourth, when Graziano merely tried to avoid trouble as his right eye was now puffed and his left pouring blood. At the end of the round the referee considered stopping the fight, but gave Graziano one more round to turn the tide.

He took his opportunity. The blood flow was stemmed, and Graziano switched on his attack with swings from all directions pounding into Zale and bewildering him. Suddenly a tremendous right had Zale all at sea and he was groggy as he went to his corner.

Zale tried to box from a distance in the sixth, but Graziano was soon piling in his rights and Zale was sent reeling to the canvas. When he rose Graziano was all over him, and eventually a helpless Zale was draped over the middle rope with Graziano pummeling him. The referee intervened and Graziano was the new champion. 'Somebody up there likes me,' he said, and this became the title of

The end of the series. Conqueror Zale is hugged by his manager Art Winch, while Rocky Graziano is receiving his handler's efforts to bring him round.

his autobiography and a film which starred Paul Newman.

Eleven months later, on 10 June 1948, in Newark, New Jersey, the rubber match was held. The younger Graziano was a 12–5 favourite to retain the crown.

The fight followed the course of the others, but some of the kick had at last gone from the big swings of Graziano, and while Zale pounded in his blows, the answering flurries from Rocky were not enough to halt him. In the third round Zale floored Graziano with a left hook. Graziano struggled up but a right to the ribs and a left to the jaw knocked him unconscious. Zale thus joined Stanley Ketchel in regaining the middleweight title.

Neither boxer achieved much in the ring after these great battles. Graziano, however, remained in the public eye, becoming a television personality and owning a restaurant in New York.

Rocky Marciano v Jersey Joe Walcott

23 September 1952, Municipal Stadium, Philadelphia

Arnold Raymond Cream was born in Merchantville, New Jersey, on 31 January 1914. He decided to become a professional boxer, and began his career in 1930. He took the name of his schoolboy idol, Joe Walcott, the former welterweight champion, and added the 'Jersey' after his own state.

He was not outstandingly successful at first and in 1944 retired for a more secure occupation (he had six children) but was tempted back by the offer of six fights from a promoter opening a new arena. This time his career was more successful, and in 1947 he challenged Joe Louis for the world heavyweight championship. He lost twice to Louis and twice to Ezzard Charles before he finally beat Charles to become heavyweight champion, at 37 years and five months the oldest to win the title.

His second defence, on 23 September 1952, was against Rocky Marciano, 'The Brockton Blockbuster', a man nearly ten years his junior, of immense strength and with a perfect record of 42 straight wins, 37 of them inside the distance. Against this Walcott could offer 21 years of varied boxing experience.

Marciano was a 9–5 favourite, but these odds looked unrealistic when in the middle of the first round Walcott's powerful left hook put Marciano on the canvas for the first time in his career. He scrambled up at 'four' and was subjected to a Walcott assault that had him groggy at the bell. Walcott continued on top. In the third round Marciano began boxing in a crouch, but still Jersey Joe caught him on the chin. All Marciano could show was his undoubted ability to take a punch.

In the sixth round Marciano had a little success with his usual powerful infighting, but it was his head which caused Walcott most trouble, opening up a bad cut on the champion's left eye. Marciano also had a cut head and in the next round the ointment used on one or other of the injuries got into Marciano's left eye and he had difficulty seeing.

In the next five rounds Walcott piled up the points, repeatedly hitting Marciano and opening a cut across the top of his nose. The three officials had him so far ahead that Marciano needed a knock-out in the last three rounds to win.

Perhaps the wily Joe realized this. He made no effort in the 13th, and retreated against the ropes whenever Marciano moved within range. This was his biggest mistake.

Suddenly Marciano threw one of the fastest and hardest punches of his career, a short right that smacked against the side of Walcott's jaw before he could sidle out of danger. The follow-up left missed, but only because Walcott was already sliding down the ropes, one arm temporarily halting his fall as it got caught on the middle rope. There was no chance he would get up in time. His handlers went to his assistance.

Walcott was 39 years old when he lost the return eight months later in two minutes, 25 seconds. He retired and became a parole officer for juvenile delinquents. He also refereed the second Muhammad Ali–Sonny Liston title fight, but made a mess of a tricky situation.

Cassius Clay v Sonny Liston

25 February 1964, Miami Convention Hall, Florida

There could never have been a man who looked so invincible as Sonny Liston before his first title fight with Muhammad Ali. Not even John L. Sullivan, the

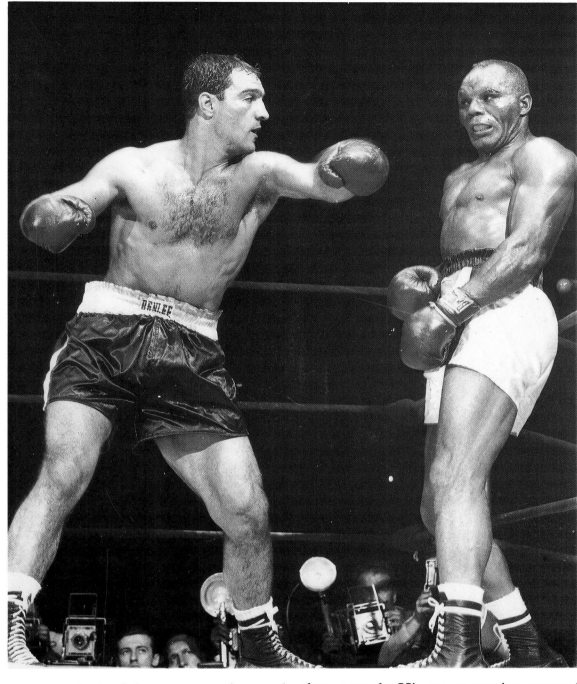

Walcott on the ropes as Marciano bores in. It was from a similar situation in the 13th round that Marciano's right sent Walcott sliding down the ropes.

taunting Jack Johnson nor the cool destroyer Louis was more calculated to strike fear into opponents' hearts.

Liston appeared to be a man with only destruction in his own heart. He was born in St Francis, Arkansas, on 8 May 1932, his father reportedly a drunkard who sired 25 children. Liston left home at 13 after arguing with his father and drifted into delinquency which ended with armed robbery and a long spell in a state penitentiary where a chaplain directed his energies into boxing. He eventually earned parole to pursue a professional career, which he began in 1953 with the early patronage of Frank Palermo, a mob figure with considerable influence in the game.

Liston dealt with all the title contenders in turn, few lasting more than three rounds. His career was interrupted when he assaulted a policeman, and received a nine-month prison sentence. For two years it seemed that his record might be all that stopped him becoming title-holder. There was talk that boxing did not need such a champion.

Liston stood 6ft 1in (1.86m) and had a remarkable 84-in (2.13m) reach. His fists were 15in (38cm) in circumference and his neck 17½in (45cm). He could take a punch without his granite features showing any emotion, and his routine blows were like the kick of a horse.

These physical assets were backed by a menacing psychology. He began the habit of staring into an opponent's eyes during the referee's instructions. He stuffed towels under his robe to make himself look even bigger. He was utterly

Clay on the ropes as the fearsome-looking Liston comes forward.

cold, boxing's equivalent of the underworld hit man.

Before the night he defended against Clay, Liston had fought two world title fights, neither lasting more than a round. Floyd Patterson had been scared and destroyed. The brash young challenger from Louisville was probably frightened of Liston, too. True, he had been taunting Liston at fights, and an attempt at psychological harassment culminated in bedlam at the fight weigh-in, where Clay and his entourage put on an act. They danced around, chanted, and Clay actually pretended to attack Liston. He had to be restrained and forced into a chair. It seemed he was demented. The commission's doctor registered Clay's blood pressure at 200/100, and the press put it down to fear.

During the referee's instructions before the fight, Liston went into his act,

and Clay called him a 'chump'. If Clay was meeting something completely new to him, so was Liston.

Liston went after Clay from the first, but Clay was too fast. All Liston's blows were missing by wide margins. Near the end of the round Clay cut loose with some rapid lefts and rights to Liston's face, then he floated off again.

Liston rushed out for the second round and managed two blows to Clay's kidneys before Clay was 'on his bike', but for the rest of the round the challenger glided about and jabbed Liston. He even opened a tiny cut on Liston's cheek – Liston was definitely in new territory. But he did at last catch his man with a good left, which Clay later admitted hurt, but Liston did not follow up.

In the third round both men landed good punches, but Clay's did more damage, opening up the cut on Liston's cheek. Liston sat down in his corner at the end of this round for the first time. The fourth was uneventful, with Clay speeding up his boxing and clearly ready to tire Liston over a long contest.

It was a very significant round, however, because Liston, who had slightly injured a shoulder in training, had used some liniment on it between rounds and some had got into Clay's eyes. When his face was wiped it got worse, and suddenly he was screaming he couldn't see and asking for the gloves to be cut off. Instead, manager Angelo Dundee pushed him out for the fifth.

In this round Clay merely tried to avoid trouble. He danced around, sometimes holding his left on Liston's forehead, trying to slip the punches from a rejuvenated champion. Some got through, especially early on before Clay's eyes began to clear. Liston could not connect later and must have guessed his best chance had gone. He had already fought about three years' quota of rounds. The doctor checked Clay's eyes in the interval.

In the sixth round Clay moved around pouring punches into Liston's face, which started to become mis-shapen and discoloured. Cassius now had the confidence to attack, and took an occasional blow from Liston without inconvenience.

At the end of the round a sad Liston sat down. He did not come out for the next. He was retired, claiming his shoulder was injured. Clay leapt about, shouting

he was 'The Greatest', saying he'd told us all. It was the weigh-in hysteria all over again.

The return was at Lewiston, Maine on 25 May 1965. Such was the power of Liston's personality that even now he was 7–5 favourite, but the fight raised questions which will never be answered fully.

A few seconds of dancing around preceded a left and right from Ali (as he was now calling himself) and a corkscrew right to Liston's head. Liston went down and lay on his back. Ali stood over him, telling him to get up, and ignoring referee Jersey Joe Walcott's instructions to go to a neutral corner. The time-keeper began the count immediately, however, Walcott eventually took it up, and pressmen estimated it reached 22. Liston got to his feet and lumbered towards Ali, and the pair began boxing again. The Editor of *The Ring*, Nat Fleischer, called to Walcott that the fight was over, and Walcott stopped it. By then it had run two minutes 12 seconds, but the official time was given first as one minute but later as one minute 42 seconds, as timed on the television replay.

The crowd yelled 'fix' and there was animated discussion for some time, and in the press for days afterwards. Many claimed there had not been a knock-down punch at all, others that it could not have been hard enough to fell Liston. The two boxers and referee claimed the punch was good, but the suspicion was that Liston, who had raised two fingers

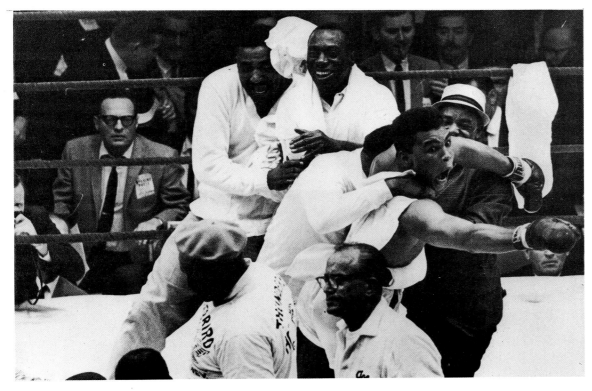

Cassius Clay dashes round the ring like a man demented after winning the world heavyweight championship from Sonny Liston.

to Ali at the first weigh-in, was now doing the same thing to the public.

It may be that Liston was just demoralized and was aiming to get it over as quickly as possible. It has been suggested that he was old and that his published date of birth might have been anything up to ten years out.

However, Liston did not retire, and fought on for four more years. A run of wins was ended when he was knocked out by Leotis Martin late in 1969.

On 30 December 1970 Liston died in Las Vegas. His body lay undiscovered for six days, until his wife found it. There was heroin in the kitchen. It had been a hard life for Liston from beginning to end.

Muhammad Ali v Joe Frazier

1 October 1975, Manila, Philippines

The 'thrilla in Manila' was the third of the Ali–Frazier fights. In 1971, when Frazier was world champion and Ali was making his comeback from his suspension, Frazier had won on points. In 1974, when neither was champion, Ali had won on points.

In 1975 Ali was world champion again, and Joe Frazier was challenging. The paying audience was 28,000. There were several hundred million watching on satellite television around the world. Ali was guaranteed a pay day of $4.5 million.

Ali built up the pre-fight publicity calling Frazier a 'gorilla' – Frazier hinted that it was not all pre-fight hype, and that he intended to make Ali eat his words.

Ali began as if he believed Frazier was past his best, although he himself was two years the elder. He scorned defensive techniques and carried the fight to Frazier, and buckled his legs in the first round with a hook. In the third he caught him again. Ali began to talk to Frazier, and if Frazier did land a punch Ali indicated to the crowd and his opponent that it did not hurt. The referee did not allow him to hold the shorter man behind the head, though, a ploy which Ali had used often in other fights.

Ali was on top, but Frazier was persistent, and caught Ali often enough in the fifth round to shade it, and in the sixth he crashed two left hooks to Ali's face, forcing him to hang on. In the sixth there was more of the same, and Ali decided to sit on his stool for the first time between rounds. He now fought in bursts as Frazier bored in. By the end of the tenth round Frazier's aggression had put the fight level. Both men were exhausted, and both knew the title could be won or lost. Ali seemed more drained, and it appeared that Frazier's non-stop forward march had taken its toll.

But Ali found some reserves. In the 11th he caught Frazier with some hard long shots. Bumps appeared around Frazier's eyes and blood dripped from his mouth. Suddenly the roles seemed reversed, and Frazier at last looked without power. In the 12th Ali turned on all his attacking power as Frazier wilted. Frazier's head changed shape and he stumbled about, unable to keep out the man who was now stinging like a bee.

In the 13th Frazier started to go backwards under Ali's slashing blows. It was a question of whether he could last the distance, or whether there was still one shot left in his locker to fire back at the champion.

Frazier's eyes were practically closed in the 14th and Ali hit him with punch after punch without reply. Frazier was led back to his corner at the bell by the referee. There was only one round to go, but Frazier's manager, Eddie Futch, would not let his man go out for it. Ali had no energy for celebrations, he sank to the canvas to rest.

Afterwards he was generous to Frazier, saying that he had nearly retired after the tenth, and that he had been 'next to death'. Frazier said Ali was a great champ. Ali said they were a great team.

Marvin Hagler v Roberto Duran

10 November 1983, Caesar's Palace, Las Vegas

Both Marvin Hagler and Roberto Duran won world titles from British boxers. Marvin Hagler won the middleweight championship of the world in September 1980, from Alan Minter, and in this notoriously difficult division was still seeing off challengers without much difficulty over four years later.

Roberto Duran was world lightweight champion as far back as 1972 when he beat Ken Buchanan, of Scotland. He relinquished this title in 1979 to have a shot at the welterweights. In a brilliant contest his aggression triumphed over the polished skill of Sugar Ray Leonard in 1980 and he won the world title.

Duran was a hero in his native Panama. He represented *machismo*. He was the man whose heart would keep him going when the rest of the body wanted to give in. He was packaged guts.

Until 26 November 1980. On that date Duran defended his new welterweight title against Leonard and this time Leonard boxed and fought and dazzled. In the eighth round the unbelievable happened. Duran turned his back on his tormentor and walked towards his corner. To save himself humiliation in the ring, he retired, and he faced the humiliation outside it. The man who represented pride to Latin Americans had given in. Idolatry turned to contempt.

Duran began a slow road to recovery, gaining scrappy wins and even registering two defeats. It seemed that *machismo* and a birth certificate over 30 years old were incompatible in the tough world of professional boxing.

In June, 1983, however, Duran celebrated his 32nd birthday by stepping up

The second Ali–Frazier fight. Frazier covers up as Ali pokes out a left.

Roberto Duran attempts to fight back from the ropes as Hagler moves in menacingly.

another weight and challenging Davey Moore for the WBA junior middleweight championship. Duran beat Moore in the eighth round at Madison Square Garden to win a world title at a third weight. He was still a world champion after 11 years. On 10 November 1983 he was given the opportunity to grab back the idolatry and more as he was matched with Marvelous Marvin Hagler, the middleweight king, in Las Vegas.

In theory a lightweight whose frame had thickened with age into the middleweight range should have no chance with a great natural middleweight at his peak. The odds were 4–1 on Hagler. But there were those who thought Duran's magic could work again.

Duran began in his usual swarming style, and accompanied his blows, legiti-

mate or dubious, with the snarl meant to intimidate. Perhaps it did, for Hagler was unusually cautious, and the match looked to be a close one. Hagler began a bombardment in the sixth round, but Duran weathered it. For the first time in eight defences (the previous seven had not gone the distance) Hagler was forced to improvise, to scramble, to scrap. After 12 rounds the fight was still there to be won by either man.

Not surprisingly, Hagler proved the stronger over the final stretch. A grandstand finish put the points decision beyond doubt. Hagler was winner and still champion, but if one man repeated his claim to be considered one of the all-time greats, it was Duran. In his 17th year as a professional he could still mix it with the very best.